The Surprising Life of Constance Spry

The Surprising Life of Constance Spry

SUE SHEPHARD

MACMILLAN

First published 2010 by Macmillan
an imprint of Pan Macmillan, a division of Macmillan Publishers Limited
Pan Macmillan, 20 New Wharf Road, London N1 9RR
Basingstoke and Oxford
Associated companies throughout the world
www.panmacmillan.com

ISBN 978-0-230-74181-2

1 3 5 7 9 8 6 4 2

A CIP catalogue record for this book is available from
the British Library.

Typeset by SetSystems Ltd, Saffron Walden, Essex
Printed by CPI Mackays, Chatham ME5 8TD

For Ben

Contents

Introduction

There was an extraordinary uproar in September 2004 when the Design Museum of London held an exhibition on the work of Constance Spry. The museum's co-founders, Sir Terence Conran of Habitat and George Dyson, of bagless vacuum cleaner fame, threatened to resign. Flower arranging, they said, was utterly wrong for a design exhibition and a 'betrayal' of the museum's original purpose. 'Design is about serious technical things, not shallow styling,' Dyson claimed, and Conran wrote to the *Guardian* to say that they were 'confused by the "high-society mimsiness" of Constance Spry and of the suitability of flower arranging for the Design Museum'. Mimsiness, a nonsense word coined by Lewis Carroll from 'miserable' and 'flimsy', is the kind of word that Constance Spry herself would have used to describe the prim, outdated flower arranging that she most deplored and did most to change. With his Habitat stores, Conran has done as much as anyone to make the British style-conscious, so it was ironic to find him so agitated about a floral designer who similarly encouraged people to feel they could beautify their homes in their own way on a modest budget. Indeed Constance Spry would have been bemused by their narrow vision, not because it smacked of sexism but because in her day design and art were pretty much regarded as the same thing.

Who was this Constance Spry who had caused such a 'storm in a flower vase'? Journalists swooped on the story and began reworking the name into a modern brand and associating it with the bland, sterile haut-bourgeois domestic perfection of the 1950s whereas in fact her greatest achievements were in the 1930s when she revolutionized the art of flower arranging – indeed, she made it an art. Nearly half a century after her death, Constance Spry was resuscitated as a household icon and taste-maker famous for doing the flowers for high society, for establishing a posh finishing school and for writing a bestselling cookery book which in 2004 *Waitrose Food Illustrated* selected as 'one of the greatest cookbooks of all time'. None of this is incorrect but it is nevertheless wide of the mark of the real Constance Spry – for she was neither the 'cookery woman' nor the grand society 'flower lady' of popular imagination.

There are few people now who can recall the glamorous days in the Thirties when Constance Spry was the most sought-after flower decorator to the wealthiest and most fashionable homes, but many more of us will remember growing up in the Fifties and Sixties when the family kitchen had a well-thumbed copy of *The Constance Spry Cookery Book*, written in collaboration with her friend Rosemary Hume. I had particular reason to be familiar with this book and these names. My mother had trained at the Cordon Bleu Cookery School in London in the early 1930s and subsequently taught there and knew Rosemary Hume, the school's founder, who later became my godmother. Rosemary, alas, was so shy and retiring that I hardly knew her, and Constance Spry was just a name on a bookcover. I was quite unaware of her extraordinary achievements, let alone her unconventional life. But as I got older and became more interested, both personally and professionally, in cooking and gardening, I began to wonder about Constance Spry and who she really was.

It has been claimed that she made the biggest impact on women's domestic lives since Mrs Beeton – though, unlike Isabella Beeton, she was a genuine original with ideas, creativity and a way of teaching entirely her own. Yet there is no evidence that Constance Spry ever tried to instruct people on how to furnish their homes, to dress, run a household or generally live perfect lives. Most of her own life was spent throwing out convention and debunking the rules of etiquette, of style – and of flower arranging too. Indeed in any one of her books on gardening, flower arranging or cookery you will find a cry from the heart for freedom of expression:

> I want to shout out: 'Do what you please, follow your own star; be original if you want to be and don't if you don't want to be. Just be natural and gay and light-hearted and pretty and simple and overflowing and general and baroque and bare and austere and stylized and wild and daring and conservative, and learn and learn and learn. Open your minds to every form of beauty.'

Constance possessed a rare combination of talents: as writer, innovator, gardener and, above all, as a floral artist. She was a gifted lecturer and at different periods in her life headed schools for the richest and for the poorest. At a time when most women's expectations were still limited she believed in instilling in girls from all backgrounds the confidence and freedom to create beauty. Similarly she showed that a woman could, if she chose, run her own business and overcome the gender and class barriers that in those days prevented most women from achieving professional ambitions. Her belief that anyone from any background, rich or poor, had the right and the ability to create beauty and derive pleasure from it reflected her own rags-to-riches story: an unhappy, impoverished childhood, then tough years in health education and teaching in the East End of London before being catapulted, in middle age, into lavish and sophisticated circles as an 'artist flower designer'. There she was transformed into a successful society 'floral artist' lionized by the chicest members of the theatre, interior design and fashion worlds.

It was a baptism of creative fire and she plunged into it with all her enthusiasm, energy and humour but also with the naivety that characterized everything she did. She rarely looked before she leaped and sometimes she landed on her feet, sometimes not. Her lack of business sense meant she never acquired much wealth and any profits from her shop were always ploughed back into her schools. Along the way was a failed marriage, divorce, cohabitation, adultery, homosexuality, an address book of hugely wealthy clients; plus high-society glamour, royal scandal and royal patronage – none of which seemed to affect her unswerving integrity and down-to-earth approach to every challenge she took on. Despite serving the top echelons of society, Constance, or Connie as she was familiarly known, was genuinely democratic, almost to the point of being blind to class differences.

She told several stories from her difficult childhood in her books, but otherwise concealed most things about herself and somehow ran her life and her business with personal secrets so well kept that she was able to do flowers for aristocracy and royalty without a whiff of scandal. Perhaps that is why she was sympathetic to other people's social disfavour. One of her most extraordinary commissions was her and her team's 'absolutely silent and loyal' furnishing of flowers for the wedding of the Duke and Duchess of Windsor.

Like many artists, Connie relied on rich patrons and so is still associated in people's minds with luxury – the grand ballrooms and elegant drawing-rooms, the fashionable weddings – but she never allowed her clients to dictate to her. Indeed, she was known to abandon a commission if she was asked to compromise her own standards and principles. The fact that Connie served high society never meant that she wished to be part of it nor that she was impressed by the breeding and wealth of her clients. She was never a name-dropper – those most often mentioned in her books are of gardeners and nurserymen whose guidance and opinions she sought. She was popular at all levels of life, from royalty and aristocracy to the 'lower orders'. The glorious flower arrangements, the friendly and inspiring books, the vivacity and gaiety she presented to the world were all genuine; she had an immense capacity for relishing life, and it was her gift to pass it on to others. But a darker current flowed beneath: she was also a woman who never knew complete peace of mind; she was wayward, nervous and highly strung. She was romantic and deeply sentimental but also tough and sometimes quite cruel when it served her to be so.

Connie was a restless spirit, always keen to move on to a new challenge – she feared criticism and was never satisfied with her work. Perhaps it was her sense of insecurity that kept her going, kept her alive to new challenges: running a huge London flower shop, creating new gardens, travelling and lecturing, setting up a cookery and flower-arranging school, writing numerous books, or doing the flowers for Princess Elizabeth's wedding and later for the coronation procession in 1953 – the grand finale of her life's work.

Everyone who worked with Connie described her as tough and funny, full of energy and originality. Her friend the writer and gardener Beverley Nichols once described the art of flower arranging as 'pre-Spry' and 'post-Spry'. In between were three extraordinary Spry decades: the extravagant 1930s' world of designers and artists breaking free from Edwardian fustiness and exhibiting their art and their sexuality with a new-found freedom; the 1940s, a period of wartime austerity and making-do, of gardening and cooking with the Blitz spirit and of refusal to compromise; then the 1950s, the last fling of English high society, of debutante balls and girls' finishing schools, and later new clients in industry, advertising and politics. Connie's success, when it finally came, was rapid and brilliant and intimately bound up with the social history of the pre- and post-war years. She designed the flowers for many of the most influential and important people and functions of the time and she made her influence felt in particular on interior decoration, especially the great rage for 'Vogue Regency', the all-white interiors of the early 1930s.

Three things made the name of Constance Spry justly famous: her creative artistry; her refusal to consider the second-rate; and her passion for perfection in detail. Nichols wrote: 'Constance has the supreme gift – which is really the core of all art and all invention – of seeing things for the first time in a new way, and seeing them whole and seeing them isolated from convention.' She turned outdated flower arranging on its ear, threw out the rules thereby liberating gardeners and florists, and inspiring designers. Her boldly modernistic approach and her theatrical effects supplanted strict Victorian and Edwardian traditions. She was most famous for freeing the flower vase from the constraints of the stiff formal arrangements of the past, did away with old ideas such as using a single type of flower or just one colour, and pioneered new ways with dynamic creations of mixed and even clashing colours.

She was very well read, possessed a vast library of books on art, cookery and horticulture, and she took inspiration from an eclectic range of sources: from Dutch and Flemish flower paintings, medieval embroidery and tapestries, old-fashioned plants and classical decoration, interpreting them in her own unique way. She was brilliant at improvisation and an enthusiastic user of new materials such as plastics and sticky tape – and she invented the use of scrunched-up chicken wire, well hidden, to anchor soaring stems and branches that would seem to fly out of her arrangements without benefit of gravity. Instead of the priceless crystal, silver, porcelain or other heirlooms that she might be invited to use at her clients' homes, she preferred baking-tins, meat plates or junk finds to put her flowers in. Her genius for creating beauty out of the cheapest and simplest materials was legendary. The most controversial aspect of her reputation was her use of all kinds of plant material. With her natural flair and remarkable feeling for the character of flowers and their potential she claimed that nothing should be overlooked, whether gathered from the flower garden, the vegetable patch, or the hedgerows and fields – branches, grasses, leaves, seeds, berries, fruits and vegetables, including her famous kale. Any plant, from the most exotic to the commonest weed, had potential for the container – anything in fact that 'excited her creative juices' to work as an artist with the freedom of her particular paintbox.

Connie's defining principle was that a flower arrangement should blend with the character of the room and the occasion for which it was intended. She demonstrated that flowers had the power to create mood and also to reflect it. It all lay in the subtlety of the material, the colours and textures, and in the complementary nature of each unique design she created:

> One arranges flowers as the spirit moves you; to obey some inner prompting to put this colour with that, to have brilliance here, line there, a sense of opulence in this place or sparseness in that; to suit your surroundings, your mood, the weather, the occasion. In a word, to do as you please, just as, if you could, you might paint a picture.

If she made any rules, she quickly broke them; she wrote that flowers should look natural, but then stripped the leaves from branches of lime to reveal the flowers, skeletonized magnolia leaves and painted branches in blue and silver. She rebelled against the fussiness of small vases of flowers dotted around a room and instead would set one or two large, dramatic displays at eye level. She shocked church authorities by decorating weddings with foaming cow-parsley and other wild flowers.

Connie always wrote with a cheerful, uninhibited directness, never afraid to debunk a convention she did not agree with or side with the reader over a problem. She never patronized her readers and offered them the freedom to follow their own creative inclinations. She opened up new possibilities for self-expression for women. Her books and ideas still seem fresh and inspirational, her flower arrangements as exciting and surprising as ever.

Her influence and artistry are still around us. Anyone who looks on the Spry era as long forgotten has only to think of Connie's original use of purple seakale, for instance, to find similar displays winning medals today at Chelsea and other flower shows.

Among the many people who rallied to defend the Constance Spry Exhibition in 2004 at the Design Museum, the poet James Fenton best summed it up in the *Guardian*:

When you visit one of Conran's shops and find some amusing table decoration – a nice little aquarium full of broad beans or whatever some zany and fetching assistant has thought up that day – all that derives from Constance Spry. You like twig bundles (I don't) – she knew all about twig bundles, their virtues and drawbacks. The exhibition credits her with single-handedly overthrowing a flower-arranging rule that insisted on one species to a vase. She pioneered the mixed arrangement, but also the eloquent use of limited materials. The starting point of her philosophy was that wild flowers and weeds could be pressed into service, just as much as tuberoses. One could indeed spend a fortune. One could also spend next to nothing. This was the source of her popular appeal.

He concluded the piece by recommending a photograph of one of Connie's arrangements:

It bears the title 'Whitewashed Leaves': a kneeling blackamoor figure in the Venetian style bears a huge display of whitened palm fronds and heaven knows what. It's fun. It's dashing, perhaps unacceptable. It's part of the uncensored history of design.

Just the kind of response that Constance Spry herself might have come up with.

Prologue

No one going up or down Bond Street during the early 1930s could have missed Atkinsons' new perfumery shop, built in the latest Art Deco style on the corner of Burlington Gardens and Old Bond Street. With its gilded 'Flemish' tower of carillon bells, it was quite unlike anything ever seen before. Inside was a fairytale setting of specially made mirror glass, crystal chandeliers and a delicate fountain. But what first attracted passers-by on crisp, dark winter afternoons were the four huge, warmly lit bay windows in which stood the most astonishing displays of flowers.

People stopped to stare at the thrilling, theatrical floral tableaux, spotlit and magnificent in soapstone urns and black marble tazzas. They were utterly different from any of the conventional flower displays normally seen in shop windows – formal and static 'shop' arrangements of stiffly wired hothouse blooms. People began to make special trips to view the Atkinsons' windows and admire the majestic yet ethereal displays. They noted the marvellous downward swoop of great trails of garlands and branches that sprang from a shallow vase on a long stem seeming to defy gravity.

How was it done? What were the strange flowers and leaves? Nothing like those they were used to seeing. It was so new, so original: the combinations of surprising colours and the blending of the materials – flowers, leaves, branches and berries – with a liveliness and freshness of line that broke all the strict rules of flower arranging. Every week new and breathtaking compositions appeared, and shoppers would press their noses against the cold window panes, discussing and arguing. They would go inside, enquire who was responsible for the flowers, then in the charming, heady atmosphere of tinkling glass and water and seductive perfume they would purchase elegant bottles of 'Love in Idleness', 'Oleander' and 'Insouciance', impossibly small pots of creams, and lotions. Atkinsons' Perfumery was soon doing a roaring trade.

Norman Wilkinson, a successful theatre designer, had been asked to design the shop. It was something he had never done before and it amused him to flout the Edwardian stuffiness of shop interiors and go for fantasy and indulgence, delicacy and surprise. Wilkinson wanted the floral displays in the four windows to hold centre stage. Above all they must possess romance, sophistication, originality and class. They should be flowers done by a lady, but a lady of quite uncommon gifts. His friend the artist Keith Henderson recalled: 'Wilkinson's designs for that exquisitely tranquil yet astonishing shop in Bond Street naturally impelled him to be eagerly on the lookout for someone of equal originality, who should be responsible for bringing them even more vividly to life with flowers. He found her. He told me about her. Her name was Constance.'

Constance Spry was forty-three years old when Norman Wilkinson found her. Yet it was the first creative challenge of her life. Indeed, life before Atkinsons' Perfumery and the numerous commissions that followed its remarkable success had been lived in quite another world – so different that it is hard to imagine how this curious, dumpy little figure could have gone on to reach such glamorous heights. Only someone with gritty determination, huge enthusiasm and a passionate desire to create something of beauty could have climbed out of the cold, grey world of her youth to conquer English society in all its complexity.

'You have no idea', Constance wrote, 'how wonderful it is to come out of the dark frustration of being unable to crystallize such visions as you may have, and to find suddenly a possible medium of expression.'

ONE

Dark Frustration

1886–1900

Our nurse would not come nettle hunting. Mary [the cook] would, and, what is more, she made and doled out the nettle beer. It was lovely to think that whole beds of nettles were entirely yours to do as you liked with and that, literally, no one cared if you picked the lot.

Old-fashioned mushroom recipes for pickling and ketchup take me back to feverish nights when I was afraid to go to sleep in case I slept beyond the appointed hour of 4 a.m. In retrospect, the fields are white with the magic fungi, and only in retrospect do I realize that we must have been trespassing.

From the few tantalizing autobiographical clues scattered like small gems in her flower books, Constance Spry reveals an irrepressible romantic streak. But her fleeting images of a wild child running free in the lush flower-filled countryside are conjured out of a childhood that was anything but carefree. From her birth on 5 December 1886 in one of the redbrick terraced houses that crammed the backstreets around Derby railway station, Connie Fletcher was caught in a tense battle between her father's passion for education and self-improvement and her mother's narrow frustrations and desire for social advancement.

George Fletcher had left school at fourteen and started work as a printer's devil, then became a telegraphist with the Midland Railway Company. His hunger for knowledge drove him to night classes at the Derby Technical School, where he gained a qualification in electrical engineering. Not content with that, he attended a range of courses in arts and sciences run by lecturers from Cambridge University – 'Studies for the History of Art', 'Sound and Music', 'Plantlife' and 'The Forces of Nature'. Connie's father always came out top in his examinations, with distinctions and whenever he had some spare time he painted in watercolour and wrote poetry. George's insatiable appetite for knowledge and his delight in everything he learned he passed on to his growing family, imbuing in them the same joy and sense of liberation that learning had brought to him.

Whereas George was tall, fair, handsome and genial, his wife was in every respect his opposite. Henrietta Maria – 'Etty' – was small, dark, pretty and sharp-tongued. She was two years older, came from a family of shopkeepers and believed she had married beneath her. Etty's fierce social ambition filled the family with tension and unhappiness. It now seems hard to understand her kind of snobbery, to appreciate the marginal, but to her very real, social differences between a shopkeeper and a railway telegraphist. Certainly, life for Etty in the early years of the marriage was very tough. They lived in a grim little back-to-back house with a tiny back yard. Some of the men filled their leisure hours nurturing prize dahlias from seeds from two-penny weekly journals. But for the women there was the endless war with the dirt and smoke from burning raw coal, the back-breaking grind of daily life and constant pregnancies.

Etty harboured her feelings of refinement and longed to move up and out to the wide Georgian streets on the edge of town with their grand houses and views of the open Peak country beyond. She struggled to keep her children clean and neat, never allowing them to play with the neighbourhood children. She can have had little contact with her husband, who was at work all day and at classes all evening, his head in his books late into the night at home. She would, though, sit on the committee of Derby University Students' Association when George became its vice-president, and she sometimes accompanied him on geological trips to the Peak District and heard him read papers to the Derby Archaeological and Natural History Society. Etty was no doubt happy to appear publicly as the proud wife, and her fierce social ambition drove him on. But if she believed in his abilities it is unlikely that she then saw in them the hope of betterment or escape.

Escape, however, was just around the corner. The instructors at the Derby Technical School were so impressed with George's aptitude and passion for education that soon after Connie's birth they invited him to join the staff. By 1891 he had become head-master and principal science teacher at a salary of £200 a year – a middle-class income at that time. It was the beginning of a long upward progress. The family of five – Connie and her two brothers, Arnold and baby Kenneth – was able to move into a house a mile nearer the centre of town. Surely now life would be so much better. The air would be cleaner, the neighbours nicer, there might be a garden where the children could play. Everyone would be happier.

Connie remembered this house, but her memories were not cheerful ones. It was a three-storey terraced house with a few shrubs in front and a yard behind, surrounded by endless streets of other redbrick houses. Some of them, though, had gardens, and for the first time Connie began to notice the common shrubs and other plants that would remain favourites – lilac, philadelphus or mock orange, dark glossy laurel, buddleia and evening primrose. Hoping to 'escape the eye of authority', she used to climb over a wall into a neglected building site to pick evening primroses. 'It was worth risking quite a deal of punishment', she recalled, 'to see its moonlight colour and to smell its heavenly scent.'

She wrote later about how small a part gaiety played in her young life, about the clumsy, ugly dresses and boring walks around the grey, dirty streets. There was very little to satisfy her hunger for 'something pretty'. On the daily city walks as she tried to keep up with her mother who was striding ahead pushing her brothers in the pram, Connie could never resist stopping to inspect a flower, however small or insignificant, growing out of a wall or a crack in the pavement.

Once, as they marched briskly through some railway yards, Connie snatched up a little posy of wild marguerites and buddleia which she offered to her baby brother. Before he could take them, their mother grabbed the flowers and flung them away, shouting that they were dirty things and now they would have to rush home and wash their hands.

They could not afford a maid, but after they moved to the new house an old Derbyshire countrywoman was hired as a nurse and took the children for walks into the countryside. Walks suddenly became wonderful experiences, as they searched on the edge of town for all kinds of flowers that the nurse identified with their old names – eyebright, ladies' bedstraw, traveller's joy. One day they stopped to chat to a woman standing in her front garden. Connie loved to listen to tales of country life, of the wild flowers that grew in the hedgerows and cottage gardens filled with bright colours and scents. The woman picked a spray of lady's locket. 'I think this might be nice for a little girl,' she said, and gave it to Connie with a warm smile. For little Connie it seemed like a miracle. She never forgot this first proper bunch of flowers – picked and given, not snatched or stolen. The woman told her it was also called 'lady in the bath' and showed her how, when the two pink outer petals were gently pulled apart, the white inner petals looked like a delicate little figure.

The children spent long winter days in the nursery. Here they did their lessons and read all the books their father brought home for them. Sometimes they would sow wheat in saucers of damp moss and put them in a dark cupboard for ten days, then bring them out into the daylight to marvel at the slender green blades that grew on for several weeks like emerald hair.

All her life Connie adored the exciting rituals of Christmas. Nothing could spoil the magic of making Christmas decorations – the 'gewgaws', as she called them. The nursery curtains were drawn, the fire glowed, and the oil lamps cast a soft light on the table, littered with gaudy tissue paper and saucers of homemade paste. Their old nurse showed them how to make hoops hung with old-fashioned 'kissing bunches'. They cut ham-frills of coloured paper, 'arsenic-green, magenta pink and wash-bag blue'. Kneeling up on chairs with paste-smeared faces and fingers they turned the frills inside out, stuck the edges together and bound them round a hoop. Bags of coloured tarlatan – a sort of coarse muslin – were filled with 'unwholesome-looking candies, sugar bird-cages, pink and white sugar mice . . . everything gaudy and gay and deliciously tawdry'. But New Year celebrations brought a 'sting in the tail' with their mother dictating their resolutions, 'an unmistakable reminder that the past year had been none too good and we had to improve'. They had to promise to be more punctual and attentive, air their beds before breakfast, keep their shoulders back and learn their French verbs. 'We rebelled and all such resolutions went with the wind.' Connie could remember the details several decades later.

The nurse fired Connie's imagination with a story about a red damask rose, so dark as to be almost black and with a heavenly scent. She wove nostalgic stories around this legendary rose – about its lustre, its beauty, its velvet blackness and musky scent – stories that Connie often recalled as 'well calculated to intoxicate a child who found heady excitement in the few flowers that came her way'. The children used to search everywhere for this rose, bringing every red bloom they could find and asking: 'Is it this? Could it be this, or this?' But the nurse would turn up her nose and, with her familiar derisive sniff, reply: 'No, no, don't be so daft, don't I keep on telling yee it were black, well nigh black?'

The children accepted old wives' tales like this with enthralled credulity until, Connie recalled,

the day she broke our belief in her for always. She had a queer, possessive sort of jealousy and she looked at us not without a touch of spite . . . One Sunday evening, getting tired of her domination, we asked: 'Where's Mother?' She replied, 'Gone for a sojer [soldier]'. At this the smallest among us began to cry, whereupon she gave vent to her irritation in vehemently Derbyshire idiom with: 'And don't 'ee be a mardi-cadi.' My mother must have been a little surprised at the unusual warmth of our welcome on her return from evening service . . . Well, that finished it. Out of the window went the myth of the old velvet rose together with other yarns concerned with the wild flowers of field and hedgerow; what you might devour or what would cause you to curl up and die; or tales of what would overtake you if you showed any great spirit of independence.

But Connie did not forget the story and spent much of her life searching for the secret of the exotic black rose of her childhood. It was the first stirrings of an artistic sensibility in her, a desire for something that would fill her eyes with beauty and her heart with romance.

As she grew up, relations between mother and daughter became increasingly difficult. Connie, the only daughter, was her father's darling. She loved to receive his praise and encouragement. In her books her mother is always referred to as 'Authority'. Connie hated the diet of snubs and coldness which years later she remembered so well when writing her books; they remained as painful as the day they were delivered, their sting still sharp and fresh. But Connie was a tough little girl full of laughter and natural wickedness. Her father gave her his life-enhancing enthusiasms and his sense of humour and she responded with a yearning to please him. But for her mother she reserved only a rock-like obstinacy and a hard, polite face.

The tensions in Connie's own personality, her headstrong energy and her creative drive, were an amalgam of both parents: her occasional sharp tongue, eye for detail and flair for unearthing beautiful objects came from her mother while her sunny optimism, her determination and passion for education came from her father. There was also a darker element of tension inherited from Etty which lay dormant, waiting to spring on her in later life.

For three years the young headmaster with no more than night-school training enjoyed his job, gaining valuable experience in teaching and school administration. George would probably have remained happily enough in this good, comfortably paid position for the rest of his life had his achievements not come to the notice of an old acquaintance with whom he had shared an interest in photography.

William Abney was by then chief of the Department of Science at the Board of Education in London. He came from a wealthy Derbyshire family; his father was the local vicar, and in his youth William had mixed easily with working lads from the parish who were interested in self-improvement. He and his father had a passion for photography; the vicar was a close friend of the pioneer photographer William Fox-Talbot, and together they encouraged a group of printers and telegraphists from the Midland Railway Company to set up the Derby Photographic Society. At some point George Fletcher joined the Society; photography was a particular 'science enthusiasm', as Connie referred to it later, which he pursued all his life. With the advantages of wealth and family connections, William Abney had left Derby for a military career instructing science and telegraphy until he was appointed Inspector of Science Schools with the Department of Science and Art in Kensington in 1877. In thirty years of work in education, he strove to improve the teaching of science in schools, waging an uphill struggle against the entrenched conservatism of the teaching profession and the dominance of the Classics-based curriculum. He kept in touch with his hometown and his fellow members of the Photographic Society, and when he heard of George Fletcher's work at the Technical School he had no hesitation in appointing him Inspector for Science Teaching in the West Country. Thus in 1894 the Fletcher family were once again on the move, this time to Plymouth.

It was a liberation for eight-year-old Connie, an escape from the grime of the Midlands and a new revelation. She described 'the almost delirious happiness remembered to this day, that was mine when I was made free of the wild flowers of the West Country lands and fields. Picking mayblobs was a foretaste of heaven even if you did leave your shoes behind in the mud.' At last she and her brothers could range over the countryside exploring. They picked white violets and hart's-tongue ferns in the lanes and enjoyed the heady excitement of crushing strong-smelling wild garlic under foot. There were several grand houses locally with huge gardens lush with trees, shrubs and flowers, and she describes their own garden in Devon as 'bathed in sunshine and filled with flowers'.

Connie later complained that as a little girl she was never taught anything about gardening or botany. But, like her father, she was clearly adept at teaching herself. At the village school she endured endless tedious lessons, but during the holidays she was free to pick flowers, climb trees and eat fruit from the garden. 'How valuable it would have been to me all my life if some of that time spent over lesson books could have been used to learn about gardens and plants,' she wrote. Most of her 'Saturday pennies' were spent on seeds, at a penny a packet. But her early obsession with growing things often got her into trouble with 'Authority'.

The family could now afford a part-time gardener – Mr Fox. Connie followed him around closely observing him and asking interminable questions. On one occasion, having noticed how carefully Mr Fox guarded his own well-matured stack of stable manure, she decided to feed her Virginia stock seedlings with the same. She hid in a thick clump of elder bushes with a toy dustpan and brush waiting for 'calling time', when visitors came in horse and carriage up the drive: 'I felt sure I should be able to salvage treasure trove from the roadway if I was quick about it.' But as she made her dash into the road to collect her steaming treasure, she was seen by 'a particularly unbending Authority, and what she had to say to me was enough to make me inhibited against the use of manure for the rest of my life'.

'If only', Connie recalled decades later, 'my wise and understanding father had been at home . . . this horrible incident would have been turned into a wonderful lesson about plants and soils, and the comforting, cleansing processes of nature.' But practical gardening was not a suitable subject for a young girl. She would simply have find out for herself, and for the rest of her life that is what she would do.

*

After two years in Plymouth another brother, Donald, was born and George Fletcher gained further promotion, this time as Science Inspector for the whole of the Midland division. The family returned to the Midlands, but this time to a pleasant house in the prosperous Birmingham suburb of Moseley where a fourth brother, Gilbert, was born. But for Connie it was the end of her idyll, of running free in flowery lanes. The country-loving girl was now ten years old and ready for proper school. She was sent to King Edward's School, and later recalled with hatred the dreary lessons and teachers, the depressing drab colours in the schoolrooms and ugly uniform. Connie was not academic and she struggled with the work, trying hard to please her father.

Every Saturday afternoon Etty Fletcher sent the children to dancing class, where the girls were expected to pirouette about in accordion-pleated dresses while the boys were made to dance with the 'directress', a short, stout lady 'who looked ridiculous whatever she did'. Connie remembered being made to curtsey, while her reluctant brother Arnold would 'fling an arm across his thin little middle as he bowed in a sort of angry abandon'. They were expected to take the lady a bunch of violets, a much-begrudged offering bought from a flower shop nearby; 'I often think that after I had unwrapped, smelt the flowers and rewrapped them a dozen times, they must have looked part-worn by the time the directress had graciously accepted them.'

Connie and the two older boys were once sent to stay with their aunts and were told to find a suitable present. With only a penny a week pocket money, they went to the penny bazaar and found an enormous and floridly ornate pot-holder; 'all pink and yellow and tricked out in bits of gold – it was guaranteed to put any plant in the shade,' Connie recalled. Proudly they presented the monster to the aunts and for a long time it served to house a succession of plants 'totally inadequate in size for such a fortress of a container'. Even at this young age, Connie was becoming aware not just of flowers, but of the right choice of pots and vases in which to display them.

Their father always made life and learning fun. He had an innate genius for making the world seem wonderful; even a bleak, snow-bound winter day was a source of joy and investigation. Sent out-doors muffled up to their eyes in restrictive clothing, they would be quickly joined by their father who would rush excitedly from the fusty warmth of the breakfast room to romp with his children in the luminous softness. He showed them the fine tracery of frost that hung on twigs and seed-heads and explained about snow crystals and how they were formed. With George, there was always something fascinating to learn and understand. For little Connie and her brothers, 'His enthusiasm and goodness shone out and wove a golden thread in our lives.'

Whenever there was an excuse for an outing, such as the half-holidays given to celebrate the reliefs of Ladysmith and Mafeking in 1900, off they went on what Connie called 'a ploy'. George would take them out into the country where they could range the fields and hedgerows like gypsies, gathering blackberries, sloes or mushrooms, and nettles when the plants were young and tender. They spent the days exploring and learning: 'without killing ourselves, we sampled leaves and berries, and would have been enchanted on return to take our full share of the kitchen end of the business had we only been allowed.' Unfortunately for Connie, it was not done for a well brought up English schoolgirl to help in the kitchen or in the task of stocking the storeroom with jams, pickles and preserves or to brew the beer from their hard-won nettles. But 'you got praise for your trepidation in picking and sympathy for stings', and later could enjoy the mild sweet drink. The important business of preparing and cooking their gathered plants, however, which in later life would be so important to Connie, remained out of bounds.

Good food and where it came from was always a source of great interest to Connie. The growing of fruit and vegetables was to her as important as cooking them properly. She had read *The Wide, Wide World* by Susan Warner, a novel about a young American girl living in the 1840s who described the communal preserving that took place in the autumn, when the pig was killed, salted and smoked and all kinds of fruits and nuts were dried or bottled. 'How I envied her share in those periodic "bees",' Connie wrote 'and though I didn't understand all of what they were doing . . . I thought the whole thing sounded grand.' In her own *Garden Notebook*, written in her mid-fifties, she wrote about the pleasure that she derived from such feasts of the senses: 'It is nice to be old enough to say lovely flowers, sweet scents and delicious foods all in one breath like that, and without apology.' In her childhood it had been considered rather coarse and unbecoming, by her mother at least, to express appreciation of food, because it might seem greedy. 'In those days no one could have confessed to any taint of greediness and held his head high.' The curious contortions of social propriety were particularly hard for children to comprehend: Connie could not see why you could say grace for good food 'but not mention flowers', or why it was not seemly to praise food in conversation at table.

> Once at a party I remember so far forgetting myself in an outburst of enthusiasm as to say I loved strawberries, and the voice of an adult from the end of the table, raised so that no one failed to hear, brought blushes from my very toes: 'Constance, I hope you don't love food, my dear; that is not the way to speak of food.' Of course I hastily denied anything so gross, but alas! I lied. I loved strawberries quite a lot. Ripe and melting and smothered, as was the fashion of the day, with icing sugar and cream.

George Fletcher continued his meteoric rise from lowly beginnings. The final thrust into the respected higher levels of education administration came in the autumn of 1900, when he was promoted to the post of Chief Inspector of Technical Education in Ireland. The family were off to a new life, in Dublin.

TWO

Ireland

1900—1910

> If I am to tell truly my own garden story, I shall have to go a
> long way back to the old Irish garden of my childhood, which
> seems in retrospect always to have been bathed in sunshine and
> filled with flowers.

Connie was already fourteen when the Fletcher family moved to
Dublin. But Ireland was no idyll. On the contrary, these were in
many ways the bleakest and most difficult years of her life. She
often wrote of Irish memories in her books, and in keeping with
the many other veiled half-truths about her she never discouraged
the popular misconception among her admirers that she was Irish
or of Irish origin. Her naivety and unconventional approach to
everything she did were often put down to her 'Irishness'. Her
clear, slightly lilting speech was probably more Derbyshire
smoothed out by her mother's attempts to make her 'talk nicely';
but to many it evoked an Irish burr – more romantic than Midlands
England – which Connie was happy to retain. She never bothered
to develop a cut-glass accent in order to ingratiate herself with
upper-class clients. Indeed, more than one person would later note
how the gentle tones in Connie's speech required one to stop and
listen, even to admire the woman for her firm but quiet manner.
It is not surprising that Connie so often drew on her fifteen years
in Ireland, for they were critical in forming much of her thinking
and attitudes. It was here that she developed her own version of
her father's liberal and practical approach to education, here that
she began to acquire her very individual taste in flowers and design,
and here that she first learned to associate with people from very
different levels of society.

The Fletcher family went to live in Ireland only fourteen years
after Gladstone's Liberal government had failed to bring Home
Rule to the country. Since then a succession of Conservative admin-
istrations had tried to keep the lid on Irish terrorism, while seeking

to prevent the country from becoming divided between the Protestant Unionist North and Catholic Nationalist South. In the long run these efforts would fail; sectarian splits would surface just before the First World War and divide Ireland in 1921. However, there was also a middle strand of official thinking which tried to steer clear of politics and instead to find the solution to Ireland's problems by improving the economic and educational condition of her people. In particular, the Anglo-Irish Conservative MP Horace Plunkett, an agricultural reformer, advocated ambitious plans that aimed to foster the development of Irish agriculture through cooperative schemes similar to those he had seen in the United States.

Plunkett had earlier organized a system of cooperative creameries among the Irish peasantry. While technical education among the English working classes was inadequate, in Ireland it had been non-existent until Plunkett forced the government at Westminster to pass a Bill which led to the formation of the Irish Department of Agriculture and Technical Instruction. The question was, though, whether the Irish peasant would take instruction from English teachers. Typical of his time, Plunkett nevertheless sent to England for his staff. A brilliant young educationalist called Robert Blair was appointed Assistant Secretary in charge of the new Department's technical instruction, and Abney, now Sir William, again recommended his protégé George Fletcher as its Chief Inspector.

Many Irishmen, seeing well-paid new appointments going to the loathed oppressor, deeply resented the attentions and interference from England. George Fletcher, however, was one of the very few English administrators who came to be accepted. As a boy from the backstreets who had come up from small beginnings, he knew how to inspire them with the confidence to aim through education for things previously thought unattainable. Successive English administrators had pronounced the Irish peasantry ineducable; George Fletcher and Robert Blair were keen to prove this was not true. 'Education cannot succeed without the interest and goodwill of the country as a whole', Fletcher wrote in one of his reports, 'and the keen enthusiasm of the individual himself.' He visited all the local authorities in the country searching for instructors in carpentry and metalwork, often resorting to crash courses to bring them up to standard. 'It was not the perfect method,' he wrote, 'but the only one possible.' There would be technical schools to take boys from the potato patch into workshop or factory and domestic science schools for girls which, although they offered no more than basic training for domestic service, gave them a certificate which afforded a better chance of a good job and higher wages than their sisters sent straight to 'the Big House'.

Hampered with inadequate finance from the Department, Fletcher and his team had to find suitable buildings in which to hold classes. Fletcher's geniality and down-to-earth nature were received far more willingly than the typical English administrator with his aloof public-school manner. He persuaded town councils to adapt disused fever hospitals and jails and took advantage of waning Protestant congregations to grab unwanted chapels. In one town they adapted an old water tower and in another contrived to create a technical school inside a disused water tank.

Etty Fletcher's own ambitions for life in a Big House were almost, if not yet completely, realized. Their new home was Dawson Court in Blackrock, a smart suburb of Dublin. It was a rambling old house, full of charm and, more important to Connie, with a walled garden. Here she remembered the 'blue hedge', a ceanothus with its 'misty haze of blue, patterned with hundreds of orange butterflies and noisy with bees'; box-edged flowerbeds planted with traditional pinks that scented the summer air, a pink May tree whose arbour shape offered a lovely haven for playing 'house' and hiding from Authority, and a Siberian crab-apple that blossomed like a wedding bouquet. Connie remembered old-fashioned rose bushes which would later become a garden passion for her. In mild winters these roses often bloomed right up to Christmas Day and, wonder of wonders, there was the lovely old bridal rose 'Niphetos', 'so white, so rich-looking, so full of romance'.

But Connie was to have little time to enjoy this garden. As soon as they arrived in Ireland, she was sent off to Alexandra College for Girls in the Dublin suburb of Milltown. Connie was happy there; she could escape from her mother's chilling shadow and make new friends. The College was founded to provide formal education beyond the age of fourteen for girls of ability. Most of the lectures were given by professors of Trinity College, Dublin, although there was no possibility that the girls might gain a degree from the university itself. But for Connie, there was one marvellous and novel thing about the school: it had a garden.

The Principal, Miss Henrietta White, who was well known in horticultural circles, invited Frederick Moore, Curator of the Royal Botanic Gardens in Glasnevin, to give classes in horticulture. Connie was his most ardent and appreciative pupil. At last she was able to learn something she really cared about – the growing of flowers, their names and their characters. School visits to the Botanic Gardens and to private gardens around Dublin were a particular delight.

George Fletcher became a close friend of Miss White and her colleague Miss Mulvaney at the College's junior school. They shared a common interest in improving the skills and general education of the rural populations of Ireland. In 1906 Sir Horace Plunkett, Fletcher's boss at the Department, would revise its programme to include a course in cookery for girls and gardening for boys. It came to be known as 'Nature Knowledge' and was fairly rudimentary. In a letter to the journal *Irish Gardening* the Department claimed: 'When the girls have learned, in our domestic science economy classes, how to cook and preserve the vegetables and fruit the boys have learned to grow in these gardens, something will have been done towards improving the now wretched and mind-and-body depressing dietary of the bulk of our people and towards increasing the happiness of their lives at home.'

But for Connie, who would one day write a book extolling the need to know and understand how food is produced, 'Nature Knowledge' was not available. She was middle-class now, a pupil at the top-drawer girls' school. Gradually she was acquiring an ability to move easily between the social strata at a time when class differences still mattered. It would be a critical factor in Connie's success and popularity in later life.

A fellow student at the College remembered Connie as a lively girl with a bright humour. She was quite fashion-conscious and made her own clothes. She always loved hats and at this time sported the fashionable wide-brimmed, shallow-crowned picture hat which she bought with saved-up pocket money. Connie could never have been described as physically attractive – she was neither pretty like her mother, nor tall like her father – but her sharp-featured little face was often suffused with laughter, her eyes bubbling with fun, though her mouth was sometimes fixed in a stubborn, even fierce, line.

Although Connie was happier at Alexandra College than she had been at Birmingham, she was discouraged by her failure with her studies and painfully aware that she was a disappointment to her father, who believed so strongly in the value of a good education. She knew she had some sort of abilities, but what were they? And why did no one value them or find an outlet for them? Her mind was filled with a miscellany of knowledge from her father, with the mysteries of science and the natural world, and the pho-tography, painting, music and poetry that he loved so much. But she always feared criticism and was terrified of exams. Throughout her life she disliked all forms of competition.

It must have been particularly galling that her now five darling brothers were turning out to be both confident and clever: Arnold, Kenneth, Donald, Gilbert and even little Lynton who was born soon after they arrived in Ireland, seemed to be moving effortlessly through school and seemed destined for careers in science, medi-cine and administration. George Fletcher had enrolled his two youngest, Gilbert and Lynton, at the junior school at Alexandra College, despite its being a girls' school. Here the little boys were petted and indulged. Lynton recalled being sent to Miss Mulvaney for some boyish crime. Instead of punishment she took him off for a wonderful afternoon at Dublin Zoo.

Thinking that Connie might have artistic talents, George arranged for her to have drawing lessons. These, too, proved a failure. Her hands, which were very dextrous with the needle and when working with flowers, could not draw a line. She did, however, hold strong views on art, and when told to copy a sinuous frieze of convolvulus in the Art Nouveau style she retorted: 'I don't like flowers made to do that.' This incident, recalled years later in her book *Favourite Flowers*, meant that 'Father's artist *manqué* was in the dog-house.' Her father subscribed to *The Studio* magazine and Connie loved to look at its drawings and reproductions – garden sketches, water-colours of herbaceous borders, and flowers painted in delicate, bright colours. In particular she sought out Flemish and Dutch still-lifes: lavish cornucopias of glowing fruits and massed dis-plays of flowers with attendant butterflies and bees, all minutely and perfectly observed. In one issue of *The Studio* she found a reproduction of a highly stylized painting of King Richard II standing in a parterre filled with exquisite flowers with the red rose of Lancaster in his hand. Connie was entranced. Perhaps this was the mysterious red-black rose that her old nurse in Derby had told her about?

In June 1904, after Robert Blair had been appointed as the first Education Officer to the London County Council, George Fletcher took his place as Assistant Secretary in Ireland. He was now the boss of his own show. Popular and well liked both in Dublin and on his extensive travels around the country, he became known as 'Fletcher of the Department'. Connie recalled that when her brothers got into minor trouble with the police, as they often did, they were let go as soon as it was discovered who they were.

Renting property in Ireland at that time was relatively cheap, and with George's promotion the family could at last move to a proper Big House, a vast Dublin Georgian mansion in fashionable Pembroke Road with numerous bedrooms, several staircases and a staff of five (poorly paid) servants for Etty Fletcher to command. She was at last in heaven, and her ambition to become a leading Dublin hostess could be fulfilled. She blossomed into a lady with charming manners and a flair for collecting interesting people. Her parties were beautifully done, and always successful. What no one knew about was the unhappy tension that prevailed outside the drawing-room. George Fletcher, though naturally hospitable, was uncomfortable with Etty's lavish displays and worried about her extravagance. The children were always on show and made to recite, sing or play the violin. The two younger boys were invited into schoolfriends' homes in the free and easy Irish way, but would never invite them back home because their mother would make an occasion of it, embarrassing them with special food and best behaviour. The public display of attending church was a particular trial; as they progressed upwards, Etty had changed the family church to the more fashionable religious denominations: Presbyterian in Derby, Methodist in Plymouth, Congregationalist in Moseley, and now in Dublin the Church of Ireland.

Arnold and Donald, who were inseparable, organized their own escape from home to a hideout in the Wicklow hills, a semi-derelict cottage reached only by foot which they named 'Araby', after James Joyce's story of that name, written in 1904, in which a youth desperate to escape from his drab and restrictive world seeks an idealized Eden at the visiting bazaar. Every weekend the Fletcher boys fled on their bicycles into the hills to their 'wild garden'. Connie, who adored her brothers, tried to escape with them. She loved to roam in the open green highlands and study the myriad flowers that grew all around their little secret paradise.

But Authority was fierce with Connie and had ambitions for her only daughter to be groomed for fine ladyhood. Connie was in danger of being consigned to life in the domestic backwater. Fortunately, she discovered the pleasures of cooking and spent many happy hours in the kitchen acquiring from Mary the cook some of the skills and knowledge that would one day make her famous. It was here that she also learned from an early age that food and class were linked in several complex ways.

Connie loved to hide away in the kitchen with Mary as she prepared for one of Mrs Fletcher's 'At Home' days – dressy affairs with tatted doilies and tiered cake stands, smart hats and best behaviour. On the morning of one of these hallowed days, Connie recalled, the kitchen would be humming with activity, the fire roaring and the oven heating up. Everyone had their task and an exciting tension prevailed below stairs. Connie and her brothers hung around hoping for 'an imperfect piece or two' of cake or biscuit, while waiting, 'unnaturally clean and restrictingly dressed', to be called to the drawing-room to say how do you do. Connie would watch with fascination as the ladies, wearing immaculate white kid gloves, balanced cup and saucer in the air while conveying a 'tremulous cucumber sandwich from hand to mouth without fault'. For Etty Fletcher, such refinement and delicate behaviour were social perfection, but Connie could not be bothered with etiquette and its 'mincing ways'; she called it 'sugar-tong manners' – though she was aware of its importance at the time, both upstairs and down.

She once described a very grand parlour maid who 'wore her hair *en Pompadour* with a high teapot handle and a haughty cap with lace-frilled ends of greater length than other maids'. She would lift her tea cup 'quirking her little finger, taking only the smallest sips', and wielded her knife between thumb and forefinger like a pencil: 'She had a special brand of gentility all her own.' But generally it was in the kitchen that the children found a safe haven: 'Downstairs was where you found a proper sort of tea: steps of bread and butter, home-made jam spooned out of the jar, watercress, perchance shrimps, and seed cake to fill in the gaps. You might blow upon your boiling sweet tea or pour it, if you chose, from capacious cup into sensible saucer.' From her mother Connie learned the fine gradations of class difference. Table manners might seem easier in the kitchen but there were nevertheless rules there too: 'you would be wrong to assume they were lax. It was just that the gentility was of another brand.' Whatever Connie's views of genteel behaviour, her familiarity with its complex rules would prove essential in her future dealings with all levels of society, from royalty and the *haut monde* to shopgirls and gardeners.

As her mother climbed up the social strata to her mansion in Dublin, she had tried, in the classic Edwardian tradition, to train Connie in the homemaking skills necessary for her daughter to live as a lady. Although Etty would never countenance the idea of her studying horticulture, it became Connie's duty to 'do the flowers', the arrangements for the public rooms of the house and table decorations for dinner parties. Connie enjoyed this and began to play with some ideas of her own. Her efforts began to be noticed, even admired by family friends. Invited to dinner at the home of an eminent Dublin QC, Connie was asked if she would like to do the flowers for the table. She took small red tulips and, to everyone's surprise, turned back the petals and floated them in wide basins of water to make them look like water lilies – an unorthodox treatment of which her mother did not approve. Etty would not permit any innovation in her house and Connie recalled how she had to 'fill great epergnes [table centres] with ferns and roses and carnations and, thinking back, I realize that a large proportion of the "creations" may have had merit as barriers during family arguments, but as beautiful arrangements they can have had little or none; they were, I fear, just grotesque.'

During his tours of rural technical schools and societies George Fletcher had become deeply disturbed by the poor state of health he had found among young people and their large families. He decided to set up a course of lectures on simple hygiene and sanitation. Connie listened to her father's descriptions of the terrible poverty in other parts of Dublin and, hoping to please him, she asked if on her sixteenth birthday she could invite a Dublin slum family to tea. Etty was horrified at the idea but George readily agreed, and a family with five children was duly found and brought home. They were so filthy that they had to be bathed on arrival. The eldest boy indignantly refused to go near Connie but finally allowed Mary, the old cook, to wash him.

George suggested to Connie that if she was interested in the poor, she might find her vocation as a health lecturer. He knew that in England local authorities were already employing women health lecturers, who toured clubs and factories. Connie was desperate to make a decision about her future and, more important, to escape from home. Despite her dread of illness and distrust of doctors, she agreed. But the training would be tough, far tougher than she had realized. It meant another gruelling year at Alexandra College, studying hygiene and physiology, plus lessons in physics from George and lectures in sanitation given by the Professor of Public Health. This was followed by six months' training in district nursing at St Lawrence's Home for Jubilee Nurses and a summer course of instruction in food analysis at the Medical School. Connie always retained a keen interest in nutrition, but her only surviving written comment on this course was the stark word 'starvation' – the common cause of sickness, even death, in Ireland in the early 1900s.

In 1905 when Connie was nineteen, she was shipped off to London to take the full health lecturers' course instituted by the National Health Society. It was still quite unusual for someone of her background to do this kind of training and one can detect her father's pioneering spirit and determination behind the project. Despite her belief that she had little academic ability, Connie completed courses on bacteriology and on the 'Art of Lecturing' at King's College, a course in local government at the London School of Economics and one for sanitary inspectors at the Royal Sanitary Institute. She spent two years living in Hopkinson House, a dreary Victorian redbrick women's hostel in Vauxhall Bridge Road. It seems to have been a grey and lonely place for the young student from Ireland. Her one friend, and roommate, was an art student called Florence Standfast, who would later play an important role in Connie's life. Her only recollection of this period, written nearly fifty years later, evokes a picture of a young woman already thinking about how to decorate a party and seeing how it should *not* be done:

I remember so well going to market with a group of fellow students to buy the flowers for our club dance. We didn't have much money, but in those days flowers were cheap, and we could have bought a car-load of marguerites or other simple flowers. But of course, we had to have roses, and even of those, we got what seem now to have been a lot for our money. It was my first experience and I was intoxicated with excitement as we carried back armfuls of long-stemmed pink roses to the rather grim building which housed us. I came down to the dance in a flurry of excitement, expecting to see a bower of flowers, only to find in an enormous room isolated vases set about here and there – all the glory departed. That was my first lesson in how not to get effects on a shoe-string.

Connie's first job after qualifying was found through her father's former boss, Robert Blair. Now Sir Robert, he secured an appointment for her as an assistant lecturer for the London County Council, demonstrating first aid and home nursing. In January 1908 she applied to the Essex Education Committee for the post of Woman Health Lecturer in elementary schools. Whether her application was successful is not known, for Connie was suddenly recalled to Dublin. Her father had found much more important work for her in Ireland.

On a Christmas visit to her family in 1905 Connie had joined the exuberant crowds watching the pomp and pageantry surrounding the arrival of the new Viceroy of Ireland. The streets were thronged with crowds eager to see the Earl and Countess of Aberdeen returning to Dublin for a second term of office. With fanfares and numerous outriders, the ornate high-sprung carriage, with bewigged postilions and drawn by gleaming black horses, proceeded triumphantly from Kingstown Harbour to Dublin Castle where the viceregal party made its state entry. Lord Aberdeen's first term as Viceroy had been cut short by the fall of the Liberal government in 1886 when he was moved to Canada as Governor-General. But in their brief period in Ireland, Lady Aberdeen, or Ishbel as she was known to her intimates, had fallen in love with Ireland and all things Irish. She determined to help the people struggling to live with poverty and sickness. During their 'exile' in Canada, Lady Aberdeen had kept up her tireless philanthropic activity in the Irish cause, fund-raising and promoting Irish produce in America, Canada and England. She founded the Irish Industries Association, to promote a variety of traditional Irish arts and crafts, in particular lace-making and tweed-weaving.

The Department of Agriculture and Technical Instruction, now very effectively run by George Fletcher, had already played an active part in the revival and renewal of Irish crafts. So it was not surprising that almost before the grand formalities and welcoming festivities were over, Lady Aberdeen made Fletcher's acquaintance, and thus began a long and close friendship. George Fletcher was a man she could deal with: he had his own concerns and ideas for improving economic and health conditions in rural Ireland; he understood what needed to be done and how to go about it.

Despite their very different backgrounds, their aims and person-alities were similar; both had an affable manner masking a steely determination and a profound conviction in what they wished to achieve. George, being closer to the people with whom he worked, was more conciliatory, whereas Lady Aberdeen would aristocratically brush aside anything that impeded her plans. Con-sequently she made several enemies. She was also criticized by many members of the conservative Anglo-Irish society, who expected a Viceroy and his wife to put on lavish entertainments – much of it paid for by the Aberdeens, who were rich, but not that rich. Although they worked hard at the social circus of formal Castle functions, their real interest lay in what they could do for the Irish working people. It was well known that, despite taking care not to get involved in politics, the Aberdeens were in favour of Home Rule and hoped to be the last viceregal couple in Dublin. They were accused by some of being mean because they economized on state entertaining, preferring to spend money on welfare work. Their guest lists began to reflect their wider, more egalitarian interests, which caused endless carping within Dublin high society.

People complained that 'very little effort was made to uphold the dignity of the ceremonial at Dublin Castle'.

Connie's tough and rather colourless life as a student in London was occasionally enlivened by letters from home. Her father described the stimulus of working with the Viceroy's wife and her mother sent cuttings from the *Irish Times* so that Connie could keep up to date with the glittering life in Dublin. One of these reported a reception in the viceregal drawing-room at the Castle: 'Diamonds worn by the Marchioness Conyngham, Countess of Annesley, Lady Holmpatrick, and Lady Guinness' made the event a 'sparkling affair', with the ladies' coiffures reflecting 'every style of hairdressing for the last half century', some adorned with ostrich plumes 'with picturesque effect'. The 'perfume of lilies, gardenias and tuberoses' was almost overwhelming in the hot rooms – it was the sort of glamorous occasion that would one day be very familiar to Connie. Her interest might have been caught by a description of the bouquets, which were criticized for being both large and heavy; and as if that was not enough, they also soiled the ladies' evening gloves. But she was more likely to have approved of the ladies who had revived the fashion of carrying just a simple sheaf of lilies or a posy of three or four large blooms tied with silver ribbon or a chiffon scarf.

The endless round of Castle Season events continued, with parades, military displays, receptions and a state ball with nine hundred guests. The Season concluded with a party at which Lady Aberdeen organized an all-Irish programme. Not everyone appreciated these unconventional entertainments. Lady Alice Howard, daughter of the Earl of Wicklow, wrote in her journal: 'We all went to a party at the Castle; Irish music and an Irish play. All too horrid and vulgar for words.' Later at a dinner party she recalled the guests were 'a very common lot . . . there was hardly a soul we knew'.

Page Dickinson, son of the Dean of the Chapel Royal, wrote in his memoirs that with the installation of a Liberal Lord Lieutenant, 'social amenities were flung to the winds, and the rag tag and bobtail of Dublin went to Court'. People of breeding gave up going to the Castle and, he recalled, 'without being a snob, it was no pleasure and rather embarrassing to meet the lady at dinner who had measured you for your shirts the week before'. Dickinson might have been describing Etty Fletcher herself when he declared that now 'only the middle-class folk liked to attend, dressing up in feathers and trains, and strutting in rarely worn evening suits and swimming in a dashing social life entirely foreign to their upbringing, but congenial to their worldly ambitions'. Etty was extremely happy now that her worldly ambitions were fully realized. Her family had arrived, they had the entrée to the Viceregal Lodge, and her husband's close association with Her Excellency meant regular invitations and considerable standing in Dublin society. Lynton, her youngest child, remembered the equerries, splendid in helmet and spurs, sitting on their horses in the drive at 53 Pembroke Road. They were not allowed to dismount, so they waited for someone to come out and receive a letter or an invitation from the Vicereine, while all the neighbours watched.

George Fletcher worked closely with Lady Aberdeen on a number of projects, including an exhibition in the Home Industries section of the 1907 Dublin International Exhibition, which also featured displays by the Women's National Health Association of Ireland (WNHA), recently created by Lady Aberdeen to fight the appalling ravages of tuberculosis in Ireland, where the death rate was twice as high as from all the other infectious diseases combined. The aim of the exhibition was prevention through education. Lady Aberdeen invited Sir William Osler, Regius Professor of Medicine at Oxford, to give an inaugural lecture. He emphasized what was already known about tuberculosis: that it was not hereditary, but it was infectious and it proliferated particularly among people whose health and diet were poor and who lived in filthy, airless conditions. With weapons such as the segregation of the infected, plus good food, good housing and pure air, the battle against the disease could be won.

Response to the exhibition was so positive that Lady Aberdeen bought a horse-drawn caravan christened Eire to take it to the most remote and poorest parts of the country. The Eire was equipped with simple diagrams, pictures and literature, pathological exhibits, a slide projector and a gramophone to liven up proceedings with traditional music. Slogans were brightly painted on its sides:

Our enemies are Bad Air, Bad Food, Bad Drink and Dirt.
Our Friends are Pure Air, Pure Food, Pure Milk and
Cleanliness.

A voluntary team consisted of a medical lecturer who spoke Gaelic, a cookery teacher and demonstrator, plus a driver. But journeys on the Eire were very hard going and volunteers did not stay long. What was required was proper paid staff. Connie Fletcher, now fully trained and working in London, was summoned home to be the first full-time paid lecturer.

Connie had barely arrived back in Dublin in March 1909 when news arrived from Donegal that the Eire had been destroyed by fire and some of the team had suffered burns. Was it an accident or deliberate? No one was sure. Lady Aberdeen's war on consumption inevitably ran into trouble; some superstitious Irish country folk feared the caravan actually carried the infection, and she acquired the nickname of 'Lady Microbe'. Politicians and Irish administrators regarded her as a 'meddling suffragette', and the Irish ruling class saw her activities as a reproach for their own neglect of the poor, which they indeed were. Undeterred, a fundraising campaign for a new caravan was got under way. Meanwhile, Connie was put to work in Dublin lecturing and setting up mother-and-baby clinics.

Connie immediately fell under Her Excellency's spell. 'Nobody who has ever worked under the influence of Lady Aberdeen is ever likely to forget it, it marked you for life.' She always referred to her informally as 'Her Ex', and their relationship was profoundly important to her. Lady Aberdeen became a mother substitute, teacher and inspiration. Connie picked up many ideas and methods from Her Ex, one of which was promoting cheerfulness and taking people out of themselves; others were how to handle people from every kind of background, how to take criticism but ignore snubs, and how to teach using encouragement, praise and audience participation. She watched Lady Aberdeen fire up her workers and make them feel they were doing something of enormous importance and, when the work was done, reward them with fun and laughter – an approach that Connie would later adopt in her own working life. Lady Aberdeen's high principles, born of her strong Protestant faith, tended to pass over the heads of her Irish audience, whereas Connie's more down-to-earth style did not.

Connie and her growing group of co-workers were ruthlessly overworked; they travelled enormous distances in appalling conditions, doing gruellingly long lecture tours. She gave ninety-five lectures in one autumn season, speaking three times a day: to housewives in the morning, schoolchildren in the afternoon and to mixed groups in the evening. Lady Aberdeen was happiest surrounded by her eager girls. One contemporary recalled that she was quite unaware that her own amazing stamina for work was not matched by her loyal workforce: 'she would sit up till the small hours rather than leave anything unfinished, while her companions were too weary to think of anything but bed' – a description that could equally be applied to Connie in later life.

In January 1909 Lady Aberdeen started a little magazine called *Slainte*, Gaelic for 'health'. Issued monthly with pretty blue covers, nice large print and some simple illustrations, it cost one penny and was distributed everywhere they went. In the first issue Lady Aberdeen wrote: 'the great thing is to create an interest in health questions and to connect them with bright little illustrated lectures and other entertainments and to make people feel how much more they will get out of life if they keep their windows open and their houses clean, and if they will eat nourishing food and practise temperance and self-control in all things.' Unfortunately this sort of advice was of little use in a world where people lived in a squalor that was largely not of their making, and were unable to afford the food that would nourish them properly. It was the kind of statement that revealed Her Excellency knew nothing of the realities of Irish life for the majority of the population at that time.

In its second issue *Slainte* reported that 'Miss Constance Fletcher's services are in constant request', and in the April issue the secretary of the Association's Wexford branch wrote:

Miss Constance Fletcher is concluding a course of eight lectures every one of which has been closely followed by highly interested and attentive audiences. Her practical demonstrations, her lucid descriptions, and above all her charm of manner, have quite fascinated her audiences, and even the most unlearned can carry away something worth remembering. Her lectures on First Aid to the Injured, and on Home Nursing, have been specially popular, numbers of people remaining behind at her invitation to learn by actual practice upon volunteer patients.

The girls of Wexford had been so impressed with Connie's lively talks that they composed a song to show their appreciation and prove they had learned their lessons:

> *We'll bravely fight and conquer*
> *In this our native town.*
> *Our work is to endeavour*
> *To keep consumption down.*
> *And we shall win the day.*
> *Our hope — fresh air and sunshine —*
> *Will sweep the germs away.*

Slainte continued to report on Connie's activities, and in July that year it was announced that she had been promoted to chief lecturer for an infant mortality campaign run by Lady Aberdeen in Dublin. In August she spent her holidays visiting children's hospitals and clinics, and so rapidly had the movement grown that by October she was heading a team of four lecturers. Lady Aberdeen's brother, then First Lord of the Admiralty, offered two disused coastguard stations to be turned into TB isolation clinics, so that patients could be removed from their homes, thus preventing further infection. This was not altogether a popular move, but *Slainte* offered several ingenious, even absurd, ideas for isolating patients in their own home: constructing small sleeping huts in the garden, hanging 'balcony rooms' outside a window or even a tent against the window inside. Amazingly, some of these makeshift methods began to work: deaths from tuberculosis dropped by a thousand in the first two years of the Association's existence, and several thousand fewer cases were reported. The medical world was surprised but impressed, and Lady Aberdeen was elected President of the Royal Institute of Public Health, the first of several international honours she would receive. The Irish ruling class, however, was still of the view that the Lord Lieutenant and his lady should be decorative and hospitable figureheads and nothing more. The Nationalist movement had been pointing out for some time that the primary cause of both TB and infant mortality was poverty; it appeared that the Vicereine was even allying herself to revolutionaries.

Violet Asquith, daughter of the Prime Minister, who would have married Lady Aberdeen's beloved youngest son Archie had he not been killed in a car accident, was often at the Viceregal Lodge. She was the same age as Connie but from a totally different world, and they can have had little in common. Violet took a more disparaging view of life with Lady Aberdeen when she dutifully accompanied her to 'busy afternoons of cattle shows, industry centenaries – tubercular congresses etc'. Violet described a woman at one particularly 'frowstyish function' at Alexandra College, quite possibly Connie herself, giving a lecture on lodging-houses with 'Zola-esque detail about lice – vice – stench etc . . . At one point it became so lurid that the Reporters dropped their pencils and wrote no more – but sat in scarlet silence.'

As soon as the new caravan, suitably named the Phoenix, was fitted out, Connie and her team were off on long tours all over Ireland. From Belfast to Galway, Killarney, Cork and Wexford the colourful caravan, with its chintzy curtains at the windows and 'War on Consumption' painted in large letters on its sides, was slowly drawn by a sturdy horse along narrow country roads and remote, almost impassable, tracks. The message was simple and effective, if crude: wash more, open your windows and don't spit – a habit prevalent in both town and countryside.

The arrival of this small travelling show was a big event in outlying country towns and villages where there was little to break the monotony. Many walked huge distances over the mountains and through rough country to stand for two hours and listen to Connie's talks and later join in the music and dancing. Lantern slides, music and cookery demonstrations were novelties that the people enjoyed after listening to the lectures on hygiene, diet and health. WNHA health lecturers never wore uniform – it smacked of officialdom – so Connie wore her own pretty, fashionable outfits that always included a large, lavishly trimmed hat. It gave the people something to talk about, and hopefully they might even remember some of the advice they were given. Not everyone, though, appreciated these interfering do-gooders. One woman sitting outside a lecture was asked by another: 'And what are they talking about in there?' 'Sure,' replied the first woman, 'they're tellin' us to be clane . . . and ain't we clane as we can be?'

The work of 'Her Ex' and her small army was nevertheless regarded by many as a success. 'If you re-visited some village in the wilds of Donegal or Connemara, that you knew a few years ago, you would probably notice changes,' Mary Fogarty wrote in her article 'Influence on Home Life' in an issue of the *Irish Educational Review* in 1910:

Houses and cabins are cleaner and better kept, windows are made to open, the manure heap is less evident to the eyes and nose, the porridge pot disputes the monopoly of the hob with the little black 'taypot', and the miller has a tale to tell of busier meal bills. If you comment on those changes you will probably learn that the health caravan has passed that way and the doctor 'that had the Irish' and the lady that had the wonderful way with the cooking, had told of what's come of keeping out the fresh air and letting in the pig and poultry, of having the manure heap by the front door, and giving the children tea and white bread instead of oatmeal and milk.

Perhaps the oddest part of Connie's experiences on these peregrinations was the contrast between her days spent travelling and meeting simple working Irish people, and the nights when, by prior arrangement with Lady Aberdeen, she slept in the grand homes of the local landowners – some of whom, she later wrote, were like fossils from a past age where 'manners and fashions had a pleasant way of lingering almost a century behind the times and formalities of an earlier era were retained'. In one particularly remote place, she remembered, the elderly mistress of the house dined in formal Victorian attire and addressed her husband as 'honoured sir', to which he returned 'dear madam'. Connie was shy and immature then; dining and sleeping in these bizarre old houses must have been quite an ordeal. But her wary eye for the social niceties was sometimes eased by her growing interest in flowers and gardening. She began observing flower arrangements and noting anything unusual or particularly memorable. One of her hostesses was a fierce amateur botanist who ruled her garden 'by remote control', but warmed to Connie when she discovered her interest in flowers. Connie recalled that the drawing-room was decorated with a 'particularly interesting flower table'. It was glass-topped and covered with an array of crystal vases in various shapes and forms, 'like a sort of altar of flowers'. Each vase held a single bloom or bouquet of something exotic, new or uncommon. The effect, Connie wrote later, 'was charming – a jewel of interest. As a decoration it lacked coherence, but it made a rich splash of colour in the room.' For Connie it was an early lesson in the value of concentrating plant material together and in the place flowers might hold in a decorative scheme.

She stayed in a house in Tipperary where 'my eyes were ravished by an arrangement of Iceland poppies in delicate glass specimen vases, set on a narrow shelf surmounting the dado; they encircled the whole room, a living garland of gold.' In another mansion she found the dining-table decorated from end to end with little mossed baskets of scented wild violets brought in by the children and their governess. And in another of those remote and extraordinary noble Irish houses she found an enormous floor vase filled with beautifully scented flowers of the giant decorative seakale, *Crambe cordifolia*. The effect was spoiled for her because the flowers were 'in a huge trumpet vase, reaching above my head, and at the base of it was all too clearly revealed the inevitable green sediment which no housemaid could reach and remove'. However, the idea of using such an unusual plant stayed with her and kale was to become one of her favourite decorative plants.

Connie was becoming adept at conducting herself in polite society and was learning how to charm people from different generations and milieux. Her real sympathies, though, were with the country people who grew their own barely adequate food and still took pleasure in a few flowers cultivated in their tiny gardens and 'wretched cottages'. While city dwellers looked down on the 'ignorant peasant' who never opened his cottage window, Connie saw lovingly nurtured flowers cramming with greedy tendrils against the pane seeking the light and felt that in their circumstances she would have done the same. But it could not be denied that in the confined space of a one-roomed cottage the air quickly became stagnant, and with some reluctance, in her role of health lecturer, Connie had to urge cottagers to remove their flowers, open their window and let in the light and air.

Most of the Irish gentry whose houses Connie had explored during her tours in the Phoenix had hardly emerged from the 'days of draped fire-places, bobble fringe and Eastern cosy corners, not to mention satin table centres over which loomed barricades of flowers'. She described how in one house long shoots of ivy growing in the garden were allowed to come through the window and trail around sofas and rustic picture frames, even trained over a 'neat arch inside, where [the] fresh green foliage softened the harsh angularities of the builder and architect'. It was a curious contrast to the sealed cottage windows crammed with imprisoned flowers; here the ivy smothered any redeeming features the room might have had.

Working for 'Her Ex' was tough and demanding but it was also stimulating, and Connie had enjoyed making new friends. Now twenty-four years old, fully trained and employed in a useful and respected occupation, she could feel that she had found her place in the world, won the respect of her father and, despite still living at home under her parents' protection, gained some degree of independence.

THREE

The Mine Manager's Wife

1910–1916

On a particularly bright and breezy day in April 1910 the Phoenix rumbled into the small mining town of Castlecomer in County Kilkenny. Connie leaped out of the caravan and put on her best hat decorated with wood anemones that she had picked that morning. She looked around her at the gloomy pitheads and the tired soot-lined faces that peered curiously from the doorways of cramped-looking cottages. She smiled and waved back cheerily, as she always did, despite feeling exhausted from long weeks on the road. Everywhere she went Connie's charm and good humour broke down reserve and suspicion, and within a few hours she was treated like a visiting celebrity. Country people remembered the personable, lively young woman dressed in elegant clothes who came to talk to them and entertain them. Despite her claims of shyness, her natural gaiety and youthfulness were often noted and always appreciated.

The Phoenix had been touring since January, starting in Armagh in the north and making a slow progress down the east coast to Drogheda, then inland to the countryside around Tullamore, Portlaoise and Kilkenny. Connie and her team planned to stop at Castlecomer for two weeks, to give lectures and first-aid and cookery demonstrations to the mining community that stretched around the Coolbawn hills. Lady Aberdeen had arranged for Connie to stay in the grand Victorian home of Captain 'Dick' Prior-Wandesforde whose family had arrived as gentlemen farmers from Yorkshire three hundred years earlier. They now owned the vast Leinster coalfields centred on Castlecomer and had amassed a substantial fortune.

Captain Prior-Wandesforde was a fairly typical landowner. Most of the miners thought of him as the lord and master; stern and hard in determining salaries and conditions, he boasted of never having yielded to pressure or to strikes. However, compared to many parts of Ireland this was a thriving community and he took an unusual interest in the welfare of his miners and the tenants on his estate. He had made improvements to the mine workings, including overhead ropeways to transport the high-quality anthracite from the pits. He had also built a number of houses for his employees, established a school for the miners' children, a basket-making workshop for the women and the elderly, an agricultural bank and a colliery Co-operative Society. And, like several of the more liberal-minded Anglo-Irish landowners, he invited Lady Aberdeen to send the Phoenix to address the villagers, the children in the colliery school and his men at the mines.

As Connie walked around introducing herself and getting to know the town and its inhabitants, she noticed a pretty little girl of about five or six trotting along with her. The child told Connie her name was Joan and that her father was the mine manager. Children often attached themselves to Connie – her easy charm and attractive clothes drew an appreciative little following that would scamper around her, demanding to see inside the Phoenix and to pet the horse. Joan was in the colliery school classroom when Connie talked to the children and set them an essay on health. In the evening, when the miners attended her lecture on first aid, Joan's father introduced himself. His name was James Heppell Marr, a middle-aged widower born in Newcastle-upon-Tyne, where he had qualified as a geologist and mine manager and worked for several years in the Durham coalfields before moving to Ireland. Connie's first impressions of him are not known, but the mine manager was clearly taken with her and he and his daughter invited Connie for tea.

After she left Castlecomer, Connie wrote a very favourable account of her two weeks, reporting that the miners had been keen students: 'Their bandaging is excellent, and I am indebted to them for the first practical experience of a pit stretcher. They intend forming a First Aid Corps, and I should like to take this opportunity of wishing them every success, and also of expressing my thanks to those whose kindness and help made the fortnight a delightful one.'

Who actually made that fortnight so delightful? The miners and their families who treated her like a celebrity, the Prior-Wandesfordes who offered her comfort and hospitality in their opulent home as though she were their equal, the adoring friendship of a motherless little girl or the flattering attentions of her father the mine manager?

Marr, it soon became clear, had fallen in love with her. He told a friend he could not get Connie out of his mind, he was fascinated by her, 'she was so gay and wore large hats with such an "air"'. He pursued her with letters and protestations of admiration and affection as she travelled on in the Phoenix, through Tipperary, Fermoy, Waterford and finally home to Dublin in July, where he visited her, bringing Joan with him to smooth the way. He met Etty and George Fletcher and her brothers, none of whom were at all impressed by this 'rough diamond' from the North East. Etty, though she no longer wielded control over her daughter, had nurtured ambitions for Connie to marry someone of good family and had been furious when she had earlier refused to marry a titled admirer. George, now full of respect for his daughter's considerable achievements and her position as Lady Aberdeen's favourite protégée, was unable to understand what appeal an uneducated mine manager could offer. He had hoped she would choose one of the bright young men working in his Department. Connie's brothers were simply bemused. But to everyone's astonishment Connie Fletcher agreed to marry James Heppell Marr.

Why did Connie choose to give up her promising career in health education? Why did she abandon her relationship with Lady Aberdeen, who must have been equally baffled by her protégée's sudden decision to marry? Did she talk to Connie and try to dissuade her? Connie was now at least partially free of her mother's authority, if not of the cold shadow of her disapproval. Perhaps she was excited by Marr's attentions and the allure of making her own home and garden with a nice little girl to care for. Was this her escape from the family to her own Araby? Many years later Connie told a friend that she had married to escape her mother, but to another she explained she had been afraid of being left on the shelf.

Whatever her reasons, on 10 November 1910, at the altar of St Philip and St James in Booterstown Connie said 'I do' – barely seven months after she and her bridegroom had met. Lord and Lady Aberdeen 'graciously' signed the register as principal witnesses. Joan was bridesmaid and Connie's brother Gilbert was page. He remembered his brothers Arnold and Donald bought a fake ink-spot from a joke shop and stuck it on Connie's wedding dress just before she was due to dress. Connie's outburst of fury was so uncharacteristic that the family were quite shaken. Perhaps she knew she was making a terrible mistake, that the ink-spot had been no joke. Amongst all the many weddings that Connie later decorated with flowers and subsequently wrote about she never once referred to her own. Her wedding flowers were never described.

Everything about James Marr was different. They had nothing in common. Whereas Connie was warm and expansive, he was dour and taciturn and had no interest in things of beauty. Was she flattered to have aroused so much passion in this strong, silent man? If she was, she quickly regretted it. As a trained health lecturer, Connie must have known the facts of life. Compared to most rigidly moral Edwardian households, her own family were fairly liberal and well read and it is unlikely she could have claimed either ignorance or surprise. It is possible that Marr was a cold, inept lover who killed off any youthful ardour that Connie might have had. The result was sexual rejection of her husband, which left him humiliated and hurt. At first he was angry, later violent. Connie's brothers recalled his temper on visits; Arnold felt that both Connie and Joan were afraid of him. But Connie could not run home to her mother, nor admit failure to her father nor appeal to Lady Aberdeen, who was not sympathetic. Her views on marriage and working women were 'Do your duty to both husband and work.' It is likely that 'Her Ex' had expected Connie to carry on her important work in the coalmining settlements around Kilkenny.

Many loveless marriages had to be endured at this time, and it is clear that Connie had not married for love. But it was not just relations with her husband that were a disappointment. On her first visit to Castlecomer Connie had been received like a celebrity. She had been admired by everyone, from the lord and lady of the manor down to the barefoot village urchins, gruff miners and timid young mothers with babies. She had probably seen herself returning as a leading figure in the town, but it proved a very different matter when she came to live there with no other social position than that of the mine manager's wife. She had stepped into an unpopular role; she could look down on the villagers now, and they would no longer either respect her or confide their troubles to her.

From her new home Connie could hear the mine buzzer go in the morning, at lunchtime and again in the evening. Occasionally it sounded 'out of turn', which signified an accident. With her first-aid training she was sometimes called to treat someone's injuries, though there were no serious accidents while she was there. Day and night could be heard the distant but constant noise of machinery, the screeching of pit wheels as they hauled the great rope round and round carrying the coal up to the surface, with the breaker, the washer and the screens all keeping time as they graded the coal for market. All day she could hear the rattle of the donkeys as they made their way from the pits to the yard with their wagons loaded with coal.

At first Connie tried to continue Lady Aberdeen's good work by visiting the miners' homes to talk to the families about hygiene, food and health. But the miners and their families had their pride, Connie's visits were not regarded as neighbourly and she was treated with suspicion. She saw families of ten or more crammed into the small houses. Life was very tough for the miners and their families; pay and housing conditions were poor, there was no union then, and the miners received no coal for heating their homes. Instead they used 'culm', which was coal dust mixed with yellow clay and lime, to make homemade 'bombs' to burn in their fires. There were no washing facilities at the pitheads, so the miners had to walk home in their wet, dirty clothes, which were then given to the women to wash. They would be hung round the fire overnight in an effort to get them dry for the next day, when the men would take them into the yard and bang them against the gable end of the house to knock the stiffness out of them before heading back up the road to the pit. There were no lavatories, so they used the 'gobbin road', a disused mine road where rats flourished and ran down into the mines to attack the 'piece-boxes', the miners' tin lunch boxes.

As for the mine owners, Connie's social position had changed there too. She was no longer the Vicereine's representative, and though the Prior-Wandesfordes did their best to be kind to her the fact remained that Marr was an employee and not of the same social class. They could not imagine how he had persuaded such a girl to marry him. The family spent much of their time improving their estates in the landscape style, adding two artificial lakes for fishing and boating and planting woodland trees – one for the birth of each of their children (one of the pits was named Vera after the eldest child). The main social activities were hunting, shooting and fishing, and though Connie loved to walk in the gardens she had no interest in country sports. Invitations to Castlecomer House were rare.

Feeling increasingly confused and isolated, Connie began to think of herself as a failure. Stoical and proud, she did the only thing she would always do in adversity: she retreated into the garden. 'I was singularly unequipped,' she wrote, 'for I lived in a very remote place many miles from village, town, station or shop. If I wanted flowers or fruit or vegetables I had to grow them' – a challenge she took up with all the enthusiasm she could muster.

She learned about gardening from catalogues sent to her by the Royal Horticultural Society, in which she read descriptions of plants, their characteristics and how to cultivate them. In those days such catalogues had no photographs; Connie recalled, 'I had a fixed idea that a viburnum would be like the snowball-tree, and could not visualize the wax-like scented blooms of *Viburnum carlesii*.'

Hers was not, however, the sedate, orderly old garden of her dreams; instead Connie was faced with a garden that had been neglected for years and was filled with a tangle of prolific weeds and old, unidentifiable plants and shrubs. She set about making her own first garden with only the help of 'a poor, delicate handyman': 'He carted water for the house, groomed a horse, carried in turf for fires, undertook dozens of chores, and, when he thought about it, did a little gardening. He had no knowledge or experience beyond growing the few cabbages and potatoes on which his large and ever-increasing family seemed to subsist.'

Her first act, in a spasm of house-proud enthusiasm, was to tear away a mass of weeds just below the drawing-room window, where she found to her delight great clumps of iris. 'The word "iris"', she wrote, 'in those days meant only one thing to me – the German flag iris – and I had a vision of a sea of pale mauves and purples lying below the windows in May and June. The untidy rushy leaves might have warned me, but I knew too little for them to convey anything.' When May came the flowers were a dirty brownish-white, inconspicuous and evil-smelling, and in a fury of disappointment she dug them all up and threw them on the rubbish heap. The following winter she saw in the house of a neighbour an old copper jug filled with brown leaves and brilliant orange seed-heads. She asked how she could grow these delightful seed-heads for winter. 'But your garden used to be full of them,' her neighbour said. 'My plants came from there.' And Connie discovered she had thrown away Gladwin irises, or *Iris foetidissima*.

Always quick to criticize her own actions, she did not spare her predecessor, Alice Marr, for planting the irises so conspicuously under the drawing-room window. 'I might have had a fine border of them for cutting in an out of the way place where the insignificance of the flowers would have been unimportant and I should have enjoyed using the seed-heads for winter decoration.' This was the first time that Connie addressed her lifelong conflict between growing flowers for cutting and cultivating them so as to create a beautiful effect in her garden. Unlike Gertrude Jeykll or the Irish gardener and writer William Robinson, both of whose ideas she admired and copied, Connie was less concerned with using her floral palette to create beauty and harmony in the garden when something more exciting could be achieved in a container indoors. If a plant like the Gladwin iris had ugly leaves or insignificant flowers or flopped untidily or clashed with its neighbours, Connie did not mind, so long as something about the plant – its seed-heads, glossy foliage or striking form – excited her artistry.

Connie was now learning fast, and enjoying discovering by trial and error how to produce structure, line and colour in her garden. Every day she escaped the dismal house and, with occasional help from the 'delicate' handyman, dug cartloads of stones from the stream bed to make a path to run under a pergola. Along its edges she set low-growing plants such as cerastium, aubrietia, alyssum and pink and blue forget-me-nots which thrived in the cool, deep root-run under the stones. The plants quickly seeded themselves in all the crevices so that her path became a sheet of blue and soft pinks. 'This, of course,' she recalled, 'is not what a path should be, since it is an essentially functional thing, and walking on this one was apt to be rather disconnected; all the same it was a lovely sight.' It was here that she first began to understand what gardening could mean in one's life, particularly the excitement of seeing plants 'luxuriating in that kindly climate . . . where rare things flourish, common ones ramp, and all the personality of a plant shines out'.

When she could drag herself away from her new garden, Connie found she also had the freedom of the kitchen to explore. She had a couple of local girls as servants, neither of whom could cook, so Connie began experimenting with homegrown vegetables and baking her own bread. Vera Prior-Wandesforde, then a schoolgirl, later remembered how impressed her family were by 'Mrs Marr's dashing housekeeping and experimental food'. Her husband's friends, however, were less keen: the estate land agent, another 'rough diamond', growled that he 'couldn't stand those sort of kickshaws', and there was much mockery locally of the strange domestic activities of the mine manager's wife. Connie became increasingly depressed and isolated. When her brothers visited they were furious with the way Marr shouted at her, and were scared of his quick temper.

Connie's closest companion was a book given to her as a wedding present and written over a decade earlier by Mrs C.W. Earle, an independent-minded woman with a dull husband and three sons. She used her shrewd, disillusioned and wide-ranging mind to escape a stultifying domestic life by writing a bestseller. *Pot Pourri from a Surrey Garden* was a jumble of personal opinions and advice on gardening, cookery, childcare, interior design, flower arranging and women's domestic and social responsibilities. Mrs Earle had possessed a remarkable library of gardening books, from the sixteenth- and seventeenth-century antiquarian herbals of John Gerard and John Parkinson to books by her contemporaries such as Canon Ellacombe's *In a Gloucestershire Garden* and Alphonse Karr's *The Garden That I Love*. Captain Earle timorously urged his wife not to publish her book. When he received his presentation copy in 1898 and had had time to read it, he decided that after all it did not disgrace him – then mounted his bicycle and rode off to meet his death in a road accident.

Mrs Earle, a widow at sixty, continued with her new career as a writer and her books achieved phenomenal success. *Pot Pourri* went into eighteen editions and the sequels were equally well received. She spoke to a generation of frustrated women, showing them how to make the best of their lot. The book was an inspiration to Connie and offered her a whole new world of gardening instruction, opinion and advice: 'It became a sort of

Bible to me.' It had a lasting effect on her ideas and her writing, and contained reflections of several of her own interests and views on both gardening and design, expressed later in her books. Some of the ideas that later made her famous may well have started with Mrs Earle. There is mention of an all-white dinner table, a suggestion for introducing a flower table 'which does flowers or plants much more justice than dotting them about the room'; plus unusual suggestions for decorations using seed-heads of honesty and large dishes of brightly coloured gourds to brighten a winter room. Mrs Earle also recommended growing and cooking unusual vegetables such as salsify, celeriac and cardoons, which she prepared herself with a 'foreign recipe' because 'Cook said she didn't know how to cook them.' Although Mrs Earle advocated growing aspidistras and India-rubber plants, both of which Connie hated, it is easy to imagine her trying the idea of floating sweet-smelling geranium leaves in a saucerful of water.

Fired with enthusiasm, Connie began sending off orders for gardening and cookery books and vegetable seeds and waited impatiently for their arrival. In reading, planting and experimenting she found a way to escape from her unhappy marriage and her loneliness. Marr was no doubt pleased to see his wife more settled, but Joan later said that she retained no happy memories of these years. Connie was concerned about how to relate to her stepdaughter, and once again turned to her 'Bible' for advice. She underlined several passages in the chapter on how to bring up a daughter. Mrs Earle's views on the thorny subject of education for women – always central to Connie's interests – were strangely inconsistent. She suggested that the kind of education that Connie's father had striven to provide was not necessarily the best. She held that a girl with a real vocation for a career might be given the same facilities to train for it as a man. 'But', she warned, 'the vote so ardently campaigned for would prove no short cut to feminine equality and prosperity'; nor would a degree, should a girl be fortunate enough to gain one, lead automatically to a good job;

and anyway, it was almost impossible for a woman to keep on with her profession after marriage.

Indeed, in Mrs Earle's view, a professional career was not much use if marriage was planned. She cited. *How to Be Happy Though Married*, written by 'a graduate in the University of Matrimony' in 1889, which claimed that the one attribute the 'lottery of marriage' required was adaptability:

> It is far better for a woman to be strong, healthy, intelligent, observant, and, above all, adaptable to the changes and chances of this mortal life, than that she should be well educated. Intelligence is no doubt inborn, a gift that belongs to no class; bad health may injure it, but no higher education will ever give it to those who are without it, nor will it ever make what I consider the ideal woman.

'The longer I live,' she continued, warming to her subject, 'the more I believe that a woman's education, if she has not to learn some special trade, should be awakening and yet superficial, teaching her to stand alone and yet not destroying her adaptability for a woman's highest vocation, if she can get it – which is, of course, marriage and motherhood.' And woe betide the disillusioned wife who did not try to make the best of it: 'For a woman to fail to make and keep a happy home is to be a greater failure, in a true sense, than to have failed to catch a husband.' This and another of her homilies must have struck a painful chord in Connie: 'No woman has a right to eat a man's food, dress with his money, enjoy his luxuries to the full, and then not in every way try to please him.'

Lady Aberdeen gave Connie a diary for the year 1912 with 'Constance' embossed in gold on its red Moroccan cover and with an inscription: 'Dedicated to the use of Constance Marr, in the hope that she may have much happiness and much blessing and much helpful service to record.' Perhaps she expected Connie to resume her work in Castlecomer. The diary remained bleakly empty; not even an entry recording the birth of her son Anthony on 23 March that year – the 'blessing' that Lady Aberdeen had been referring to. At first it hardly seemed much of a blessing to Connie. The labour was agonizing, long and frightening. She struggled on the same bed in which Joan's mother had died in childbirth and, after she had recovered, she was determined never to go through it again.

A baby improves relations with everyone – at least for a while. Lord and Lady Aberdeen stood as godparents and even after they had left Ireland remained in close contact with Anthony. James Marr adored his son – a consolation perhaps for the lack of love from his wife. George Fletcher was an equally proud and devoted grandfather and even Joan seemed happier with a baby brother to cosset and play with. Connie, though not a natural mother, did her best. A photo from this time shows her looking tired, thin and dispirited.

Life, however, had to go on. Every day Connie would walk out into the countryside pushing baby Anthony in a beautiful, elaborately woven wicker pram made in the Arts and Crafts basket-making workshop established in Kilkenny town by Captain Prior-Wandesforde and his 'progressive' Anglo-Irish neighbour Lady Desart. She also visited the Arts and Crafts model village built by Lady Desart for her factory workers. It was Connie's first real introduction to interior design, and here she discovered the idea of a unified design style. The Arts and Crafts movement, which rejected modernity and industry, had been founded by the socialist William Morris in an attempt to reclaim the pre-industrial spirit of medieval English society. Utopian in theory, Morris's intentions were to create affordable, handcrafted goods that reflected the workers' creativity and individuality, qualities not found in industrially produced goods. Ironically, in the end, high manufacturing costs made the objects too expensive for many to purchase. In her books Connie cited the views of both her mother and Mrs Earle on the Arts and Crafts style. Etty, who had natural good taste and

loved fine things, especially Georgian furniture which she collected, disliked the fussy detail. Mrs Earle's views were more
favourable:

> The first time I went to Mr Morris's old shop in Queen's
> Square was a revelation. It had the effect of a sudden opening
> of a window in a dark room. All was revealed — the beauty of
> simplicity, the usefulness of form, the fascination of design, and
> the charm of delicate colour. Added to this came the appreci-
> ation of things that had gone before, and which in my time had
> been hidden away.

Years later, when Connie herself visited the William Morris
gallery in Walthamstow, she wrote that she was unable to
understand Mrs Earle's sense of 'revelation'. She particularly
disliked the objets d'art so loved by the Arts and Crafts movement.
Whenever her mother received gifts of fashionable bowls and vases
of this kind, they were hastily rewrapped in their tissue paper and,
Connie wrote, 'I remember the light of disapproval in her eyes.'
Her mother could not reconcile these 'tortured objects' with the
fine traditional furnishings that graced her own rooms. Unusually,
mother and daughter even agreed that the arsenic green and fierce
magenta wallpaper of this period was over-busy and that 'nothing
will go against it'. But her father was enormously influenced
by the movement and for her twenty-seventh birthday gave Connie
a copy of *The Man of Sorrows* by Elbert Hubbard. An American
writer, publisher and philosopher, Hubbard was inspired by
William Morris to found the Roycroft Arts and Crafts movement
in New York. Whatever Etty Fletcher and Connie felt about the
latest mode in interiors, other, more enlightened Dubliners were
embracing the change. 'I remember', Connie wrote, 'artistic friends
of my parents who chose pale cream distempered walls and dark
brown paint with lots of blue and white plates and reproductions
of pre-Raphaelite pictures on the walls.'

*

For both Connie and James Heppell Marr the outbreak of war in August 1914 was the opportunity for release. There was no conscription then but Marr immediately volunteered, along with Connie's brothers Arnold and Donald, and in March 1915 he was given a commission as captain in the Royal Irish Fusiliers. Soon afterwards Connie abandoned her isolated life in Castlecomer and with her son and stepdaughter returned to Dublin, where Lady Aberdeen's magnetic influence quickly swept both Connie and her father back into her orbit. There was then no Red Cross in Ireland so Lady Aberdeen naturally established herself as president of a new branch in Dublin, and convened a meeting attended by representatives of all the voluntary societies and medical associations. She explained to everyone present that George Fletcher, head of the Department of Technical Instruction, was now undertaking to organize classes in first aid and ambulance work. In a letter to Lady Aberdeen, Fletcher later recalled 'how you pressed a somewhat unwilling Department into service, and how in spite of lions in the path you were the cause of our training nearly ten thousand VADs', as the members of the Voluntary Aid Detachments were called. Connie was appointed Honorary Secretary for the City of Dublin branch of the British Red Cross Society (BRCS) and Assistant County Director of the joint Voluntary Aid Detachment selection board, with an office in the Castle where the state apartments were converted into a Red Cross hospital. She and her team collected and distributed tons of clothing and food, and organized clubs for soldiers' wives and work-rooms for unemployed women. They continued to set up children's playgrounds, mother-and-baby clinics and pasteurized milk depots – for, as Lady Aberdeen wrote in *Slainte*, in time of war there was an even greater need to save the country's babies.

Etty and George had moved from the Big House out to Shankhill on the outskirts of Dublin, so Connie and the children lived in a small flat in Leeson Street which she quickly made pretty and homely. All day was spent in arduous work: lecturing, fundraising, planning subscription concerts and dances. At night she was responsible for a canteen at the National Shell Factory. Everyone who had contact with Connie in the early years of the war remembered her as a wonderful organizer, always inspiring, elegant and gay. 'I think we all had a bit of a crush on her,' recalled Eva Hackett, who trained under Connie as a young VAD. This period marked a radical change in Connie's life: she no longer lived under the protection of either parents or husband; she was independent, earning her own salary, and she had become a team leader with responsibilities, no longer merely an acolyte of Lady Aberdeen. This was particularly significant because, suddenly, the Aberdeens were given their marching orders. The Prime Minister Mr Asquith decided that nine years as Viceroy was long enough and it was time for them to go. The King handed them a consolatory marquisate, and they set out on a two-year fund-raising tour of America.

It was a terrible blow. But although there were protests from the viceregal couple and their many friends and supporters, Lady Aberdeen had made too many enemies in high places, so there was also considerable jubilation. Nonetheless, her influence and legacy remained for years after their departure. She retained a private apartment at the headquarters of the WNHA, which kept active, and she left behind the Peamount Isolation Hospital near Dublin plus numerous projects such as a children's playground, mother-and-baby clubs and milk depots – and, more significantly, a considerable drop in the numbers of people suffering from TB. The Aberdeens' formal departure took place on 15 February 1915 with all the usual pomp and ceremony of a state occasion. George Fletcher and Connie Marr said their goodbyes privately and remained in touch with the Marquis and Marchioness of Aberdeen and Tara, as they styled themselves, for the rest of their lives.

Almost exactly one year later, when Connie was still working in the Red Cross offices at Dublin Castle, she found herself caught up in a brief and bloody event which was to change the course of Irish history. Irish nationalism was now vigorously asserting itself and British domination slowly coming to an end. On 24 April

1916, Easter Monday, the streets were almost empty as most people were on holiday enjoying the bright sunny weather. Just before noon a group of men and a few women left Liberty Hall and began marching determinedly up Sackville Street. They were an oddly assorted group: some wore the dark-green uniform of the Irish Citizen Army, others wore the grey-green of the Irish Volunteers, but by far the majority were in their ordinary clothes. Armed with rifles, shotguns and handguns, they headed straight for the General Post Office. When they arrived their leader, James Connolly, gave the order to charge. The guards were taken completely by surprise and the rebels quickly took control of the building. They pulled down the British flag and replaced it with two others – a plain green one emblazoned with the words 'Irish Republic' and a green, white and orange tricolour. Meanwhile, small groups of rebels had taken control of other key buildings in the city. The rising had been planned for some time and was originally to be supplied with German weapons. Although these weapons had been captured by the British, the rebellion went ahead, ill-equipped and undermanned.

Working at Dublin Castle, Connie was one of the first to hear of the Rising, and over the following five days she found herself actively involved. The British authorities acted quickly: troops poured into the city and surrounded the rebel strongholds, which were hopelessly outnumbered but put up a fierce resistance. For two days Connie and the Red Cross staff prepared to receive wounded at the Castle hospital, while ambulances drove round the bullet-swept streets and volunteers went out under fire to find and bring in the wounded – soldiers, rebels and numerous civilians hit either by stray bullets or deliberately shot by British soldiers, who also fired on Red Cross workers. The injured had to be pulled on makeshift stretchers along the ground under fire as volunteers crawled about on the rubble and tried to avoid burnt-out cars and broken tram wires lethally coiled in great loops. On the Tuesday a British machine-gun crew positioned themselves on the roof of a hotel at the top of Leeson Street, near Connie's flat, and began firing into the city centre. Connie took Joan and Anthony to a large Georgian mansion on neighbouring Fitzwilliam Street where she had orders to set up a temporary hospital to receive the wounded. People outside Dublin were blithely unaware of the full horror of the events; Connie's schoolboy brothers Gilbert and Lynton, living out at Shankhill, thought it a lark. They crept into Dublin to watch the fighting from the Leeson Street Bridge and were lucky not to have been killed.

By the Wednesday the city centre was surrounded by mounted howitzers, and a British patrol boat stationed on the River Liffey shelled the rebel positions. More and more victims were being brought into the hospitals while building after building was burned or shelled and the streets littered with broken glass and blood. Food, medicine and linen were running short, and the gas had been cut off. Connie got volunteers to visit private houses and beg for supplies of coal, food and bedding. The VADs slept in chairs and worked round the clock, baking bread, washing linen, making bandages and preparing soup. Dr Ella Webb and her colleague Dr Lumsden, the energetic leaders of the St John Ambulance Brigade, cycled through the firing line to reach the hospitals that had been set up around the city.

By Friday afternoon the roof of the GPO was ablaze and the rebels were forced to evacuate. General Lowe, commander of the British Forces, ordered a savage frontal attack on the rebels that lasted until the Saturday morning. The British soldiers, unused to fighting men not in recognizable military uniforms, took their wrath out on the civilians. After five days of mortar shells, gunfire, street fighting and burning buildings, four hundred and fifty rebels had been killed and the survivors had surrendered. They were taken to the gardens of the Rotunda Hospital where they gave up their arms and spent the night in the open, huddled under guard. Meanwhile, Connie returned to the Red Cross hospital at the Castle.

In the morning as the surviving rebels were led away to jail, many locals sided with the British, shouting abuse and hurling rotten fruit and vegetables at the ragged army that had wrecked their holiday, left blood on their streets and almost destroyed their city. But the British response was so brutish that public opinion quickly changed. Every day people became increasingly disgusted by news of further executions of rebels after notional trials – almost one hundred men were shot. The most shocking news was of James Connolly, whose leg had been so badly wounded that he had to be strapped to a chair to be executed. The British Army came out of this with no credit. Indeed their actions made martyrs of the republican leaders and revived the spirit of separatism.

There is no evidence that Connie ever wrote about her experience of this bloody week. But later in life she told friends that she had been horrified by the violence and by the executions of the Rising's leaders. However, her humanitarian work and her courage, along with those of Dr Lumsden and Dr Webb, were recognized. All three were awarded silver medals for their services during the week of riot. Connie's citation said: 'Mrs Heppell Marr . . . was at her post at 29 Fitzwilliam Street each day, along with many members of the BRCS Detachments who took their share of carrying the wounded in under fire and caring for them . . . and treated casualties on both sides and fed and cared for evacuees.'

In the summer of 1916, Captain Heppell Marr returned home on leave and Connie took time off to go home to Castlecomer; perhaps she planned to try to make her marriage work. Relations between James Heppell Marr and Connie's brothers seemed to have changed. They were now fellow soldiers; to Donald and Arnold, Marr was a comrade in arms, to the younger brothers he was a hero, and Etty suddenly decided she liked him after all – perhaps he looked more gentlemanly in his uniform. 'Never liked your husband till you'd left him,' she is alleged to have said. The family no longer sympathized with Connie and were keen to see reconciliation. Her friend Eva Hackett records that when Connie knew Marr was coming home on leave she seemed excited, even pleased. But the reality was that the situation was as bad as ever;

Joan remembers the rows starting up all over again. Connie was no longer prepared to be shouted at; she felt that her marriage was beyond saving. She had her own flat in Dublin as well as responsibilities and plenty of work to give her financial independence and confidence to lead her own life. In September 1916 she answered an advertisement for the post of welfare officer to women employees at the Vickers armaments factory in Barrow-in-Furness. With her excellent training and references, she got the job. She handed Joan back to her mother's family, 'tucked her son under her arm' and left for England. It was the end of her marriage and of her life in Ireland.

FOUR

The Freemasonry
of Flowers

1917–1928

After life in provincial Dublin, Connie's first day at work at the opulent headquarters of the Ministry of Munitions in January 1917 must have been quite a shock. Before the war the Cecil Hotel had been one of the most popular and fashionable hotels in London. It stood on the Strand between the Adelphi Buildings and the Savoy Hotel. Its monumental façade and imposing courtyard boasted of elaborate accommodation and luxurious 'appointments' covering three acres. 'Very few buildings so impress the visitor with a sense of amplitude and security,' it claimed; it was perfect for American tourists, to whom particular attention was paid. But now the tourists had gone and the hotel had been requisitioned by the Ministry for its aircraft production staff. Military personnel of every rank plus clerks and secretaries, including a surprisingly large number of women, were housed in the vast warren of offices and carpeted corridors. The glittering public rooms became canteens and meeting-rooms; people scuttled back and forth across the marbled entrance halls and up and down the imposing staircases. But the constant activity and the general air of wartime utility never quite expunged the tasteless Edwardian lavishness.

After the introduction of conscription in March 1916, the government encouraged women to take the place of male employees released to serve at the Front. They ranged from working-class women who took jobs in factories and on the land to educated ladies who worked as clerical and administration staff. Women such as Connie with professional training found themselves quickly elevated to jobs with considerable responsibilities and good pay.

After fleeing Ireland, Connie had spent a few months with Vickers in Barrow-in-Furness, where she proved her competence reorganizing the work and living conditions of Irish 'munitionettes', who had been risking their lives and their health handling poisonous substances without wearing protective clothing or taking safety precautions. Connie's ability was quickly noted and she was transferred to London to be appointed director of women staff at the Ministry of Munitions. She was now thirty-one, an independent woman living alone but for her son and responsible for the welfare of several thousand female workers. Once again her job took her around the country – this time, though, visiting aircraft production factories to inspect their health-and-safety conditions, which were often poor. But the women workers were paid good wages and were glad to escape the drudgery and poverty of home or domestic service. With a female doctor and nurses Connie organized medical treatment for them at their workplace. She established rest and recreation rooms, got up a sickness benefit scheme and found a holiday cottage for girls in need of rest or convalescence. She planned training classes for the clerical staff, and it was on her advice that women personnel officers were appointed in all branches of the Ministry. Connie's confident good nature and easy, unaffected manner were welcomed by both factory workers and employers, and at her office in the Cecil Hotel she made several good friends, two of whom were to have a lasting influence on her life.

Marjorie Russell, known to everyone as 'John', was the public relations officer. She had come from a good job in advertising, 'knew everyone' and was generous and sociable. Her husband, 'a distinguished literary man', was away serving in the war and she invited Connie and baby Tony to share her flat in St John's Wood. Strangely, one of Connie's closest friends at this time was Jos Cook, her estranged husband's sister-in-law. Alice, Heppell Marr's first wife, and her sisters Josephine and Enid had been brought up on a large farm in North Yorkshire to which Tony and his stepsister Joan were sent for summer holidays; both remembered very happy times there. They were particularly fond of Aunt Jos, a beautiful and gifted woman who had studied music. The Cook parents were authoritarian and none of the sisters pursued careers, although Jos would spend a good part of her life working with

Connie. When she heard that Connie was working in London and had no one to care for Tony during the day, she joined them in St John's Wood and looked after little 'Toto' until he was packed off to prep school at the age of only six.

In April 1917 Connie received the news that everyone dreaded: her brother Arnold had been wounded and was in the Red Cross hospital at Rouen. Her father hurried out to be with him, but Arnold died a few days later. Before George could return from France, Connie received another telegram: Donald had been killed, on almost the same day, in Salonika. Gilbert, who had been was staying with Connie in London, now made the long night journey to Dublin to break the news to their mother. The death of two sons was such a terrible shock for Etty that she did not speak again for two years. Indeed, everyone in Dublin was horrified by the tragedy. In Ireland, where there was no conscription, family losses of this kind were relatively rare. The front page of the Dublin papers carried the news, and the poet Katharine Tynan, who had been a close friend of Lady Aberdeen and the Fletcher family, published a poem recalling the boys' 'Araby', their hideout in the Wicklow hills. She described the brothers:

> As oft before, breasting the Wicklow hills,
> Light-foot and leaping
> Over the bog-pools and the singing rills,
> Side by side keeping.

These deaths were a terrible blow. Connie began to feel increasingly guilty about escaping and leaving her family in Dublin. She missed her father very much and she knew that her little boy also missed *his* father. But she was determined not to go back. For Connie retreat was never an option.

In March 1918, the House of Commons passed a bill giving women over the age of thirty the right to vote. But when the hostilities ceased, huge numbers of women who had worked during the war and earned a good wage found themselves reluctantly driven back into domesticity. Those who managed to stay in the workforce were criticized for competing with the men for a diminishing number of jobs. Postwar women's magazines tried to elevate housekeeping to a more professional status. 'We are on the threshold of a great feminine awakening,' gushed the editors of *Good Housekeeping*, while offering readers a correspondence course in managing home resources, improving cooking and needlework and advising on how to take advantage of the new mechanical household aids being tested by the Good Housekeeping Institute. Women were encouraged to make their own furniture polish and buy seasonal foods for bottling and jam-making; and the better-off, now coping with fewer domestic servants, were advised to 'be kind to servants as that way one can get the best out of them'.

The magazine also urged its readers not to allow drudgery in the house: 'There must be time to think, to read, to enjoy life', sentiments of which Connie would have approved. She supported the idea that women's role in the home deserved proper training – it was an idea she nurtured until it bore fruit many years later. But, for now, satisfaction through domesticity and motherhood was not for her. Connie was a single working mother at a time when a woman was either a spinster, married or widowed, but she somehow always managed to keep her status and the whereabouts of her 'Irish husband' rather vague.

After the war the more independent-minded women were busy grasping new opportunities in order to realize at least some of their professional ambitions. But Connie was not sure what her ambitions really were. Was she determinedly heading towards senior positions in personnel and management, or did she still nurture her father's enthusiasm for work in education? Perhaps she had dreams of doing something creative. Her flower arranging was still a hobby, something to enjoy and develop outside her career. One thing was very clear: if she was to remain independent and support herself and her son she would have to earn her own living. In 1919 she applied for the post of deputy principal of women staff for the Inland Revenue. Her boss in Munitions wrote a glowing testimony describing how her patience, sympathy and wisdom had smoothed over difficulties, righted injustices and ensured a high standard of efficiency and morale. He deeply regretted losing her 'in every respect'. It was a moving tribute from someone with whom Connie had come to form a very close relationship while working at the Cecil Hotel. It was signed H.E. Spry.

Henry Ernest, known to his brothers as 'Shav' or 'little Shaver', was thirty-nine — six years older than Connie. After public school and Cambridge, he had gone to India's warm climate because of poor health and had joined the Indian Civil Service, where he was quickly promoted through the legal and financial departments. He returned home at the outbreak of war and was seconded to the Ministry of Munitions as head of personnel. Charming, with the classic arrogance of a colonial civil servant, Shav was cultivated, witty, erudite and attractive. At least, Connie found him so. He loved the same things that excited her: beautiful design, gardening, antique furniture and good food. He was in every way the antithesis of James Heppell Marr. Connie was lonely living in London with a small child, even with several good friends for company. And despite successfully holding a well-paid job she craved security and stimulating male companionship of the kind her beloved father, whom she still badly missed, had provided in her youth. For his part, Shav Spry had fallen very much in love with Connie. But she was still a married woman and it is unlikely that their relationship was more than platonic. Shav was also married, with two young children, but had reached that stage in life when some men seem to have more in common with the bright female colleague than with the devoted wife at home.

By April 1919 Connie and Shav had become so close that they decided that one day they would be married. Connie left the Ministry to work for the Inland Revenue. Shav, however, now that the war was over, was obliged to return to India and put in a further two years with the Indian Civil Service in order to be eligible for his pension. They would be separated for a very long time.

Connie soon tired of being a civil servant and wrote to her father that she wished to devote herself to working in education. George Fletcher was of course very pleased, and contacted his old boss. Sir Robert Blair, now Chief Education Officer for the London County Council, offered Connie the headship of a pioneering new school. It was one that would embody the principles that both she and her muse Mrs Earle espoused: that education should directly prepare children for the life they were going to lead.

The 1918 Education Act, passed under the auspices of Herbert Fisher, President of the Board of Education, was intended as a radical approach to education that would give children in the aftermath of war a better chance in life. (In 1920 only 12.6 per cent of children leaving elementary school continued in full-time education.) Fees were abolished in state elementary schools, the leaving age was raised to fourteen, and teachers' salaries were increased. The great novelty of the Act was Section 10, which provided that all boys and girls between fourteen and eighteen who had not gone on to secondary schools should compulsorily attend day-continuation schools, their employers giving them leave from work for one whole day or two half-days per week. The curriculum was designed to prepare a child for a working life in a factory or workshop.

Sir Robert Blair, also chairman of the Liberal Party's advisory committee on education, was able to exert a significant influence on Fisher's Education Act which gave day-continuation schools a central role. Since his spell in Ireland, Blair had remained a strong advocate of educating adolescents for employment, particularly through technical instruction. But the training in these new schools was not to be entirely technical. It also aimed to open the young person's mind to wider aspects of life beyond the workplace: to the theatre, the art gallery and the concert hall, and to an aspiration to enjoy and even create a better and more pleasant living environment – concepts that became the cornerstone of Connie's own principles of education. Elementary school staff tended to be rigid disciplinarians used to teaching the three Rs to huge classes in grim surroundings; Blair's advisory committee recommended that the new schools should train their own staff and urged the local authorities, which would run the schools, to look for men and women with experience of a world beyond textbooks.

But the day-continuation schools were no more than a half-baked idea, with an inadequate budget, unsuitable buildings, untrained staff and, apart from Blair, few who actually believed in or supported the scheme. The failure of most of these schools was the result of postwar economic depression, a lack of vision and the opposition of vested interests. London, however, under Blair's energetic direction, set an example to the rest of the country, and two of the schools proved successful because they were set up and run by individuals with the right vision and ability. One, in the East End of London, was the Homerton and South Hackney Day Continuation School. Its headmistress, appointed on Sir Robert Blair's recommendation, was Mrs Constance Marr.

The concept of the schools was so novel that, much as George Fletcher had in the Department of Technical Education in Dublin, Connie found herself making things up as she went along. It was exactly the sort of challenge that she thrived on. Everything she had learned from her father and Lady Aberdeen, plus her own creative ideas and her determination to produce something worthwhile from very little, spurred her on.

The grimness of the East End, even after Ireland, was nevertheless quite a shock. The building, in a tree-lined avenue, was a Georgian mansion with an imposing portico, a relic of the days when Homerton had been a smart area where wealthy City merchants built homes. But it had recently been used as a teachers' training college and the interior was dark, dingy and institutionalized. Connie wanted the school to be an oasis of pleasure and beauty, so she immediately set about making it inviting and attractive to the young people living in the decaying slums that surrounded it. She had the classrooms painted in cheerful, bright colours and made regular visits to County Hall to demand more equipment, books and furniture. If the supply department failed to produce what was needed, Connie would breeze into Sir Robert Blair's office, perch on his desk and argue her case. They were well matched. Blair, an impressive figure with 'a magnificent leonine head' and a forceful personality, admired Connie's resolve and good humour, and she usually left with what she wanted.

Putting together the right team proved equally challenging. Connie was supposed to recruit suitable men and women from business and commerce rather than traditional teachers, but instead found herself luring the best teachers she could find in the elementary schools. She was able to offer secondary-school salaries, which caused considerable ill-feeling. Florence Thurston, then a young sewing teacher in a Stoke Newington school, later remembered an inspector coming round to tell the staff of the new project and asking for volunteers. The headmistress had gloomily remarked: 'The head of that queer new school is coming to pinch you.' For an extra hundred pounds a year, Miss Thurston moved to a far more interesting job with Mrs Marr – 'a charming headmistress'. Typically, Connie also drew on her friends and relations, quickly persuading Jos Cook to come and teach music and drama.

The Homerton school was officially opened in 1921 by Mrs Herbert Fisher, wife of the President of the Board of Education. Jos had trained her small choir to perform a medley of songs, including 'Forty Years On':

> *Forty years on, when afar and asunder*
> *Parted are those who are singing today,*
> *When you look back, and forgetfully wonder*
> *What you were like in your work and your play.*

Mrs Fisher was heard to observe in the staff room afterwards that the public-school ethos of this song could mean little to children from the slums. Connie quickly replied that she could not see why stirring words and a fine tune should be the exclusive property of Harrow School.

The lethargic attitude of many local authorities to funding and running these 'compulsory' schools was reinforced by pressures brought to bear on them by local employers. Lloyd George's hard-faced businessmen who had done well out of the war detested the scheme: young labour was cheap labour, and if it had to be freed from the shop or bench for a whole day a week, it ceased to be as cheap as all that. Many even refused to employ children attending the schools. One of the tasks that Connie most feared was having to go round the shops and factories making it clear that she *would* have the law enforced. Many parents, too, were opposed, and Connie was also obliged to knock on the doors of tenement homes and confront enraged fathers who saw no point in educating a child who should be out earning. Some actually encouraged their children to behave badly in the hope that this would finish the school.

With the parents, Connie won her own victory. She issued an open invitation to them all to come one evening and hear her point of view and why she and the children needed their support. A surprising number turned up and listened while she explained the practical and personal advantages their children would gain from the school. Though hostile at first, gradually the mood of the meeting swung round and when she had finished she announced, 'Now we'll have a concert . . . you all know "Old Folks at Home"?' Jos Cook struck up on the piano and suddenly the East End was singing along and the parents, at least, were on her side.

The pupils might have been obliged by law to attend, but most had to be charmed or coerced into doing any work. No punishments or sanctions were allowed and many of the children, used to Victorian class discipline, were rebellious or larked about. Connie and her team faced the challenge of making every task so interesting and attractive that the children wanted to do it. Lily Cullen, one of the first pupils, recalled how the school treated the children like adults and made them 'feel alive and free'. Here in the cheerful, busy atmosphere Connie created, Lily and her school-friends found themselves far removed from the harsh realities of their daily lives, and only occasionally were they 'suddenly brought back to reality with the smells of a pickle or glue factory which penetrated the school'. Connie's policy was and always would be to praise first and comment after. She was particularly horrified by the treatment of the 'truancy boys', most from violent and unhappy homes, who came to her from a special school for con-sistent truants. They were treated as potential criminals, segre-gated from the other children and made to wear humiliating short trousers. Connie soon put a stop to all that, and the sense of failure and injustice that many felt began to disappear.

Her firm belief that gardens and flowers had healing powers took shape at this school; in the harsh postwar environment it seemed more important than ever, and not just for the children. She described interviewing the mother of a particularly unmana-geable boy. 'I confided in her,' Connie wrote, 'telling her of the efforts we had all made to do anything with him; all the while she remained silent and wooden-faced. At last she spoke, looking me coldly in the eye. "Jim is a perfectly good boy at home," she said. "We don't have no trouble with him, none at all. Every time he opens his mouth his father hits him over the head."' Gradually Connie discovered that the father's nerves were so bad that even the noise of a chair accidentally scraped back from the table was a signal for an outburst of anger. 'He can't help it,' the mother said tearfully. 'It's his nerves; he's bin like that since the war.' Connie was sensible enough to know that gardening would be an unreal-istic option for such war-ravaged people. Nevertheless, the healing powers of gardens and gardening are today generally acknowl-edged.

If Connie could not help the adults, she could at least make a difference for the children. She used her instincts and imagination to humanize the curriculum and relate it to daily life. As well as literacy, numeracy and bookkeeping, she believed in the importance of good manners and good social behaviour generally, and got Jos to run drama classes to improve her pupils' confidence in their speech and deportment. Dance classes and 'socials' were organized to which staff and parents came. In their carpentry classes the boys made attractive objects for the home, while the girls did dressmaking, copying the latest styles, though the materials available were very limited. All her life Connie showed a mastery in producing something beautiful out of very little; she had an extraordinary flair for 'making a purse out of a pig's ear', as she put it. On one occasion she and Miss Thurston made themselves each a dress with some horrid bright-green material. Miss Thurston worked a daisy chain into a yoke; Connie embroidered hers with brilliant small flowers. They modelled the dresses in class and the effect was electric. 'The memory that is still vivid in my mind,' recalled Lily Cullen, 'is of Mrs Marr sweeping into the school full of zest and flamboyance, always dressed very, very smart and modern which to us being young was a thrill, especially after our ordinary LCC teachers who were very Victorian and dowdy.'

Connie was determined that all the children should experience the pleasures of beauty. She described one girl being hauled up before her for stealing a shilling. The child had spent the money on coloured paper flowers. 'I only wanted something pretty,' she wailed. Nothing could have brought home to Connie more clearly the hunger for beauty in the grimy homes set in those wretched surroundings; it was reminiscent of her own childhood, and she remembered so well her own desperate search for flowers to please the eye and gladden the heart. From then on she ensured that every classroom was generously decked out with fresh flowers; she got the children to colour-wash old earthenware crocks for vases – a technique she was to use later in her shop.

After a long, tough schoolday Connie longed to escape to somewhere peaceful. Early in 1921 she and Jos took a cottage in Billericay in Essex, an easy bus ride from the school, where they set up home for Tony, now aged ten, and shared their passion for gardening. This was Connie's second garden, and she crammed it with a great bounty of colourful flowering plants whose blooms she cut and piled into baskets every day to take to school: 'according to the season the basket would be filled with pansies and pinks, roses and phlox, sweet rocket and wallflowers, primroses and daffodils; whatever might be in bloom.' But she never reached school with a full basket:

> One way or another they used to be scattered along my route: the bus conductor who had to have a pansy for his buttonhole because his grandmother grew them in the garden when he was a little boy, and the ticket collector who hadn't smelled a mignonette for he didn't know how long, and quite a few 'give us a flower lady' urchins and some shyer ones who only asked with their eyes. And so, little by little, the contents of the basket dwindled. The journey ceased to be dreary and was enlivened with garden chat, homely personal memories of an earlier, more sunlit world, which were added to day by day, grew into sagas, nostalgic human stories. That is one of the things flowers do for you.

She even turned a blind eye when itinerant hop-pickers grabbed flowers from her garden. 'You might call it the freemasonry of flowers,' Connie wrote thirty years later in 1953, when she was running quite a different sort of school but with very much the same beliefs and values – personal fulfilment and the appreciation of beauty, whatever one's background.

Connie visited the National Gallery and Burlington House (the home of the Royal Academy) for inspiration and ideas for the school. Reproductions in *The Studio*, which she read as a child, had familiarized her with the paintings which she now saw as potential inspiration for her students. She bought postcard reproductions and stuck them around the classroom walls. Her favourites were the flower compositions of sixteenth- and seventeenth-century painters such as Cornelis de Heem, Jan Davidsz de Heem, Justus van Huysum and Jan Brueghel the Elder, which were once popular with wealthy patrons across Europe. Many of these paintings were rather stiff and unnatural; some were carefully arranged to give prominence to the highly valued tulip, while many of the earlier ones carried symbolic and religious significances in which Connie had no interest. They often featured an idealized or imaginary still-life composition that could never have worked as a living arrangement – gravity was defied, branches and tendrils poised without means of support, and flowers from different seasons were mixed together.

Nevertheless, these works had an enormous influence on Connie's developing ideas about flower arrangement. From them she took some of the essential characteristics that she carried into her own creations, their feeling for mass and line and their contrasts of texture and colour. She was inspired by their opulence and the care with which the individual personality of a leaf or flower was highlighted. But she rarely tried to translate flower paintings into her own living arrangements, because in her view they were quite separate art forms.

While Connie was struggling to bring a sliver of enlightenment to the East End, in other parts of London the rich young things who had survived the war were swept up in a wild upsurge of fun and frolicking. They danced new dances, drank cocktails and held fancy-dress parties, bathing parties – any kind of parties, just as long as they broke the old pre-war conventions. Connie was not herself a party person, but she always enjoyed good food, cheerful, stimulating company and beautiful, though preferably informal, surroundings. Connie's great friend from 'Munitions', Marjorie Russell, returned after the war to her job in advertising at J. Walter Thompson. Marjorie did like parties, and she had numerous wealthy and cultivated friends. She was always trying to drag Connie out of her country life or sweep her away from her 'slummy school' in the East End into her own glamorous West End milieu. Connie would sometimes be invited to make up the numbers for a dinner party while Jos babysat in Essex. London was full of 'war widows', respectable women on their own who needed a bit of fun and entertainment, some light relief from their lonely lives. No one enquired where Mr Marr was, and her relationship with Shav Spry, who was still in India, was a carefully kept secret. It is unlikely that Connie told anyone, except possibly Marjorie, about her past life. Friends often confided in her, but Connie mostly kept her personal problems to herself.

When Marjorie's friends heard that Connie liked arranging flowers as a hobby, they would beg and cajole her into decorating their homes when they were entertaining. Connie enjoyed the challenge and the freedom to experiment, using flowers picked from her garden or bought by the hostess. She was beginning to realize that she had considerable creative skills, which friends seemed to recognize and appreciate. Also, there were several people Connie had known in Dublin who were now living in London, and they too were asking for her flowers. Gradually she began to expand her social circle and her repertoire. Every weekday she spent at the school, but many evenings and some weekends she could be found at smart houses in town. It was a crucial further step from being a mine manager's wife in Ireland to entering English society. It was almost as if Connie didn't see herself actually belonging anywhere.

Despite her professional and social success, Connie was missing Shav desperately and found their separation very hard to bear. Florence Thurston the sewing teacher, who was sometimes entrusted with posting a weekly letter to India, recalled that although Connie was always cheerful and bright with staff and children, when she was alone she often looked sad and anxious. In her office she kept a large box, crammed with hundreds of letters on fine India paper tied with pink ribbon. Despite their time apart, Connie and Shav forged a strong affectionate relationship through the regular exchange of news, views and descriptions of their very contrasting lives and surroundings.

By 1923 Shav was at last due to come home. His two years in India had been spent as financial adviser to the government of

Bengal, and on his return he was offered a job at a firm of London chartered accountants if he qualified, which he did.

In the meantime Connie had been seeking a divorce from James Heppell Marr. Divorce in the 1920s was still relatively rare and could only be granted when one party was found guilty of adultery. If the husband was a gentleman, it was up to him to do the decent thing. James Marr took the blame for their divorce so that Connie's career would not be affected; his own was already in ruins. He had returned from the war with a DSO but found himself, like thousands of others, unwanted and forced to tramp the streets of London looking for a job.

Shav too was trying to organize a divorce from his wife Claire, for whom the news that her husband was leaving her and their children came as a complete shock. Connie and Shav between them were wrecking two families and the lives of four young children. Connie's family was horrified. Indeed, Etty refused to stop thinking of Marr as her son-in-law and told Connie that if she divorced him she would never speak to her again; it is possible that she never really did. Connie might perhaps have felt she had little cause for self-reproach over the failure of her marriage, but her lack of consideration for Claire Spry was another matter. Although usually generous and kind, Connie also possessed a ruthless streak, and when she fixed on something, or in this case, someone, she was prepared to take what she wanted whatever the cost. It could be said that she paid for it later.

While Connie's divorce went ahead, there are no records of either a divorce between Claire and Shav Spry or of a marriage between Connie and Shav. Indeed, Marjorie Fletcher, Connie's sister-in-law, later confided to her daughter the carefully guarded secret that Connie and Shav were in fact never married. 'He just gave her his name,' she told her. Divorce was a demeaning business that still carried a social stigma of disgrace and failure, and it is most likely that Claire Spry, to protect herself and her children, refused to grant Shav a divorce.

Despite not being able to marry, Connie may have thought that her relationship with Shav would continue in the same spirit as during the years they were apart. Neither of them had found success in marriage, so perhaps they could just continue in an informal relationship. They were both middle-aged, with little prospect of further children, and Connie imagined she had found a relationship based on companionship rather than passion, a marriage of minds, if not in law, of mutual interests and support; a calm, peaceful place where she could be herself, living with a man who respected and loved her and understood her creative longings.

Typically, she had not thought through the implications of 'living in sin' at a time when it was regarded as unconventional, if not downright unacceptable, especially for two people holding respectable jobs in education and accountancy. If the truth had come out, they would most certainly have lost their jobs. Of course, no one at Homerton School was ever aware of any changes in Connie's private life; it was generally assumed that she was a war widow and she continued to be addressed as Mrs Marr. If she and Shav were to be together and remain employed, the only option was for Connie to change her name to Spry and for them to live together as though they had married. How many people were party to this deception is not known. Were Connie's parents aware of the fact that their daughter was not only divorced, but now openly living with a married man? Did her son Tony know? For the rest of their lives Connie and Shav Spry kept up the pretence that they were a legally married couple. It would not be the only scandal in their lives that had to be kept under wraps.

In 1925 Connie and Shav moved into a small Essex farmhouse. They both loved being in the country and it never occurred to them to set up home in London, which would have been far more convenient for their jobs. Since they now shared two good salaries, they soon found a larger home, the Old Rectory at Abinger, set in one of the most charming 'mountain' parts of Surrey. The house and garden were in a poor state of repair, which was just the challenge they wanted. They could indulge their passions for hunting for furniture in antique and junk-shops, and for gardening. They moved in on Boxing Day, ready to start a new life together and to look forward to what Connie hoped would be lasting happiness.

She felt sure that the 'strange little garden' was haunted by the ghosts of nuns who had once walked inside its high-walled enclosure. The garden had been neglected since the war and was badly overgrown. It seemed grey and sombre, but Connie could see its potential and believed she could make it beautiful. She was single-minded and enthusiastic but realized that the Herculean task would require some strong young muscle-power. Walter Trower was a local boy who was engaged to Connie's parlour maid Gladys. Though he had little knowledge of gardening, Trower was keen and needed a job. He applied to work for Connie and she took him on after agreeing to teach him all she knew. Like dozens of friends and employees who came into Connie's orbit, he remained at her side, running her gardens for almost thirty years. They learned together, developing their knowledge of horticulture and growing in confidence and skill. Their relationship was not always harmonious: Trower's passion for the plants in his garden was often at odds with Connie's cutting raids. But they had a great mutual respect. Nothing Connie grew was wasted. When she moved, as she often did, the whole garden had to be moved too, a challenge Trower was expected to face each time without complaint.

At Abinger they set about double-digging 'three spits deep' and filling the trenches with well-rotted manure. Soon their labours were wonderfully rewarded: 'Never in all my gardening experience', Connie wrote, 'have I had such flowers.'

Long borders of old-fashioned deep-red carnations scented the air with their clove-like perfume; tall Madonna lilies gently swayed in the evening light like the ghosts of the nuns. Much of the garden was on unworkable heavy clay. Connie recalled reading how Dean Hole, one of the great rose-growers, had improved his heavy soil by burning it. She would try that. When the bonfire was sufficiently hot, they damped it down with lumps of clay which gradually disintegrated into more friable material; this was then mixed with lime or sand. It was a long and arduous task, but once again Connie's energy and resolve paid off and she and her new gardener were able to 'raise some of the finest chrysanthemums and roses she had ever grown'. Connie and Shav had little money to spare for the garden, but as Trower recalled, 'if there was a plant or bulb she wanted she'd go without things for herself or for the house'. She fell in love with the parrot and lily-flowered tulips that had recently come onto the market and rushed out and bought just two of each – all that she could afford. They grew their own vegetables and salads; the garden luxuriated with roses, flowering shrubs and herbaceous borders, while the house was filled with Connie's experimental flower arrangements. As long as she continued to run the school at Homerton, flowers from the Abinger garden went up daily to decorate the classrooms. Every morning the clothes basket, filled with flowers, was strapped onto the carrier on the car and driven up to London by Shav.

Word of Connie's skills in flower arranging was continuing to spread, and more often than not the clothes basket also carried flowers earmarked for her private commissions – blooms for dinner parties, birthdays, weddings and cocktail parties. Connie loved doing them and was also glad of the money. She never charged very much, saying it was a wonderful opportunity to do what she most enjoyed, so why charge for it? These small commissions helped pay both for new plants and Trower's wages.

Daily life was tightly packed. Each morning Connie and Shav were up with the lark for the long drive to his office and her school in London, returning home 'only just in time for dinner' prepared by Gladys who had been upgraded to cook. At weekends they were free to indulge in gardening, country walks and entertaining. The Sprys were keen and hospitable hosts; every weekend there were lunch parties for their growing circle of friends from London and their new country neighbours. Shav, who had enjoyed several comfortable years of colonial life, had high standards. Like most men of his kind, he liked to live *en grand seigneur*, presiding in the dining-room at the head of a generous and tastefully laid out table. Connie on the other hand always preferred what she called her 'kitchen suppers'; they were beautifully done, with delicious, fresh, often homegrown food enjoyed in the cheerful, gossipy, everyone-mucking-in atmosphere on which she thrived. Shav appreciated her homemaking skills and particularly admired her flower arranging, a hobby which always made the house so fresh-looking and beautiful – though as Connie liked to recall in her books, he was often alarmed by her predatory raids on the garden, armed with baskets and secateurs.

Winter evenings were spent cosily by the log fire with Shav while he did the crossword out loud or read her 'thrilling bits from the evening paper' or regaled her with exotic stories from his time in India. As soon as the Christmas cards had stopped dropping through the letter-box and the seed catalogues began to arrive, Connie became totally absorbed. Armed with last year's garden notes and with a good garden encyclopaedia to hand, she made lists of annual and vegetable seeds followed by biennials and perennials: 'With these I am busy and utterly content.'

Someone noted that there was little sign of children or teenagers in the home. Shav's children never visited; Tony, now fifteen and away at school, often spent his holidays with the Cook family in Yorkshire. His father, unable to find employment in England, was obliged to take a post as a mining geologist in India where he would remain for many years, cut off from the one thing that mattered in his lonely life, his children Joan and Tony. Heppell Marr would sometimes join them in Yorkshire when he was home on leave, and they would spend idyllic days riding in the pony and cart that he bought for them. These were the few precious weeks when Tony and Joan enjoyed something resembling normal childhood.

According to his second wife Vita, Tony was a very unhappy child who hated being sent away to school and longed for his father, whom he adored.

Shav Spry was never a substitute for Heppell Marr. He had no strong paternal instincts and Tony would not accept him as his stepfather. In 1927 George Fletcher retired and left Ireland, with an honorary degree from Trinity College and considerable praise and affection from his peers in Dublin. George and Etty bought a near-derelict Elizabethan farmhouse at Great Hallingbury in Essex, which Etty made into an elegant and tasteful home, while George, who refused to stop working, became a member of various English educational committees and chairman of his parish council. If he was not with his beloved Cook aunts, Tony would go to stay with George and Etty in Essex rather than spend time at Abinger – which he never felt was home.

One fine summer Sunday in 1927 Marjorie Russell brought a new lunch guest down to Abinger. Sidney Bernstein was a young, handsome, exquisitely dressed bachelor, a showman and the leading figure behind the exotic-looking new cinemas that were springing up around the country. Bernstein was entranced by the wild, rambling garden; he admired Connie's flower decorations and listened approvingly to her very individual views on interior design and gardening. He was working at the time with a team of successful professional designers to create several new cinemas, but he saw in Connie the touch of an inspired amateur, a true artist.

Bernstein invited her to lunch at his flat in Albemarle Street in London, where he complained that the flowers supplied by a West End florist bored him and begged Connie to take on the commission herself. At first she demurred – she had never accepted a regular commission before, and how was she to fit it around her school work? Another guest at the lunch was the theatre designer Norman Wilkinson, who was equally enchanted by Connie's simple and direct views on flowers and design. It was a meeting of true minds. Norman was soon telling her about his commission to design the interior of Atkinsons' newly built perfumery shop in Bond Street. He told Connie he planned to fill the shop windows with unusual displays of flowers and did his best to persuade her that she was just the person to take up the challenge. By the end of the meal both Bernstein and Wilkinson were cajoling Connie into thinking about turning professional, maybe even setting up her own little business. Bernstein decided to put on the pressure, announcing that if Connie accepted Wilkinson's request to do the perfumery shop windows, he would give her the commission to supply flowers and pot-plants for the foyers of his new London cinemas – how could she possibly refuse?

Connie was both elated and terrified. She was flattered and stimulated by the encouragement she had received from these creative and confident men. Wilkinson urged her to think of the Atkinsons' windows as works of art rather than as a conventional florist's commission. This, therefore, was what Connie saw in her mind: not a business deal but a creative challenge. Those cinema foyers and those enormous, empty shop windows were blank canvases on which she might at last realize her long-suppressed artistic ideas. She rushed home to discuss things with Shav, hoping he would give her good financial advice about the probable pitfalls of setting out on a new career. It was a considerable risk, even with the promise of two commissions. It is possible that Shav agreed to it initially because he liked the idea of Connie giving up her work at Homerton School and becoming a 'housewife'. With his Civil Service pension and accountancy work, he was earning enough – even after payments to his wife and children – to keep them both. He thought her flower arranging was an 'artistic' ladylike hobby; it eased her restless spirit and kept her amused. It is also possible that when Connie told him about the idea she underplayed the whole thing: just two little jobs that would take her to London for a day or two in the week with plenty of time spent at home and in their garden.

Shav had no idea that servicing Atkinsons' Perfumery and the Granada cinemas was going to be such a demanding full-time commitment that it would lead to a radical change in their lives. Had he firmly put his foot down and said, 'No . . . stick to doing flowers for your girlfriends', Connie at that point might have quietly acquiesced. But he did not. And Connie had made up her mind. Whenever she was fired up with something new and exciting, she revealed a fiercely stubborn streak; nothing was allowed to stand in her way. She was ready to move on, to face a fresh challenge and a new adventure. Somewhere, always at the back of her mind, was the knowledge that she was not his wife, not subject to his wishes and demands. She had long since discovered the taste for independence and for freedom to pursue her own inclinations, and she could, if she chose, disobey him. It is doubtful if she ever did openly flout Shav's wishes, but the strange situation and its accompanying secrecy sometimes led to disloyalty on both sides.

Connie's teaching colleagues were appalled by her resignation and considered her departure a serious loss to the profession and a sad waste of talent. But Homerton School was in trouble; its champion, Sir Robert Blair, had retired in 1924 and the local authorities decided that these schools were totally uneconomic and should be closed. Homerton was the last surviving day-continuation school and Connie's resignation spelled its end. To her parents her behaviour was incomprehensible. Her father had been immensely proud of her achievements at the school. Along with the shame of divorce she was now recklessly giving up a fine career in education for a ridiculous little job doing flowers for shops and showmen.

Connie realized that she was abandoning all that her father and Lady Aberdeen had trained her to do. She was leaving behind the slums with their poverty and disease, and perhaps she did feel some regret. But perhaps, too, she could argue, filling shops and cinemas with flowers was no less useful in showing people the healing power of natural beauty. No doubt she was seduced, as anyone might be, by the prospect of finally being able to crystal-lize those creative visions she had nurtured for so long. But she never abandoned her belief that beauty was not a privilege for the rich but, like good health, something everyone could and should enjoy.

FIVE

*Ensnared with Flowers**

1928–1930

* From Andrew Marvell's poem 'The Garden'

Connie visited Norman Wilkinson at his riverside home Strawberry House, by Chiswick Mall, and was delighted to find ducks and swans standing by the door. Before she even entered the house she noted the pots of daisies on the stone terrace, formal hyacinths in Bristol Blue glasses on the window sills where the sunlight made 'a deep rich note of blue'; shallow, straight-edged dishes tightly packed with narcissi – the flowers and the receptacles perfectly complementing each other. 'The effect of these solid masses of flowers was quite beautiful,' Connie recalled.

Wilkinson grew delicate camellias in his tiny greenhouse and old roses, stocks and laced pinks – simple flowers that would then have been spurned by florists' shops but which Connie saw had decorative potential. The house seemed equally lovely. Wilkinson was a passionate collector of antiques and filled his home with 'a delightful clutter' of Art Nouveau, 'Gothic' and Tudor furniture and furnishings. In every room flowers were arranged with originality and a keen colour sense; in particular, Connie observed, set in alcoves in the dining-room, two large shallow marble bowls generously filled with close-packed flowers – scarlet geraniums, red camellias and dark-red roses lay in a pool of light from spotlights hidden in the ceiling. Wilkinson was an artist who understood not only colour, form and lighting, but also the vital integrity of flowers in the scheme of a room. This, Connie told him, was precisely what she too believed in: flowers used as materials, like paint on a canvas, 'for something truly creative, truly artistic'. To her immense relief Wilkinson did not laugh at her, but understood what she was struggling to express.

As she explored and admired the house, Connie came across something that suddenly jogged her memory: hanging in the sitting-room was a copy of *Richard II Holding the Red Rose of Lancaster*, the painting that she had seen as a child in *The Studio* magazine. She explained how she had been so excited by it, the lavish richness combined with austere formality: 'I remember to this day', she wrote, 'the parterre of delicate, exquisite even strange flowers: flaked and ticked pinks, curious foxgloves, *pana-chée* roses . . . the minute and elaborate detail of the smallest flower.' She told Wilkinson that this painting had inspired in her a creative interest in all kinds of flowers, whether wild, exotic, rare or commonplace. The artist was pleased when he heard that she had liked it so much because, he told her, it was he who had painted it when he was very young. He quoted some lines of Milton from 'Lycidas' which had inspired him:

> Bring the rathe primrose that forsaken dies,
> The tufted crow-toe, and pale jessamine,
> The white pink, and the pansy freaked with jet,
> The glowing violet,
> The musk rose, and the well-attired woodbine,
> With cowslips wan that hang the pensive head,
> And every flower that sad embroidery wears.

Wilkinson, like Connie, had spent much of his childhood in the Midlands, but in a cultured and wealthy family of textile manufacturers who owned 'a sort of Selfridges'. He grew into a precocious young man with evident musical and artistic leanings – though he was quick to point out he was not the distinguished marine painter of the same name, and liked to be known as 'Norman Wilkinson of Four Oaks' to emphasize the difference. He persuaded his parents to commission the architect William Lethaby to design a magnificent new house in the William Morris style and laid out the gardens himself. Later he studied art in Paris. He shared a studio in the Latin Quarter with his friends the artist Keith Henderson and the theatre designer Lovat Fraser. Henderson recalled how every day Norman bought huge bunches of flowers from the flower women in the 'Boul' Mich' and filled the studio with their scent. 'I can see him in the studio, touching the flowers gently, as though they were human . . . It was a perfect setting for his slender Roman elegance.'

Wilkinson went on to make his name designing costumes and sets, mostly for Shakespeare productions. His memorable design for *A Midsummer Night's Dream* at the Duke of York's Theatre in London in 1914 featured an iridescent forest and 'gold-faced fairies, their eyebrows picked out in crimson'. Increasingly his designs put him in the vanguard of the rebellion against nineteenth-century stage realism and won for him an international reputation as a stage designer. He went on to work with Granville Barker, the theatre actor and director, and later became a governor of the Stratford Memorial Theatre.

Connie always claimed that Wilkinson was her most important teacher and source of inspiration. He was shy and self-conscious but had a generous spirit and taught Connie all he knew about design. She made several trips to his home, where they discussed art, poetry and flower arranging, and studied drawings and plans for Atkinsons' Perfumery. Sometimes he visited Connie at Abinger, where they searched for suitable plants and ideas in her garden. With a comfortable private income and plenty of work designing for the theatre, Wilkinson claimed that he took on the Atkinsons' commission only because it amused him. The notion of doing a scent shop took his fancy, and he wanted to get away from the traditional 'fake Pompadour or dolled-up chemist'.

His concept for the decor was a fairytale setting: the walls would be covered with specially made mirror glass with a grey antique finish that gave a soft reflection of subdued and tremulous light, 'creating an almost insubstantial air'. Cascading crystal chains, representing fountains of perfume, would be subtly illuminated from above by spotlights similar to those he had in his home. For the windows, Wilkinson told Connie, he had in mind dramatic flower displays that stood as if on the stage of a theatre, full of character and romance. He wanted flowers that were reminiscent of the old herbals – scented if possible – and absolutely no common 'shop' flowers such as carnations, ferns and gypsophila.

He suggested old-fashioned roses, striped pinks, single marigolds, mignonette, sweet william, honeysuckle, auriculas, wild flowers and 'country bunches', with occasional bursts into the richness of camellias of the kind he grew in his greenhouse. Connie was charmed and flattered. Wilkinson was offering her a tantalizing window of opportunity, but could she live up to his exacting standards?

On Monday 15 November 1929, Atkinsons' opened its doors and the twenty-two carillon bells in the gilded tower that soared above the new and elaborately decorated Art Deco building rang out a 'delightful and delicate medley of tunes'. For Connie, doing the flowers at Atkinsons' for the first time was a day of mingled excitement and panic: 'Yawning emptily were several very capacious urns to be filled by nine-thirty on that Monday morning.' The vases had been provided by Wilkinson out of his junk-shop finds, so Connie felt at home. They were exactly the type of container she herself loved to use, soapstone and metal urns, marble tazzas, carved wooden angels holding aloft cornucopias and some 'particularly fine majolica'. But it had almost ended in disaster when she realized that Covent Garden in November could offer only 'chrysanthemums, chrysanthemums all the way, with not even a snippet of myrtle, which would have fitted the picture so well'. The only 'drieds' were the ubiquitous Chinese lanterns, helichrysums and dyed statice. If she worked with this sort of shop-worn material she would produce the very effect of déjà vu against which Wilkinson had inveighed.

What was she to do? Her heart sank, and she felt herself entering a dangerous world about which, she suddenly realized, she knew nothing at all. She was saved from disaster by a friend returning from a country walk with arms filled with a bundle of old-man's-beard covered in silvery seed-heads, various copper-coloured leaves and great trails of hops turned to strawy gold. 'The bunch lived and glowed,' she wrote, and the thought of it in the gentle soapstone was exciting. I had a niggling fear that the authorities at Atkinsons might feel that to furnish them with weeds was not part of the contract, so when I saw in the market a few stems of a rather clumsy heavy green orchid, I bought them, because they looked as though they might fit in with the strange assortment lying in the van, and also perhaps soften any disapproval waiting round the corner.

After a childhood in which disapproval was always waiting round the corner, this was something Connie was particularly anxious to avoid.

Those first unconventional displays of leaves and berries, seed-heads, trails of wild clematis and the gloriously heavy cascade of golden hops with the central cluster of strange, exotic green orchids were an immediate success, 'and I was not cast out with ignominy'. It was, she wrote, her first lesson in the use of plant material that was usually discarded, 'gone with the wheelbarrow', and her first success with what was to become one of her most famous principles: that wild and cultivated flowers displayed together could be both beautiful and dramatic.

It was not the most auspicious time to open a grand perfumery. The Wall Street crash that October was the harbinger of a decade of financial stress, and even the very rich had to cut back on houses, horses and servants. But there was still a steady supply of wealthy customers willing to treat themselves to small luxuries, and Atkinsons' were so delighted with Connie's arrangements and the resulting publicity for their products that she was given a permanent contract. Other fashionable stores followed suit, and Connie was soon asked to do the windows for Drage's furniture store in Oxford Street, Elizabeth Arden's showrooms and Hatchet's Restaurant.

But it was the world of the theatre that swept Connie up on a wave of glamour and success and where she would make some of her greatest friendships and triumphs. Norman Wilkinson was part of the predominantly homosexual set of young theatre talent and it was through him that Connie was introduced to the most gifted designers, writers and actors, several of whom had their careers launched by Charles B. 'Cocky' Cochran, the leading showman in the Twenties and Thirties. Cochran's skills were described as a combination of Diaghilev and Ziegfeld, 'with a touch of Barnum'. The best talents were attracted to work for him, among them Ivor Novello, Cole Porter, Roger Quilter, Norman Hartnell, Paul Nash, Lovat Fraser, Leonid Massine, Frederick Ashton, George Balanchine and the Diaghilev ballet company. Cochran liked a 'dash of the Continent' in his shows, with 'rows of chorus girls with gorgeous legs, tits and tinsel'. His revues, staged at the London Pavilion Theatre, which advertised itself as 'the Centre of the World', were a medley of sketches, colourful 'turns' and musical numbers; the best had wit, charm and pace, plus style and elegance. If the revues lacked the earthiness and gusto of the music hall they appealed to the wealthy middle-class audiences, who adored the glamour and lavishness.

Connie, who loved the theatre, often accompanied Wilkinson to see new Cochran productions. They would go backstage where she met several people who would become her closest friends and collaborators, such as the costume and set designers Oliver Messel and Rex Whistler, the writer Beverley Nichols, the photographer Cecil Beaton and the actors John Gielgud and Charles Laughton. After his huge success in *Richard of Bordeaux* Gielgud spent lavishly on flowers for his dressing room, and Connie would continue to provide them for many years. Wilkinson was busy spreading the word about his wonderful new discovery – 'Connie Spry and her marvellous flowers' – among his coterie of theatre friends. Word of a new talent or fashion quickly spread, and Connie was soon in great demand.

Meanwhile, she had another commitment to honour – her contract with Sidney Bernstein to provide plants and flowers for his Granada cinemas, which were nearing completion. The Bernstein family, along with the Ostrers, the Woolfs, Oscar Deutsch (and later the Grades), were the children of Jewish immigrants who came to prominence in the entertainment industry and were the British equivalents of the great Hollywood moguls. Sidney Bernstein's father moved to London from Latvia in the 1890s and had a somewhat chequered business career. On his death in 1922 he possessed a collection of properties which included a small but important chain of about twenty film theatres which Sidney, with his brother Cecil, was now enlarging. Bernstein had planned their opening at a particularly propitious time: in September 1928 the film *The Jazz Singer* with Al Jolson opened at the Piccadilly Theatre – the 'talkies' had arrived. Theatre entrepreneurs scoffed and tried to make light of it. Cochran claimed the talkies were a passing phase, a novelty of which the public would soon tire, but the public flocked to the cinemas. 'The theatre is dead . . . quite dead,' the theatre critic Hannen Swaffer wrote. It wasn't, but it started to change. Cochran fought back with *Bitter Sweet* by Noël Coward and *Wake Up and Dream* with music and lyrics by Cole Porter, starring Jessie Mathews, Sonnie Hale, Tilly Losch and Anna Neagle; and soon everyone was singing 'Let's Do It' and 'What Is This Thing Called Love?'. Indeed, new theatres were still being built at a great rate during this tug-of-war to win the public. Had the theatre managers had any idea of the grim times ahead, they might have thought again.

In 1928 three million cinema tickets were being sold every week in London alone, and it was growing clear to Sidney Bernstein that, despite his own personal passion for the theatre, the future lay with the movies. Early that year he announced in the trade press that he planned to build a new cinema opposite Sadler's Wells, to rebuild the Empires at Edmonton, Willesden and West Ham and the Rialto in Enfield, as well as taking over the lease of the Lewisham Hippodrome. These cinemas would reappear as elegant places of entertainment, completely redesigned and fully equipped for sound. Several would also have dance halls, tea rooms or cafés. The age of the supercinema was about to be ushered in.

Bernstein knew exactly how he wanted his picture palaces to look — they had to be perfect, the best. Each would be totally individual and full of original ideas. They would be palaces of the imagination where people who led lives of drabness could find escape and fantasy, glamour and drama. They would be called Granada Cinemas, after a happy walking tour he had had in southern Spain.

Bernstein invited his friend Theodore Komisarjevsky to become the art director of all his theatres and cinemas. Komisarjevsky was a brilliant architect, theatre director and designer; a slight, balding man with protruding eyes and immense charm, he was renowned for being unreliable, sometimes plaintive and, unusually in the mostly gay world of theatre design, a womanizer (his theatre friends who found his name difficult to pronounce nicknamed him 'Come and seduce me'). He had trained as an architect in Moscow before the Revolution, risen under Lenin to be managing director of the Moscow Grand State Theatre of Opera and Ballet, then founded his own acting school. He also made a number of films which were praised for their originality and beauty. In 1919 he left Russia and settled in Paris where he started the Arc-en-Ciel Theatre. It was here that Bernstein met 'Komis' and they became close friends, sharing a passion for both theatre and films. Bernstein persuaded him to come and work in England, where they joined forces with the writer Arnold Bennett to stage a number of new plays. Both showman and businessman, Bernstein was in every way Komisarjevsky's opposite, but it proved a hugely successful and creative partnership. Influenced by the marble and gilt American dream palaces of the 1920s, they set about creating a chain of cinemas the like of which had not been seen before in England.

Komis was immediately charmed by Connie and offered to take her on a tour of the London Granadas, which were receiving their finishing touches before opening. The Granada at Walthamstow looked like a Moorish court, with wrought-iron columns and a fine metal canopy over the entrance. Inside were heavily patterned walls, three thousand seats upholstered in alternate deep-claret and dark-orange corded velvet, and stage curtains of a delicate pale-green silk with a 'deep embellishment of orange, black, green and white'. In each cinema, expensively re-equipped for the new talkies, a Mighty Wurlitzer rose silently out of the depths and burst into sound, filling the vast auditorium, while in the foyer someone played popular songs on a grand piano, so that patrons could listen to music as they stood waiting for their seats. Connie was to supply sweet-smelling pot-plants such as orange blossom and myrtle to line the walls, Komis told her. Then they visited the Granada at Woolwich, which was quite different: a delicate, almost medieval confection of colours based on early church manuscripts with lines of gold, grey and red. Connie decided that the plants here would have to be quite different: dainty ferns, handsome, red-plush-coloured coleus and heavy, polished leaves of anthurium.

Bernstein was a perfectionist who daily fired off telegrams and nagging memos to his staff: to one cinema manager – 'A man who sells the Ice-Cream is still in a white overall. This looks horrible and must be stopped'; to Connie – 'All theatres should now be hanging baskets of greenery and flowers outside their canopies', to all managers – 'Regarding rubber heels for the staff . . .' And so on. No detail was too small to escape his attention.

Connie and Shav were invited to attend the grand opening of the Granada, Tooting, in South London in September 1931. At 7 p.m. sharp, sixteen trumpeters from the Life Guards blew a fanfare from the steps of the brilliantly lit Italianate façade, and while the public looked on from the chilly streets four thousand invited guests surged inside. Komisarjevsky had designed the immense foyer after a medieval baronial hall, with minstrels' gallery, carved panelling and heavily beamed ceiling from which heraldic Venetian lions stared down on the milling crowd. Lining the wall were oak and gilded Gothic side-tables on which Connie had placed giant urns of exotic plants and vases containing large displays of sweet-smelling flowers. A 150-foot-long hall of mirrors, with Italian Renaissance marble columns, led the guests on through an arched cloister to the vast splendour of the auditorium. Here everything was the colour of antique gold: the ceiling was embossed in rose and gold mouldings; the walls lined with row upon row of cloistered arches and delicate tracery. A series of cusped Gothic pendants, shrouded in rich draperies, were clustered on the proscenium. The floors were either of marble or covered in deep carpets of rose and mauve, and in the recesses were murals of courtly fifteenth-century figures such as troubadours and damsels in wimples, while above were stained-glass windows and wall paintings simulating illuminated manuscripts.

As part of the opening show, Bernstein ordered all those who had worked on the cinema to parade onto the darkened stage as their names were announced over the loudspeakers. He did not join them, and neither did Connie, who had fulfilled her commission for these wildly theatrical picture palaces with enormous skill and enthusiasm but was too nervous to make a public appearance. Her name, though, was passed around the elegant and wealthy guests as the woman who had 'done the flowers'. The experience was overwhelming, and the following day a stunned press described the Tooting Granada as the 'Cathedral of the Talkies, and one of the seven wonders of London'.

Connie's little order book was rapidly filling; suddenly she was finding that she had neither the time nor the flowers to fulfil all her commitments. She desperately needed a base in London to work from, and proper staff to help. Perhaps the answer was a small office or shop where she could also sell flowers. With somewhat reluctant support from Shav, Connie found herself hurriedly setting up a flower business to cope with the demand. It was hardly a good time to open a flower shop. Factories were closing down and banks refusing to lend money to finance new ventures. But, Connie argued, she had secure commissions, the rent would be low and the staff would be paid very little.

Shav, in the meantime, was becoming increasingly alarmed by these developments. Connie's flower 'hobby' had blown up into a considerable undertaking and he was concerned about the financial risks. Even though they were not married, he was afraid that both he and Connie could find themselves legally responsible for bad debts and overstretched budgets. He was right to be concerned; as would become increasingly clear, Connie was no businesswoman, had no head for figures and seemed barely aware that she was engaging in a commercial venture. But as usual, she was already forging ahead, stubbornly refusing to listen to sense, blind to possible risks and blinkered to suggestions that did not suit the direction in which she wanted to go. This was the Connie that Shav, her friends and employees would have to learn to accept. She was not going to change now.

Connie flung herself into the challenge with characteristic verve. Although this was not how she had planned it, the idea of owning a small shop appealed to her. She could hear her mother's disapproval: here was Connie, now reduced to the level of shopkeeper from which she, Etty, had struggled to raise herself all those years earlier. Connie found a shop that suited her in modest rented premises, consisting of ground floor and basement, in Belgrave Road – nowhere near the fashionable Belgrave Square but near Victoria Station on the way down to unfashionable Pimlico. It was, as she later wrote, a terrible mistake to start in such an out-of-the-way place. The shop was called Flower Decorations, which she hoped would distinguish it from the common florist. (She always preferred to use the term flower decorating instead of arranging; perhaps in some snobbish way she believed this distinguished her 'art' from 'business'.) At first she tried to run the shop almost single-handed, doing all the marketing and the flowers herself. She was used to hard work, but now she had taken on something entirely new for which she had neither training nor experience. It was the most critical year of her career, the year in which she made her name; it was also the year in which she dreamed of bringing a new art form to fruition. But it came with the risk that her 'art' would be superseded by the demands that accompanied commercial success.

A steady stream of old friends came through the shop door offering help and advice, from painting walls to bookkeeping. This was always her way of creating her team: picking people up en passant, firing them with her infectious enthusiasm, then simply telling them to 'get on with it'. Connie's young brother Gilbert, who worked abroad in colonial administration and was home on leave, came to help get the shop ready. He was dismayed to be told to stipple the walls, a novel painting effect of the time. 'Nonsense,' said his sister, 'anyone can stipple', and Gilbert got on with it.

Throughout her life Connie would gather up people she liked and find them jobs, whether or not they were suitably trained. She seemed to have a nose for talent, always confident that her protégés had only to 'give it a try' and, with a little guidance from her, would blossom and 'do brilliantly'. It had worked with the assortment of friends who became her team at Homerton, and would do so again in creating her staff for the shop. One day she came across Florence Standfast, her old student roommate, working nearby in Belgrave Road restoring and painting furniture for an antique dealer, who paid almost nothing. Poor Flo was half-starved. 'We can't have this,' Connie declared, 'you must come and make artificial flowers for me.' A department known as 'Arts' was born out of Connie's wish to help her old friend and, like so many of her 'workers', Flo remained there, loyal and successful, for twenty years.

Marjorie Russell sent over some out-of-work Civil Service colleagues, and teachers from Homerton School offered themselves, including her devoted friend Jos Cook, and Mr Phippen, the school instructor in bookkeeping, who came in the evening and did the shop accounts. Gilbert had to return to Africa but his wife Marjorie stayed behind with her baby Norma, to help get the little business on its feet, and became its first saleswoman. Marjorie and Norma lived for a while at Abinger with the Sprys, where Norma later remembered she was looked after mostly by Gladys the cook and only saw her mother, Connie and Shav briefly in the evening. Connie was a tough taskmaster and always led by example. She had a genius for getting everyone enthused and involved so that they would do anything for her without complaint, and often without pay. Above all, what Connie really loved was having a team, and she took an almost schoolgirlish delight in heading her various teams.

As demand grew, the need for yet more cut flowers increased. The indomitable Walter Trower laboured in Connie's Surrey garden, sending up vanloads. But even more flowers, and in greater variety, were soon required. Connie started making daily sorties to the London flower markets, getting up at 5.30 each morning to visit Covent Garden to get the best and the freshest. She always loved the market and had a good relationship with the dealers. Her favourite haunt was the French Department in Covent Garden where, even on the drabbest day, Mediterranean flowers and plants formed an oasis of sunshine. Flat French bamboo baskets would be filled with exotic and wonderful surprises: lavish quantities of deep-cream, double-flowered tuberoses and tightly furled buds of the rare *Iris susiana*. There were golden French ranunculus, anemones, eucalyptus, masses of small, white, wild Roman hyacinths, and lily-of-the-valley, 'smelling gloriously and carrying one straight to the steps of La Madeleine'. Parma violets, which were especially favoured by ladies for their corsages, were sent to England in slatted wicker baskets like picnic hampers. Stacked at the station or quayside waiting to be shipped, they would have been hosed down to keep fresh for the several days it would take for them to arrive at the flower markets.

Connie also adored exotics with their dramatic and unusual forms and colours: 'Huge clumps of palm-tree fruits, looking like fantastic bunches of grapes, their small, hard, black fruits on thick, canary-yellow stems; hard to arrange but dramatic in the right place.' There were branches of pepper-tree that might have come straight from a Tunisian market-place, the delicate pink berries hanging in graceful racemes that lasted for weeks. Many flowers arrived at the shop beautifully packed in wooden boxes, which were chargeable, and money recouped on yesterday's returns was spent on more flowers. To unpack and search through deliveries sent up from the English gardens produced an almost unbearable feeling of excitement. From the hothouses camellias and gardenias arrived in special cases beautifully lined with cotton wool, as well as 'all manner of exotic flowers, blue water-lilies, scarlet passion flowers, and strange lily-like and waxy blooms'. It was wonderful in summer to find scented sweet-peas and moss roses, stately spires of delphiniums, foxgloves and eremurus.

The market traders soon learned Connie's likes and dislikes; they knew her *bête noire* was chrysanthemums, but if they had anything new or strange such as a rare orchid, a richly coloured anthurium or a fine passion flower, they kept it back for her. At first she was a curiosity at the market and nobody took her seriously. 'I'll give her a fortnight,' laughed one market official. But Connie passed effortlessly through the fortnight, meeting buyers from old-established florists in the breakfast room at Covent Garden which Munro, the great wholesale flower business, ran for its customers.

Here Connie loved to sit and listen and learn. Basil Unite, who had just completed his training at Munro's and was in charge of the lily department, remembered his surprise when the first walked into his office. Covent Garden was hardly a ladies' world. But there she stood, chatting away to him and humming with vitality 'like a little transistor set that you tuned into immediately'. Although she was not a big customer, Connie's influence on the London flower scene was soon reaching back to the markets. She had an insatiable appetite for lilies and white arums, and Basil Unite persuaded James de Rothschild's head gardener to grow extra quantities for his demanding new customer. Connie knew exactly what she wanted, and she got it. When she wanted big branches of magnolia and camellia, rare species rhododendrons or exotic shrubs, orders went down to plantsmen's gardens in Devon and Cornwall such as Caerhays, Glendurgan and Trebah and to the Rothschild garden in Exbury, Hampshire. They would always do their best to supply her.

When the breakfast ritual was over, Connie would sit on the pavement surrounded by her purchases and wait to be collected (she never learned to drive). The little green Austin van would eventually arrive and be loaded to bursting – including its canvas carrier on the roof where thickets of branches would protrude fore and aft – before Connie and her assistant sped back along the Embankment. The policeman on duty at Westminster Bridge got to know the van with its thatch of green, and would hold up the traffic to let them through. It was the sort of thing that Connie loved and they would arrive back at the shop in good humour and gales of laughter, which would carry the overworked and under-paid staff through the long, arduous day and 'make it all seem so worthwhile'. To get the best plant material meant going very early to market, but Connie's clients were not such early risers and so with the flowers plunged into buckets of water she and her assistant would rest in a couple of deck-chairs until the time came to set off on their rounds.

In the early days there were the regular bread-and-butter jobs: Atkinsons' windows done on Mondays and visited daily to check nothing needed renewing; four big windows at Drage's in Oxford Street, the Elizabeth Arden salons and the dining-rooms at Hatchet's Restaurant. Because these places were so hot it was difficult to keep the flowers fresh, and they tended to wilt; Connie gradually developed her own special methods for ensuring her flowers survived all kinds of maltreatment.

In order to get the best out of her material, Connie found certain methods worth using to ensure long vase life and reduce the trauma which often resulted in drooping and wilting blooms: 'Some of the most exquisite flowers are the most fleeting, but I find that no reason for disregarding them . . . I would like to say that there are ways and means of prolonging the life and freshness of many flowers that are regarded as being too short-lived to be worth picking.' She always picked her own garden flowers at least a day before they were needed, and put them in deep pails of water in a cool place. This enabled them to absorb plenty of water before being exposed to the rigours of travel, warm rooms and over-handling during arrangement. There are several kinds of cut flow-ers that will not last in a vase at all unless they have been first almost submerged in water – for example, arum leaves and maid-enhair fern, bougainvillea, violets and annual sunflowers. A few plants such as hellebores, Connie suggested, last better if allowed to 'swim' in water before being arranged. Some types of flower are unable to absorb enough water to support both blooms and heavy foliage – for instance, lilac and some philadelphus: 'You may prolong their life and also gain a greater decorative effect, by removing a good number of their leaves', she wrote. Some of the most difficult flowers were also her favourites: cow-parsley, lime flowers, euphorbia, wild willowherb and garden lilac, which all require special attention including the stripping off of nearly all the leaves.

Some of Connie's methods might sound rather extreme but she was convinced of their efficacy. For example, in order to enable hard-wooded material such as fruit-tree branches and woody-stemmed chrysanthemums to absorb enough water to keep them alive, the cut ends of their stems should be bruised, or crushed with a wooden mallet, several at a time. Very tough stems can be hammered or split for three or four inches. Soft-stemmed flowers can be helped if split with a knife at the cut end to about one inch. Dahlias, hollyhocks and poinsettias should have the ends of their stems either charred or dipped into boiling water for a few seconds before being soaked, while poppies and bluebells should have just the ends of their stems dipped. To restore flowers wilting in a vase she suggested using warm water and, to keep it clear, putting a lump of charcoal in the bottom of the vase. If flowers such as tulips or rosebuds show signs of wilting they can be lifted out of the vase, have their stems re-cut, be rolled up in newspaper to keep them straight, and plunged to the neck in water in a dark, cool place until they revive. Care must be taken that no leaves ever touch the water, and one should never disturb an arrangement after it is done – just top up daily with tepid water.

Servicing the pot-plants for all the Granada Cinemas required much driving around and heavy lifting and carrying. Then there was the increasing list of clients wanting flowers for parties, dances and weddings. Contracts for flowers for shop windows and cinemas were gradually superseded by private orders for regular floral decorations in the smart society houses, for parties and weddings, or for any special public occasion where an eye-catching display was required. Commissions piled up and more staff were urgently needed. Connie requested help from an agency and, one Monday morning, a rather plain young woman arrived.

Valmar, or Val, Pirie was from an old Franco-Scottish family. Her grandfather had married a Frenchwoman who insisted on living in France, so he bought a chateau near Angers and transported his entire family, livestock, furniture and possessions by boat from Aberdeen, across France, then up the Loire to his new home. Her father was the MP for North Aberdeen and a passionate gardener, her mother a daughter of the 17th Baron Sempill. The Pirie children were mostly brought up in France and French was their first language, but with the outbreak of the First World War they had been sent back to Scotland to be educated. Val was musical and had hoped to become a concert pianist, but soon decided she lacked the necessary talent. She also had a flair for fashion and loved dressmaking and was accordingly apprenticed to a tough London couturier, where she was treated more as a general slave than a trainee. After a few years of snubs and scolding, she walked out and signed on at an employment agency. There she was told about a job with a small florist paying just £2 10s a week; she must be good with flowers and gardening and be able to drive a van. Val had been a keen gardener as a child and though she could only name flowers in French, she could drive. Connie felt she had the right instincts and enthusiasm for the job and immediately took her on. For the business it was a decision that would prove unerringly correct. For Connie personally, it was disastrous.

On her first day Val arrived at the shop at eight o'clock. Flo Standfast shouted to her to hurry and drive the van to the market, where 'Mrs Spry had expected you at six!' Val leaped into the van and drove hell for leather to Covent Garden, where she found an anxious little figure on the pavement surrounded by boxes and baskets. 'Just get me to Atkinsons' in Bond Street,' Connie cried, and off they roared. The boxes were unpacked and Connie started to work on one of the big soapstone urns. 'You do the other to match,' she told Val. With trembling fingers Val did her beginner's best, and presently Connie came over. She thanked Val, praised her work and then slightly retouched it; Val was completely hooked. Working with Connie, she recalled, was always delight-fully warm and friendly. From the beginning, one was treated as a colleague of equal status, not as a lowly trainee: 'Everyone's ideas were encouraged, and it was always praise first and gentle criticism after.' Connie had the instincts of a good teacher, always patient, never negatively critical but absolutely demanding of complete dedication and effort.

As commissions piled up, more experienced staff were needed. When Connie heard that a West End flower shop had gone out of business, she quickly pounced on the head saleswoman, a Miss Oldfield, a large, calm and dignified lady who was initially dubious about exchanging the smart West End for a shop on the wrong side of London. Connie also hired Miss White, the firm's head florist. 'Whitey', a jeweller's daughter, did floristry work with a jeweller's precision, taking on the most delicate tasks, such as separately wiring each bell of a bunch of hyacinths to form a wedding spray. It was largely thanks to her skill that Connie was able to offer innovative crescent-shaped sprays for brides to carry instead of the traditional bunches tied together like a miniature broomstick.

*

Connie had always been rather ambivalent about traditional floristry, and it has been customary to think of her as the woman who set flowers free from such artificial constraints. The term 'floristry' in those days meant the art of wiring flowers and leaves into ornate bouquets, garlands, wreaths, headdresses, buttonholes, pins and corsages. It was both fashionable and very popular, and Connie had the highest regard for those with the necessary speed and skill for this kind of work. It was essential for weddings and funerals, the bread and butter of many flower shops and, as Connie herself remarked, 'the sentimental young thing who wants only natural flowers at her wedding is likely to be disappointed by the result.' Her own requirements in floristry were exacting: if any wiring showed she would complain about the 'ironmongery'; the end result had to be jewel-like.

In many of her books Connie claimed to dislike artifice, anything that seemed unnatural, particularly wiring – 'do not wire flowers for a vase, it takes away the natural grace of the flower' – and she usually rejected artificially dried or coloured flowers. Yet in later years she created extraordinary dramatic effects by painting and gilding leaves and using artificial 'drieds'. She loved to create her Christmas 'gewgaws', and was often seen happily wiring and waxing in Flo's 'Arts' department. Connie knew the difference between these sought-after products, which were fun and very necessary to her business, and the serious art of decorating with flowers.

Soon an assistant was also found for Flo, whose skill in making artificial flowers was proving very successful; her 'Flemish pictures' made out of perfectly fashioned flowers of waxed paper sold for high prices and were kept by customers until they gathered dust. She also became adept at working with papier mâché, and made boat-shaped and wall-mounted vases which she varnished or coated with plaster, then painted. Later, Flo made models of vases designed by Connie which were then made up by the Fulham Pottery and sold as collectibles.

Connie always took great care with her choice of receptacles for her flower displays, which in her view was as important as the choice of the flowers themselves. Having inherited from her mother a passion for ornaments, she could never resist the junk-shops that proliferated at the time, where real bargains could be found. Travelling on a bus, she would often spy something in a pawn shop or junk-yard and leap out to buy another treasure. Driving around in the van made such acquisitions even easier. Connie would suddenly shout at her assistant, 'Stop, I've seen something!' and return triumphantly carrying some quite filthy and unpromising-looking object. 'Never mind,' she would say. 'Wait till I've got it cleaned up.' Often these finds would turn out to be copper or alabaster, but even if they were only wood or pottery she might see an interesting shape that had potential. She particularly loved giant vases that she could barely carry. This growing assortment, including jugs, tins, boxes – anything that could be made to hold water – became an essential part of her work, and both her shops and her houses would always be crammed with pieces waiting for their moment. Connie's private clients often wanted her to use their own cut-glass vases and silver rose-bowls, but instead she would throw open their cupboards and bring out old heirlooms in bronze and marble, silver cups, tureens and sauceboats, and even bread bins, pottery dishes and meat plates from the kitchen. Once the ladies had got over the shock, they were usually delighted with the results.

Connie's little shop gained an element of masculine resourcefulness, stability and humour with the addition of George Foss. 'Fossey', then only twenty-four, had ambitions to be a head gardener but his father said they were a dying race and sent him to Drage's department store where his brother worked. When Fossey saw Connie's dramatic flower arrangements in the store's windows, he was hooked. With his horticultural knowledge and experience in retail, he was an ideal flower buyer. The only problem was that he could not drive. Val put him in the van and made him drive round and round nearby Vincent Square until he ran into a lamp-post, after which he was considered qualified. He was willing to turn his hand to anything, or, if it was beyond him, to find precisely the chap who could do it – such as the craftsman who made the watertight tin linings for Connie's junk-shop finds, or the chap who could construct pedestals, screens and backgrounds for her displays. Fossey accepted with amusement his position as the only man in a small and decidedly feminine world. He was infinitely kind and helpful to the beginners and always had a shoulder for anyone to cry on. Over thirty years later he was still there, as Managing Director, and like so many of her devoted staff remained working with Connie for the rest of her life.

Connie listened to her clients, learned from them and tried to interpret their wishes and preferences – only steering them away from things that seemed dull or 'unsuitable'. Happily, many of her private clients were discerning, cultured people from whom she could learn as well as share her own novel ideas. There was the client who wanted vases of 'old roses' the same as those in her Aubusson carpets, another who wanted the greens and greys and crimsons of a wonderful tapestry to be emphasized, an artist who wanted flowers that did not look 'too real' and was given urns of sculptural-looking arums. Each commission was personal and individual; and gradually Connie developed a deeper understanding of how to use flowers to suit both an individual room and the character of its owner. From the peaceful atmosphere afforded by fresh greens and soft plums to the simple prettiness of pinks and blues to lively scarlets and acid yellows, she demonstrated vividly that flowers had the power to create mood and also to reflect it.

Connie's first grand customer was Lady Winnifreda Portarlington, the wife of an Irish peer. Lady Portarlington was driving home from a Royal Horticultural Show in Vincent Square when she saw the little shop, and something 'novel and exquisite standing in the window'. The chauffeur stopped the car, came into the shop and asked for the owner. When Connie appeared, Lady Portarlington leaped out of the limousine with cries of delight, amazed to find that Constance Spry was the little Connie Fletcher who had worked with her old friend Lady Aberdeen in Dublin.

She immediately invited Connie to do regular flower arrangements in her home and became her lifelong friend and patron.

Grander still was Molly Mount Temple, mistress both of the vast Broadlands estate in Hampshire and of a superb London house. She was a domineering and exacting woman and not popular with the staff at Flower Decorations. She would phone the shop in the morning and order flowers for the dinner table to coordinate with her chosen gown. But she was also dynamic and amusing, and there were times when she even laughed at herself. 'Exit tornado!' she would cry as she got into her car, knowing she left behind her 'gasps of relief'. But she had a genuine feel for good decor and was a passionate gardener. She did not, of course, soil her own hands with actual gardening (she is said to have been the first person in London to paint her fingernails), but she was a knowledgeable garden designer who broke away from the old Victorian 'blaze of colour' borders and planned her planting in harmonizing tones – blue and grey, or all-red, or silver and white. She employed ten male gardeners and two girls who were students from horticultural college. Two of Connie's best flower decorators, Margaret Watson and Joyce Robinson, came ready-trained from Broadlands. They shared a bothy in the grounds and were paid very little while they were training. Their chief work was to pick and arrange flowers for the large weekend house parties. They also made up baskets of cut flowers for Connie's shop, to be sent up to London early on Monday mornings. Over the years Molly Mount Temple and Connie became close friends, sharing an interest in interior design and gardening – although, according to their mutual friend Beverley Nichols, there was a certain rivalry between the two ladies which, 'in Molly's case, grew into a positive animosity'.

As her reputation grew, Connie found herself being taken up by society women who wished to be her patron; she was their very own flower decorator, a 'special discovery' whom they could recommend to their friends. Her easy charm and ability to move effortlessly between different social circles meant that she was even invited to luncheons and occasionally to parties. She was, however, always very wary of combining business with social life, declaring that she was 'a shopkeeper, and shopkeepers do not attend customers' parties'. She hardly ever accepted dinner invitations. Exhausted after a long day, she far preferred spending a quiet evening at home with Shav in the garden or playing Scrabble or doing the crossword puzzle. Occasionally she went to luncheon parties where she could see her flowers 'in action' and make useful contacts. She was always a popular guest, keeping everyone laughing at her stories and her mimicry, though she still claimed she was shy with strangers.

Back at home, friends were always welcome in the rambling old house and the semi-wild garden at Abinger. Marjorie Russell was a regular visitor, bringing her theatre and 'arty' friends who enjoyed the relaxed atmosphere, good food and far-ranging, sometimes racy talk. Sidney Bernstein had rented a cottage nearby from Vita Sackville-West and visited with his own weekend guests such as Oliver Messel and his sister Alice, Norman Wilkinson, John Gielgud and Charles Laughton. Connie particularly adored Theodore Komisarjevsky, not because of his famous sexual allure but because, like him, she loved to make something out of nothing. Komis could design stage sets out of the most unpromising materials and make them look remarkable by his artistry and his supreme ability in lighting. Given a few second-hand flats, an old back-cloth, some paint and a modest lighting set, Komis would give you beauty. And it cost almost nothing at all. In the course of their long association Connie learned many valuable tricks from Komis, which she developed in her own way for parties and weddings.

Similarly, her long and enduring friendship with Oliver Messel brought her numerous important commissions and she took many valuable ideas from his theatre designs. Talented and precocious, Messel was in his early twenties when Connie first met him. His family was cultured, wealthy and artistic; his grandfather and father, of German extraction, were the knowledgeable plantsmen who created the famous gardens at Nymans in Sussex. Messel, whose mother was a daughter of the artist Edward Sambourne, studied at the Slade School of Fine Art in London under Professor Henry Tonks. He so impressed his teachers with his extraordinary and original masks modelled from wax and papier mâché that, while still a student, he held an exhibition of them. This led to his first professional commission to create masks for Massine's ballet *Zephyr and Flora*. 'Cocky' Cochran, alert as ever to young talent, engaged Messel to create masks for his *1926 Revue* at the London Pavilion. During this time Messel designed costumes and scenery for a succession of Cochran's revues, including, in 1928, the setting for Noël Coward's song 'Dance, Dance Little Lady' from *This Year of Grace*.

One weekend Val Pirie brought an old schoolfriend who had recently finished a cookery course at the famous Cordon Bleu School in Paris. Rosemary Hume was one of the first women to have gained the coveted diploma. She had been taught by Henri-Paul Pellaprat the repertory of French dishes derived from the great Escoffier.

Rosemary was born in 1907 near Sevenoaks, Kent. Her father, Colonel Charles Vernon Hume, was in military intelligence and had recently served as military attaché at the British legation in Tokyo during the Russo-Japanese war. Her mother Ursula was from Keswick in Cumberland. Rosemary and her sisters grew up in several homes, often staying with family or friends in large country houses where she quickly found her way to the kitchen and wheedled the cooks into teaching her their skills and recipes. She had failed to shine at school but instead became passionate about cookery. Connie took to her immediately.

It was the beginning of a lifelong friendship which eventually became a professional partnership too. Since her return from Paris Rosemary had often been asked to cook special luncheons and dinners for friends and pass on a little of her expertise and knowledge in French cuisine to their somewhat reluctant cooks (some of whom so resented the idea that they required any instruction that one woman threw a saucepan at Rosemary's head). Nevertheless, one of her elder sisters recalled that she was astonished to see such 'a shy, unassuming girl gain such rapport with these old pros'. Connie was sufficiently impressed with Rosemary to persuade her to give her cook Gladys Trower some lessons. Happily Gladys proved to be a keen and talented pupil. Connie herself was always present during these sessions in the kitchen, watching, tasting, learning and taking note of every detail.

In 1931 Rosemary borrowed £2,000 from family friends and set up a cookery school in London with Dione Lucas, a fellow student from the Paris Cordon Bleu. They rented two ground-floor rooms in Jubilee Place, Chelsea. The larger room was the kitchen, the smaller the office, and in a corridor to the street, according to Rosemary's niece Griselda Barton, 'they set up a few tables and chairs for passers-by to partake of the more edible results of their students' efforts'.

Val Pirie was now spending almost every weekend at Abinger, helping in the garden and relaxing after the long, arduous week. Sunday afternoons were spent gathering in the garden, woods and hedgerows enough to fill the huge hamper with flowers, leaves, seed-heads and branches to be driven up to town early on Monday. Although Connie sometimes took her friends for granted, her friendships were always intense and close, very trusting and generous. She regarded Val as part of the family and the most important member of her team. She relied on her for her loyal support and unfailing good advice on running the business. Whereas Connie, as already noted, had neither aptitude nor interest in the business side of things, Val showed considerable talent for it.

A few days before Christmas, when Connie, Gladys and Rosemary were up to their elbows in mixing-bowls preparing puddings and pies, Connie sent Shav and Val off for a walk in the woods with instructions to collect some branches of larch well-studded with cones. They claimed they could not distinguish a larch from a pine and their search took them a long time. They returned home several hours later, giggling conspiratorially at some intimate joke. Their arms were laden with all kinds of greenery. Long trails of creeper wound all around them, tripping everyone up.

SIX

All-White

1932

The late 1920s and early 1930s were a golden age for party giving despite the fact that the country was in the grip of a depression. Wages fell and prices rose; there were strikes in the coalmines and hunger marches on London. More and more people were beginning to experience the kind of poverty Connie had seen in the East End: the long dole queues, the apathy, the clothing clubs, the undernourished children forced to give up their education and work for a pittance.

But the rich seemed barely to notice, and continued to spend with extraordinary abandon, lavishing fantastic sums on entertaining. The Season of 1932, everyone agreed, had been 'every bit as amusing as previous years'. The society pages of newspapers and magazines reported in every trivial detail who was where, with whom, what they were saying and what they wore:

> But really [exclaimed one social diarist], how does anyone stand the whirl of the London Season or hope to keep up with it? There were so many interesting things going on: Ascot and Henley, the Tattoo at Aldershot, the Test matches, a show of 19th-century paintings at the Lefevre gallery, the Opera at Glyndebourne, *The Dubarry*, playing at His Majesty's Theatre, with Margaret Yarde giving a vigorous performance as a hard-boiled lady of unimpeachable lack of virtue . . . Really, Londoners are spoilt. And that is before one mentions the parties.

Lady Rothschild's ball was the most magnificent of the year, 'with live, powdered footmen in yellow plush; with so many guests, Hyde Park was opened specially for parking cars . . . Mr Jimmy Rothschild, complete with eye-glass, and Mr Winston Churchill were amongst the interesting older men while all the household names among the girls and young men were there,' gushed *Vogue*, while *The Times* reported: 'The debutantes, for all their tulle and simpering organdie, are much better made up this year; some of them can even dance the tango, though the current favourites are "She didn't say Yes" and "I want all of You".'

Fashions were carefully noted: for example, at a private view at Tooth's Galleries guests were given 'a novelty' in the form of cardboard cylinders through which to peer at the pictures – 'An excellent idea, but which did not prevent one noticing that the chicest woman present was Mrs Charles Winn in a red and white dress with a little white cap.' At one society luncheon it was reported that Mrs Vreeland, 'who is the last word in polished American chic, was wearing a small black suede beret with a black quill at a daring angle and a coat of black pony cloth, so smooth it looked like patent leather'. Other guests included Lady Lister-Kaye who wore red, Lady Chamberlain in brown, and Lady Carisbrooke in black. Lady Juliet Duff was draped in a cape of nine silver foxes – 'we counted them' – and Madame de Polignac 'appeared magnificent in apricot satin and the loveliest ermine and pearls'.

Party decor and floral displays were accorded equal critical attention in the press. For Lady Astor's ball, the house was 'literally lined with lilacs'. Lady Anglesey's dining-table held irises floating in shallow silver dishes, and Lady Ribblesdale had her lunch tables decorated with bowls of flame-coloured azaleas and delphiniums. The triumph of flower arrangements that year was the decoration at Simon Marks's dance at Prince's Gate: 'In a niche in the hallway there was a magnificent "set flowerpiece" such as one sees in pictures, and in one of the drawing-rooms stood a huge bouquet of pink azaleas and pink wisteria.' 'Of course,' the writer concluded, 'all the flowers were done by Mrs Spry.' Anyone who knew Connie's work would have recognized the classic Spry principles from these descriptions: her novel use of colours and containers, the single dramatic 'flowerpiece', and the influence of paintings.

Connie had by now become the most sought-after and most

fashionable florist (or 'flower decorator', as she always preferred) to the highest echelons. Recommendations from clients such as Lady Portarlington and Molly Mount Temple had permeated through the London (and country) social sets until it became the chicest thing to employ Mrs Spry and her staff at Flower Decorations. Connie quickly learned that success with 'artistic' decoration relied on the wealth of patrons; on their glamorous lifestyle, their tight-knit milieu and their competitive socializing. Connie's ascendancy into the most exalted and privileged ranks of fashionable society was remarkable, and she now found herself being lionized by clients desperate to be on her waiting list. But for all the admiration and the constant stream of invitations to the grandest parties, Connie was still 'trade'. And in 1933 *Vogue* was quite clear in describing her as 'one of the essential figures behind the scenes in social life'. Polite society might have become more open, but however charming and skilled one was, breeding still mattered.

Four London hostesses occupied centre stage at that time. The Hon. Mrs Ronald Greville, a down-to-earth Scotswoman from a hugely wealthy brewing family, specialized in royalty – Queen Mary, a personal friend, often came to tea. Lady Emerald Cunard, an American socialite, collected ambassadors, cabinet ministers and other eminent figures such as Lady Diana Cooper, Sir Thomas Beecham and Winston Churchill. Lady Sybil Colefax assembled the pick of the brains: George Bernard Shaw, Max Beerbohm, Duff Cooper and Virginia Woolf.

The guests of Syrie Maugham, the 'Queen of White', ranged from the scandalously unconventional to the fascinatingly rich and rare: 'Not at all the same crowd as you'd meet at Emerald Cunard's.' She captured her own splendid list of young lions, mostly theatre people, café aristocracy, editors of fashion magazines, writers and artists such as Arnold Bennett, Cecil Beaton, 'Cocky' Cochran, Noël Coward, Rex Whistler, Oliver Hill, Rebecca West and the Prince of Wales, who was said to have enjoyed the 'mock-virgin pallor' of Syrie Maugham's white rooms.

Her parties had a brilliance and glamour that others could hardly equal, and when she entertained everything else had to be cancelled in order for one to be there. 'She had a secret recipe,' recalled her friend Oliver Messel: 'The stage was set with infinite care, so that as you arrived at the door it was magic . . . She had an individual way of entertaining – creating an atmosphere of delicious charm and comfort and the exquisite flower arrangements concocted by Constance Spry for every occasion made their first appearance in her house.'

In the early Twenties there had been a momentary attack of black – black-lacquered furniture, black fabrics and objects. Then came a craze for silver-covered surfaces: silver gilt on furniture, silver paint on walls and silver threads woven into drapes and fabrics. After Howard Carter discovered Tutankhamun's tomb in 1922 there was a passion for everything Egyptian, while Diaghilev's newly arrived Ballets Russes and the pre-war Oriental style together evoked Arab and Eastern mysticism and exoticism.

But now everything was white: white decor, white clothes and white flowers. The all-white 'Baroque' style that Osbert Lancaster described as 'Vogue Regency' swept through both the fashionable theatres and the houses of the rich. Theatre people like Messel and Norman Wilkinson were trying their hand at interior decoration, and interior designers flirted with theatre and costume designs. Parties too were regarded as a form of theatre. First-night and after-theatre parties were choked with celebrities, and 'bright young things' could be seen enjoying a table at the Trocadero in Shaftesbury Avenue where they watched cabarets called *Champagne Time*, *Supper Time*, and *Going to Town*. Messel claimed that it was his designs for the extraordinary all-white scenes in the smash production *Helen!* premiered at the Adelphi in January 1932 that 'were carried into the home by Syrie'. But long before then, Syrie had 'turned everything white'. After the triumphant first night of Cochran's *1931 Revue* she threw a party in her newly decorated 'sumptuous home with flower decorations by Constance Spry'. Syrie's all-white drawing-room appeared to guests, as they entered, like a 'stage on which they were to act and watch others act for them'. Her guests were astonished by the revolutionary room, decorated entirely in off-white and beige or palest green – but never dead-white or cream. A reporter for *Vogue* wrote: 'Ever since Mrs Somerset Maugham made her white room in Chelsea one has felt that parties require to be bathed in light: white satin drapes, mirrors in white rococo plaster frames, dining chairs in gold and white, white ceramic cockerels, white electric candles, white birds on rings in the windows, silver and white ceramic ashtrays and white flowers.'

White made Syrie Maugham famous, and it drew Connie into a different, dramatic and creative world; a new departure from shop windows and the homes of the rich.

Syrie's father was the philanthropist Dr Thomas Barnardo, who founded the famous Barnardo Homes for boys and girls. A man of evangelical correctness, he was severe with his children: socializing, books and the theatre were forbidden. Syrie escaped into two disastrous marriages, first to the much older Henry Wellcome, American founder of the great pharmaceutical house. After an affair with Gordon Selfridge, another American and the founder of the London store, during which she picked up an interest in furniture and decoration, she met and fell in love with William Somerset Maugham. During the war Maugham had served as a driver in France, where he met his American lover Gerald Haxton. It is said that Maugham only married Syrie in 1917 as a cover for his relationship with Haxton. Although her friends always claimed that Syrie continued to love Maugham, the marriage was clearly doomed, though it did produce Syrie's much-loved daughter Liza.

To survive both financially and emotionally, Syrie turned to her own talents and resources. She threw herself into a decorating business and in 1922 opened her own showroom 'Syrie Ltd' in Baker Street. She borrowed £400 from her friend Mrs 'Winkie' Phillipson, wife of a wealthy coal merchant and herself an amateur artist and keen exponent of white. Norman Wilkinson had taught Winkie to paint flower pots white for her white flowers and, as a result, Cecil Beaton recalled, she had 'allowed her mania for no colour to spread indoors, and the house, too, became all-white'. Some would suggest that Syrie Maugham had borrowed more than just the £400. Oliver Hill, another designer friend, wrote that Syrie once said, 'I am off to India to paint the Black Hole of Calcutta white', and when she later went to Hollywood Oliver Messel joked, 'Now she's white-washing the whole of the film colony.' There the white craze seemed to be embodied by Jean Harlow, 'who appeared to have been constructed of equal parts snow, marble and marshmallow'.

When Connie and Syrie Maugham first met they immediately found mutual interests and sympathies; they became firm friends and collaborated on projects for several years. Despite different backgrounds, there were many similarities in their unconventional lives. Both women were in their forties, had difficult relationships with their mothers, had married to escape unhappy homes and had been divorced. And they both ran their own businesses. *Vogue* rather perceptively noted: 'Someone once said that a woman is either happily married or an Interior Decorator. Whether or not the rise of the Society decorator can be attributed to the present slump in married felicity, it is certain that it is as fashionable now to be doing up the house of one's acquaintance as it was to open a hat-shop in pre-war days.'

Connie began supplying flowers for many of Syrie's luncheons and dinner parties, where the table decorations might include a central group of white flowers and individual bouquets in white china cabbage leaves at each place setting. One guest remembered pillars of white blooms in the dining-room lit from within. Swept up in the 'all-white' craze, Connie's novel designs became an integral part of Syrie's decor. She was at last able to put into practice her long-held conviction that flowers are an ephemeral but essential dimension to interior decoration. James Amster, an American interior designer, recalled that Connie showed Syrie how 'when you do a room, you must "over-scale" it'. He was referring to her practice of using one or two oversized and dramatic displays of flowers instead of several small vases dotted around the room. Thanks to Connie, flowers were no longer the finishing decorative touch but an intrinsic part of the decor. She had come a long way from painted clay pots of marguerites in an East End classroom.

As the craze spread, more and more of Connie's clients asked for white flowers to complement their new decor. Her close friend Lady Portarlington was one of the first to decorate her drawing-room in white. It was a superb setting, and Connie responded with all her artistry and skill. She shared the current passion, believing that white and green flowers were the ideal complement to a white room: 'their infinite gradations of green or cream standing out against white walls, with the right lighting, [appear] almost sculpted.' Outline and setting, as well as scale, were what mattered, Connie wrote, and if the container and background were right, then 'all kinds of strange combinations could be achieved. It is in the interplay of light and shade, colour and shape in a thousand variations, that the delight of white flowers lies. It is subtle and distinct, cool yet brilliant, and is a matter for endless experiment and pleasure.'

Connie used Lady Portarlington's magnificent collection of celadon vases to build breathtaking groups of white lilies set off with eucalyptus, green hydrangea heads and lichen-covered branches with perhaps one brilliant spike of a scarlet anthurium for drama. The nurserymen who supplied the white lilies and arums were astonished by the sudden increase in demand for flowers more traditionally used for funerals. For one party Connie bought quantities of *Lilium giganteum*; they had as many as twenty great flowers to a stem and were so tall she had to cut them down to size. The only place they could be successfully accommodated was in a huge Chinese vase at the foot of a wide stone staircase. After the party the hostess gave a stem to each of her guests, who found it necessary to dismiss their cars and send for taxis, which could be opened in the front, in order to carry home their single splendid lily.

As more and more extravagant parties were held Connie was increasingly called in, often with Oliver Messel or Syrie Maugham, to decorate the venue. One of the most extraordinary was given by the journalist and investor Ronald Tree at his Sussex home. Messel decorated a tent of white muslin with 'Negro' heads sporting red and white ostrich plumes and ropes of pearls, Connie filled the drawing-room with huge vases of green and white flowers until 'the scent of lilies was almost overpowering', while on the terrace a giant birdcage festooned with white roses housed the orchestra. Every room was lit and the whole house 'looked like a giant liner, its lights shimmering across the blackness of the ocean'. Guests were asked to wear red and white – Oliver Messel arrived in a white suit with a red tie. His sister Alice heard an outraged peer muttering: 'Bugger ought to be thrown in the lake.' The evening ended with a magnificent red and white firework display. The landscape architect Geoffrey Jellico remembered driving back to London in the dawn 'wondering whether we should ever see the like again'.

It wasn't just the fabulous parties that were being noticed in the popular press: fashions in interior design were going through radical changes, and demand for individual forms of expression was growing in the homes of those wealthy enough to satisfy it. The big London stores such as Fortnum & Mason had always supplied expert but conventional decorative services, but now it was considered the height of fashion to invite a leading artist or a personality with creative flair to redesign one's home. For the first time women were finding greater freedom and responsibility in decorating their own homes, previously the prerogative of the master of the house. Sybil Colefax had joined her neighbour and rival hostess Syrie Maugham in the new profession of 'lady decorators', as Madge Garland, then editor of *Vogue*, called them. But there was nothing ladylike about it. It was a cut-throat business and required the tough-mindedness of a Syrie Maugham if one was to make one's mark.

Before starting her business Syrie sought the advice of the

American decorator Elsie Mendl, who had introduced the craze for chintz and antiques to America and was thus nicknamed 'the chintz lady'. 'You're too late, my dear, much too late,' Elsie told Syrie. 'The decorating field is already overcrowded.' But Syrie was not too late. Her Baker Street shop was so successful that she opened others in New York and Chicago and went on to decorate some of the grandest houses and country estates in both England and America.

The art historian Martin Battersby described the small handful of ladies who led the design revolution as ruthless and often unscrupulous in their dealings. They 'all had an unshakable belief in their own taste and talents', and 'Woe betide a client who bought anything from a rival decorator – by the lift of an eyebrow they could insinuate that the object was a shoddy fake, an error of taste, absurdly expensive, and that the morals of the rival decorator were highly suspect.' Syrie certainly fitted this description. Unlike Connie, she was not a team person: she was high-handed and imperious, with a brusque way of demanding people do what she required. She could be unscrupulous and formidable, but with a steely wit and quick temper, the sort of woman you either loved or loathed. Like Connie, Oliver Messel was an excellent mimic and particularly loved to imitate Syrie with her clipped high-pitched voice – 'Go and pick up those pelmets *at once*, please.'

Connie, though, enjoyed working with Syrie and found her open and experimental mind stimulating. And as the smartest interior decorator in London, Syrie's support for Connie was invaluable, opening many doors that might otherwise have remained closed.

Connie adored Syrie's beautiful house in Chelsea with its huge white salon and pine-panelled dining-room, the pieces of old Chelsea porcelain and other ornaments, any of which could be used for flowers. For one party in Syrie's drawing-room Connie used a set of large pearly cockleshells. She filled them with masses of Roman hyacinths arranged in a sort of fringe emerging from the shells and drooping onto the tables. The shells were set in informal groups around the tables and in the centre of each table she placed a large green papier mâché dish in the shape of a leaf, made by Flo Standfast. Each one was heaped with fruit – green and black grapes, passion fruit, fresh lychees, plums and peaches – and among the fruit Connie put gardenias and white and purple hellebores. The grapes were raised from the centre of the dish and allowed to fall over the edges; she mounted the passion fruit into loose racemes by fastening their short stems on to thin green twigs. The hellebores emphasized the purple note of the passion fruit and grapes, while the gardenias and green grapes lightened the whole.

Syrie knew nothing about flowers, but she knew what she wanted; she liked colours to be either muted or brilliant, as in nasturtiums or 'pegaloniums' (her floral mispronunciations were a constant joy to Connie). Later, for Liza Maugham's coming-out party, Connie decorated a room with wild fireweed, which looked exquisite but 'gave far more trouble than conventional flowers would have done'. Syrie shared Connie's magpie skills and together they combed flea-markets and junk-yards on the lookout for pieces to transform into their own creations. Syrie is said to have coined the term 'distressed'. She 'pickled' antique furniture by dipping it into a bath of lye or acid solution, which stripped the heavy patina of dirt and wax polish and revealed the pale, raw wood grain. She took Chippendale furniture and 'painted the hell out of it!' Her speciality was 'antique white', a sort of amber glaze on white, with gilt. Some people thought the results were elegant while others regarded her wild methods as vandalism. She was accused of ruthlessly stripping, bleaching and waxing Chippendale, Biedermeier and black coromandel screens. She stripped a French provincial fruitwood commode with a marquetry top and painted it white, with details picked out in gold. Once, when Syrie brought home a Provençal armoire, Noël Coward was a weekend guest; 'She'll pickle it before you can say knife,' he moaned. And Elsie Mendl was heard to say, 'One day darling Syrie will arrange to be pickled in her own coffin.'

Syrie introduced Connie to Victor Stiebel, an exciting young couturier. Stiebel had been brought up in South Africa and had studied at Cambridge where he designed costumes for the university theatre, and in 1932 he opened his own fashion house in Bruton Street in London. It was so successful that within the year he expanded his showrooms into an adjoining elegant Georgian ballroom, to which Syrie applied one of her classic all-white schemes: bone-white walls, white curtains and carpets. 'You must have Constance Spry to do the flowers,' she told Stiebel. 'She's a genius and you'll adore her.' He did, and soon became one of Connie's dearest friends. His first dress show was launched with a lavish midnight party. Cecil Beaton photographed the mannequins for *Vogue*, which reported that Connie's 'bouquets of golden roses and corn bloom together against white walls'. From then on Connie would provide the flowers for Stiebel's twice-yearly shows; her classic long trail of flowers, usually with lilies among them, flowed down each side of the Adam mantelpieces which stood at either end of the vast ballroom. Like Norman Wilkinson, Stiebel provided Connie with inspiration. She shared his love of unusual colour combinations and his sense of drama, which he expressed with simple elegance and good taste. *Vogue* wrote:

Stiebel has taken the lives and hearts and aspirations of English-women and transmuted them into clothes, adding that touch of the artist, something that is rich and strange and exciting – like the sweeping scarlet cloth cape over a black dress that makes so dramatic an entrance – and the town suits made exciting by scarlet braid, or stripes of Persian lamb, plus absurd bonnet hats. He builds unusual and lovely colour combinations, such as a dark, slatish purple chiffon scarf and a bunch of violets with ash-pink crêpe, or adds a spangled scarf and a charlady bonnet.

Stiebel often joined Connie and Syrie in their junk-shop raids and the trio made many discoveries, 'either delightful or valuable!' They found two marble-topped tables 'for a song' in the

Caledonian market and spent 'hilarious hours' rummaging around the furniture storage warehouse off Tottenham Court Road. Although Connie was never as ruthless with antiques as Syrie, if an object had potential to hold flowers she would strip, paint and re-cover with as much brio as her friend. If something was not waterproof she would get her 'chap' to fit a special lead lining inside. Connie's ingenious improvisations were a great wonder to Stiebel, who was extremely fond of both of his 'lady companions in style', despite thinking that Syrie had 'a vulgar streak'. Connie, however, was 'without a flaw' and he loved her talent for making life civilized – whether with food, furnishings or, of course, flowers. He once said she had 'started something which was spreading over the country like a wonderful euphoric disease'.

Connie had already demonstrated her ability in the commercial world with her work for Atkinsons' and Drage's. Now Heals, a leading London furniture store and one of the 'cathedrals of consumption and barometers of fashion and style', approached her. The most fashionable shops had begun to use top designers to attract customers with eye-catching window displays, state-of-the-art interior decorations and modernist advertising posters. Prudence Maufe, wife of the architect Edward Maufe, was a trained decorator. She had had an affair with Ambrose Heal, whom she persuaded to let her create entire rooms of furniture and furnishings in the store's Mansard Gallery, quite a novel idea in those days. In order to show the full lived-in effect, Maufe asked Connie to do displays of flowers to fit the scheme. 'It was a weekly masterpiece,' wrote Maufe, 'and I used to look forward to meeting a genius every Monday.' However, her first sight of Connie was a disappointment: 'I had pictured someone as tall and elegant as her own lilies; instead a short, and by now plump middle-aged woman arrived wearing an overall, an outsized hat and an armload of incongruously jangling bracelets . . . One's impression was of a fussy little dowager duchess.'

As with Atkinsons', word spread among Heals' customers and many came especially on a Monday just to see Connie's floral 'weekly masterpiece'. Connie was now firmly linked with all the big leading names in decoration and design. For one King's Road drawing-room Syrie Maugham provided a carved wood console table painted white; the textile designer Marion Dorn designed the rugs in white and beige; Oliver Messel created a draped white plaster female figure which hung on the wall; and Connie arranged white lilies in a huge white ceramic vase that stood on the console table.

In addition to her Chelsea house Syrie owned a villa in the fashionable French resort of Le Touquet, much favoured by the rich, who went for long weekends to play polo or take the sea air. It had been a sanctuary from her unhappy marriage, and since her divorce it had become another place in which to show off her latest designs. Weekends at the Villa Eliza, named after her daughter, were filled with interesting and influential guests who admired her styles and spread the word. Magazine editors had discovered that their readers gained vicarious pleasure from a peep into the homes of the famous and, although this meant original creations were widely plagiarized, it did afford decorators considerable free advertising. For example, *House and Garden* described Syrie's villa in great detail: the drawing-room was decorated solely in tones of white and beige, it said, with peach-coloured silk curtains and beige sheepskin rugs, white leather on natural oak chairs, white lampshades, white gesso mirror frames and white porcelain. 'All this white and beige', the reporter wrote, 'can only mean a great deal of cleaning and maintenance', which for those who could afford an army of servants was half the point. Connie was among the guests who crossed the Channel for these rather wild and eccentric weekends. During one long summer house party Beverley Nichols recalled her bowls of white roses on the Provençal sideboard, adding that they were 'so overblown that one had to be somewhat adroit in lifting the silver lids on the hotplate, lest the petals should fall into the kedgeree'.

Syrie never failed to go home without booty bought in the French flea-markets. The artist Paul Nash sourly complained about formidable designer ladies such as Syrie 'hopping backwards and forwards between England and the Continent on the benefit of the Exchange. In their homeward flight they seldom failed to carry back something for the nest, a piece of stuff from Paris, a German lamp, a steel chair or just a headful of other people's ideas.' In Syrie's case this included the work of the French minimalist Jean-Michel Frank. Connie's booty, with the exception of a vase or container that caught her eye, was usually botanical; she would comb the beaches and dunes for grasses and wild flowers growing along the seashore.

Three years after creating her first Atkinsons' window displays, Connie was successful and famous. She had found a new clientele and new openings for her business, and she could now add the cutting edge of fashionable interior design to her portfolio of shop windows, theatres, cinemas and private patrons. What makes her achievement particularly extraordinary is that she managed to do it with a handful of staff in a backstreet flower shop in Pimlico. Its small door became increasingly battered as customers, staff, buckets of flowers and delivery boys passed in and out throughout the day. The telephone rang shrilly non-stop, and one girl had to be deputed just to answer calls and take orders. It wasn't quite how Connie had imagined it, but as long as the thrill and the rush were on, she thrived on it.

Gradually the little staff at Belgrave Road increased. When the young actor John Gielgud, whom Connie had been providing with flowers for his dressing rooms for some time, suggested that she might give his sister her first job, Connie typically agreed. Eleanor Gielgud was quite a colourful character. Though she showed little interest in flower arranging, she was deft with her hands and learned to wire, and sometimes helped the florist out in a crisis. Nell had a racy tongue and a whiff of stage glamour about her that everyone loved. Her nicknames for the staff were always apt. Some of her 'resting' actor friends would help out in the shop for pocket money, just for the fun of it. Charles Laughton used to come in; he would grovel about among the discarded twigs and leaves on the floor because, he said, it was where he found the best things – he rather fancied himself as a flower arranger who could make an effective vase out of almost nothing. Connie, of course, adored him.

Nell Gielgud was told that part of her responsibility was to keep the books, which terrified her as she had only an elementary knowledge of bookkeeping; it was enough, however, for her to see that things were not looking good.

One evening Shav found her weeping over the accounts, unable to make them add up to a profit. She knew that Covent Garden wholesalers' bills allowed no credit and would have to be paid by the end of the week. When Shav went over the accounts, as he should have done regularly, he got quite a shock. Only the floristry and cut-flower sections were making a real profit. In spite of the long hours worked by Connie, Val, George Foss and the junior decorators, the decorating side barely broke even. Connie, who worked solely out of passion and the creative urge, was ignorant of proper costing and kept her prices far too low, often failing to build in costs such as transport.

For the displays at Atkinsons', retouched two or three times a week, she charged a mere £5, and for Heals' 'weekly masterpieces' only £1. Sidney Bernstein's cinema contract required long journeys and that too was priced far too low, as were the lavish parties and house decorations. Commissions brought valuable publicity and business but were of little use if the extra work failed to profit the shop. No one, it seems, had realized that the bills had to be dealt with on a proper basis. Having no sense of the cost of things, if Connie suddenly decided that an arrangement needed a rare orchid or some other exotic and expensive addition, someone would be sent round to a rival florist's to buy it at retail price and any profit would be gone. Flo Standfast, too, was incurring serious losses. Shav discovered that one creation priced at thirty shillings had actually cost the business forty-two shillings' worth of Flo's time to make. At this stage Shav Spry did not have an active full-time hand in the business that bore his name, but it seems extraordinary that Connie's 'helpmeet and support', a trained chartered accountant, had not kept his eye on the ball. Just as Connie and her team were doing so well, it seemed as if they might have to restrict themselves to more modest activities until they got the shop back on an even keel.

Connie, the eternal optimist, rarely saw the sensible way forward. When she heard that a shop next door to Atkinsons' Perfumery was vacant she decided that this would be the obvious move. They would leave the backstreets of Pimlico and set themselves up in the fashionable centre of the West End – surely then business could only get better. A Bond Street address would enable her to charge the same prices as established commercial florists like Edward Goodyear, Moyses Stevens and Felton. The leading flower shops in the West End were highly efficient, well-established businesses. They constituted formidable opposition for a small, barely known firm run by a person with amazing artistic ability and an impressive clientele but little business sense. Connie nevertheless believed that they could improve turnover by selling cut flowers to passing customers, instead of clients having to send their chauffeurs out to Pimlico. The premises were larger, so they could employ more staff there. The windows of Flower Decorations would complement those of Atkinsons' next door and would draw even greater numbers to see Connie's dramatic arrangements; together they would dominate Burlington Gardens and bring new customers streaming through the doors. Even Shav acknowledged that it was an opportunity not to be missed. Somehow they found the money to prime the failing accounts and took the lease. It proved to be a risk well worth taking.

No. 4 Burlington Gardens consisted of an elegant showroom with offices behind. Syrie Maugham and Norman Wilkinson helped design it, adding mirrors, white walls and bamboo screens. Connie, with her eye for new or unusual materials, used dull white surgical rubber sheeting pleated on screens to divide the front window from the interior. She made grand-looking gesso-style tables at no cost by draping half-moons of wood with swags of hessian, then plastering the whole lot and painting them white. Down a murderously steep flight of outside steps was a roomy basement where they installed a huge refrigerator to keep the cut flowers. Since they still had the Pimlico lease, Connie initially decided to allow Flo and her assistant to remain there; Flo had always enjoyed special protection from Connie, who treated her as a great artist, which sometimes caused jealousy among other members of staff. But Shav, who had now become more involved in decisions, vetoed the idea. It was no use, he pointed out, for Flo to work as though each piece was intended for the British Museum; praise-worthy it might be, but it wasn't commercial. The 'Arts' department had to be with everyone else, under Connie's artistic eye and Shav's financial monitoring.

Soon everyone was rushed off their feet, and a new decorator was urgently needed. Sheila Young was walking down Burlington Gardens with her mother when she saw in Atkinsons' window an urn of dried leek heads and old-man's-beard in a brown ceramic cylindrical vase. 'That's the sort of thing I want to do!' she exclaimed, and entered the shop to enquire who had done it. Directed next door to Flower Decorations, her mother told Connie that Sheila came from a family of keen gardeners and longed for a career in flowers. Sheila had that very day just been for an interview for an apprenticeship in floristry, which had depressed her. Could she not work and train in this shop instead, where the flowers looked so natural and were done so creatively? Connie was immediately taken by the eager girl's delight and agreed to take her on as an apprentice for a monthly premium which her mother was very happy to pay.

On her first day in the shop she was mystified when Val set her to strip sloe branches of their leaves, but laboured on until she heard an amused voice behind her: 'You need only bother with those that have fruit.' Connie explained how the glowing colours of the fruit on the branches would create character in an arrangement she was doing. For several days Sheila painted earthenware jugs until, at last, Connie allowed her to try her hand at a display in the Atkinsons' window. Sheila recalled that Connie had a particular technique for instructing her pupils, putting in two or three stems or branches herself to start it off, then handing over with a 'Now finish that.' After the first month Connie informed Sheila's mother that she expected no further payments – the girl had such an outstanding natural flair that she was already a valuable member of staff. For the rest of Connie's life Sheila Young, along with Joyce Robinson, whom Nell had nicknamed 'Robbo', were her chief decorators.

Connie could no longer do every arrangement herself, but her creative eye saw everything that was done by her team. She kept them alert, demanding new things, never happy to see the same effect twice, instantly pouncing on and dismissing anything that looked formulaic. Connie would sometimes quickly glance at a completed group and then drop some tiny comment like 'Lime green in the middle'; it always lifted an ordinary arrangement into something special. 'Suitability' was her key word for a really good arrangement. 'Most suitable' was her highest praise. Connie's trainees learned by looking, feeling and learning to relax, and they gained confidence by following their instincts and natural spontaneity. They learned from her, slowly absorbing the look of the things she did and the way she did them. The effect created at a church wedding or in a ballroom, for instance – how it blended with the place and the spirit of the event. Afterwards they would sit and analyse, criticize and discuss, thinking up a fresh approach or reworking something already successful; nothing could be repeated or be allowed to go stale.

As a welcome break from the hothouse atmosphere of shop work, demanding hostesses and society functions, Connie had begun making monthly visits to the Swanley Horticultural College in Kent to give a flower-arrangement class. It helped her retain her interest in education. She would wander round the large college gardens with her class of fifteen girls, collecting materials, often from the

vegetable garden, looking for shape and colour, texture and character. Then they would set about creating outsize and lavishly
flowing arrangements *à la* Spry. Even the least talented student
was caught up in the enthusiasm and gaiety and blossomed under
the individual attention that Connie gave to each of them. The
principal of the college, Dr Kate Barrett, had been a lecturer in
botany at Imperial College and her most successful students there
included the garden designers Brenda Colvin and Sylvia Crowe.
Connie lunched with Dr Barrett and picked her brains about all
kinds of horticultural matters; she liked to tell people she was
entirely self-taught and not at all infallible. She described how one
day at Swanley College a student brought in a tall stem of a white
umbrella-shaped flower of great delicacy, which Connie did not
recognize. After some discussion about its identity, the student
took the class back to the experimental garden where she had
found it, 'and there discovered it was the flower of the ordinary
cultivated carrot gone to seed!'

Through teaching at Swanley Connie grew increasingly interested in educating and training new staff. Whenever a new girl
was taken on in the shop, she was paired with an experienced one
and told to copy her work for a while until she could begin to
evolve her own personal style. Connie encouraged her decorators
to develop their own styles, but their work would nonetheless
retain the intrinsic character of Connie's pioneering artistry. When
any of them walked down Bond Street they could immediately tell
which of them had done Atkinsons' windows that week; at the
same time, everyone knew a Spry arrangement, whoever had
made it. Connie's displays at the perfumery grew ever more daring and unusual, and she had a totally free hand to use any plant
materials she wanted. On one occasion she created a jaw-dropping
display of red kale and scarlet roses, which drew such large crowds
that the police were called to move the traffic on.

Younger decorators remained for a while under Connie's
immediate supervision. She went with them to every new client
and personally planned every large-scale commission. She studied

each new interior: 'My first instinct', she wrote, 'is to seek some note round which to plan a scheme.' For example, 'Lady Howard de Walden's green marble staircase in Belgrave Square could best be emphasized by mixed foliage arrangements, while Mrs Ashley's onyx table lit from beneath gave a water-lily quality to any white flowers.' A blank canvas was her ideal, which is why she loved the all-white schemes so much. But more often she was confronted with an ugly or cluttered room which, as she said, made her 'think with longing of what could be done with a whitewashed barn'. Her tact on these occasions was an object lesson to her staff. Without offending the house owner she would contrive to suggest that a curtain or swathe of fabric should be hung over the garish wallpaper or deplorable picture, and the flowers set against it.

Mrs Spry's 'young ladies', as they were known, worked to an accepted routine. They always went to the front door – not the tradesmen's entrance; always assembled the arrangements where they were to stand, not in the pantry or scullery; and spread dust-sheets around them as they worked, then cleared up immaculately, leaving not a single leaf. This routine applied to church decorating as well (except at St Mark's, North Audley Street, where there was a strict rule forbidding it). If Connie and her team were decorating for a country party or wedding, they would travel down and stay the night; sometimes they were treated as guests, but were often relegated to the servants' quarters, which the girls claimed was far more amusing. On one of these occasions, gleefully remembered, the hostess, who had treated them with considerable *hauteur*, was mortified to find her guests falling upon Connie with cries of admiration and warmth.

Connie particularly enjoyed walking around a client's garden discussing their borders and shrubs. Several invited her to use flowers from their own gardens, and she loved to have the run of a new garden for picking. Sometimes the head gardener would at first be less forthcoming, but then soften when he got talking with Connie who was so evidently an expert gardener. She admitted, though, 'all the time I have an eye on the flowers that will be useful to cut for the house.'

These were happy times, when the business was still manageable enough for Connie to know most of her customers. There were the inevitable difficult ones, however, all of whom Connie treated with courtesy and kid gloves, 'as a shopkeeper should', for the customer was always right – or nearly always. Once, the owner of a grand house in Curzon Street called in Spry flower decorators, then decided she did not care for the style of the finished display. She would have preferred some carnations, Connie's most despised flowers, with asparagus fern. Connie and Sheila returned to the house and immediately dismantled the vases, piled the flowers into a taxi and drove back to the shop. Connie was white with fury: 'Any ordinary flower shop would do it for her,' she snorted. 'I won't. I only want to do exciting things.' Within a couple of years she was invited back, and arranged for every party held thereafter.

Connie had a gift for relieving tense situations, and her sense of humour was legendary. She often impersonated a difficult customer, to gales of laughter, after he or she had left the shop. But sometimes her delight in the absurd would fail her. On one occasion she was asked to do a 'divorce party' with flowers arranged inside plaster skulls. Connie was disgusted, and politely declined the commission. But appreciative and loyal customers were treated impeccably. If one of them decided at short notice to throw a party, the team stayed on to get the flowers done. Nothing was ever too much for Flower Decorations, even though the hours were impossibly long and the pay was still terrible. According to Sheila Young:

Someone once asked us if we felt bitter that we were paid so little whilst seeing so much affluence. It is true we were paid little, and we worked hard, but I loved to watch the expansion of the firm and to become part of the creative art that was developing. Working with flowers and in such good company gave rise to a great deal of pleasure, laughter and companionship.

Connie praised, charmed and encouraged her team, mostly young girls, and kept them in love with her and their work – 'a thrilling occupation, continually doing what you really enjoy with a perpetual change of material', as Robbo described it. Connie was always there working alongside them, twisting wire, clipping, stripping and dunking. She produced delicious cream cakes to make up for missing meal breaks, and entertained everyone with stories and jokes. Sheila recalled: 'It was one perpetual party, she made everything seem such fun.' Several of them, Sheila in particular, were so skilled and well trained that they went on to run their own successful businesses.

If anyone had suggested to Connie that she was exploiting her staff, she would have been horrified. She paid what she could afford and she trained and cared for them, if not financially, at least by making them feel appreciated and fulfilled in their work. Her standards were extremely high. She took immense pride in her team and would defend them against any criticism. Her instinct for finding the right people was rarely wrong, and in the one or two instances when it failed her she was ruthless in dismissing the person concerned. But she could never do the unpleasant task herself; any disciplinary action was deputed to Val Pirie, who was known to be a strict disciplinarian and regarded with equal measures of fear and dislike.

Val, who had less talent for flowers than the others, began to concentrate on running the business with Shav. The two were often closeted together at weekends when he instructed her in accountancy and business management, while Connie spent nights away in London working or as a weekend guest. The relationship between Val and Shav, which began on that Christmas walk two years before, had developed into an affair. It is hard to see quite what her attraction was. Although Connie was utterly immersed in her business, it must be assumed that by this time she was aware of the affair, but it is not known what she felt about it, or how she handled it.

Connie was never open or honest about her private life – it had become too complicated. Shav had not anticipated that the lively and creative woman who had first attracted him would become such a driven, single-minded person. He had no wish to enter high society and did not want to hang around at parties while Connie was fêted and praised. He liked to work in his office and then return to his quiet life at home in the country. Most of all, he loathed the homosexual clique in which Connie found so many of her closest friends. She was caught in a trap of her own making, a divorcee living with a man to whom she was not married, who was now conducting an affair with her business assistant and friend. Even her name, by now so well known, was not actually hers. If 'Mrs Spry' left Shav, the whole story would come out and the scandal would ruin her; besides which, she sincerely loved Shav and their life together, and it appears that he loved her. Taking a lesson from her upper-class customers, Connie turned a blind eye. This sort of thing was not uncommon, after all, and she kept her own counsel, pouring all her passion and energy into her work.

Despite any friction caused by Shav's affair with Val, when the lease on Abinger expired and they were forced to move, Connie and Shav opted to remain in the country rather than move up to town. They found a house on a much grander scale at Colney Park near Aldenham in Hertfordshire. The garden, which was also much bigger than at Abinger, had been planted by a connoisseur and Connie recalled the thrill of exploring her new garden and finding all kinds of rare and delightful surprises. In the rough grass in the wilder parts she found unusual autumn crocuses and colchicums. 'It seemed', she wrote, 'as though the original owner had purposely tried to forget he had made these plantings so that he might have the pleasure of coming on the flowers unaware.' There was a pergola of *Clematis montana*, woodland filled with flowers in spring and, overhanging a stream, alder trees whose stems Connie would pick in the depths of winter, bringing them indoors where the catkins came out: 'the arrangement had the beauty of an etching.'

Nearby at Aldenham Court were the famous garden and nurseries of the late Vicary Gibbs, who had collected plants from all over the world. When they heard that the nursery was closing down and there was to be a plant sale, Connie and Trower, who with his wife Gladys as cook had followed the Sprys to Aldenham, rushed over and acquired several rarities including some mature magnolias and two 'very beautiful, rare and unusual plants': a Chinese shrub, *Decaisnea fargesii* or 'dead man's fingers', which Connie was particularly attracted to for its strange fruits 'like purple broad beans'; and *Sinofranchetia chinensis*, which bears long slim bunches of amethyst-like fruits. She also found a wonderful stock of snowberries in the sale which, she noticed, were much more thickly clustered with white wax-like berries than the usual type. She had found a unique variety, eventually marketed by her friend Mr Beckett at Sunningdale Nurseries as *Symphoricarpos laevigatus* 'Constance Spry', an honour of which she was immensely proud.

The gardens at Colney Park were reorganized to include well-managed cutting beds and Trower was at last given two under-gardeners to assist him. But Connie was still very much a hands-on gardener and she and Trower still argued ceaselessly. She would snatch the spade from him and move a plant herself to make a point, or chop away at some poor plant she thought had 'got too big for its boots'. She often wrote about the comfort she found in getting earth on her hands or in holding a bundle of dripping flowers in her arms. She would be out in the garden in all weathers – in soft 'Irish' rain, sharp white frosts, full blowsy sunshine – and only reluctantly came in to change for a meal. Guests were amused to find Connie serving dinner still with traces of earth under her nails and muddy shoes peeping from under her evening dress. Nobody minded, as she kept up a vibrant conversation on the merits of some new plant she had found, a new way to 'murder slugs' or the eccentric behaviour of a client. She was an inveterate gossip, indiscreet and cheerfully outspoken about most things and most people. However, friends who knew her well were aware that behind her outgoing cheerfulness lurked all kinds of fears and worries. Beverley Nichols wrote:

> She was almost painfully sensitive because she always had an extraordinary illusion that she might be boring people when, in fact, she was bewitching them. When she forgot to be nervous she lit up and twinkled all over so that you felt she was dressed in sequins . . . oddly enough, she had a spark of naughtiness – as though she had sometimes lingered outside the dining-room door to listen to the gentlemen when they were letting their hair down over the port.

Only her own private life was kept firmly behind closed doors.

The demand for flowers for the shop and for her clients was insatiable, and Connie found that even with what she grew in her own garden, the commercial flower markets and private estates, they were only just keeping pace. She and her 'buyer', George Foss, were constantly looking for new sources and together they attended as many Royal Horticultural· Society shows in Vincent Square as they could. Connie adored these annual 'great floral festivals' and was a keen active member from early on. She would tour the stands of specialist nurserymen, many of whom became regular suppliers and friends with whom she kept up lengthy correspondence. Connie and Foss would stay until late in the afternoon of the second day's showing, when many exhibitors sold plants off cheaply rather than have to cart them home again. They would buy, say, a whole stand of lilies; the flowers would adorn the next wedding or party and the precious bulbs would go into the borders of the large walled garden at Colney Park.

For Connie the Chelsea Flower Show was the great event of the year. She and Shav had been attending ever since their mutual passion for gardening began. The RHS had held shows in Chiswick and later Kensington since 1833, but later it was decided that these venues were not sufficiently central to attract enough visitors. In 1913 the first Spring Show took place in the grounds of the Royal Hospital, Chelsea, where it proved a huge success. It continued there even through the war, except for 1917 and 1918, and was back in full swing in the 1920s when the famous Chelsea tea parties were introduced and royal visits resumed. As her business increased, Connie found many new suppliers through flower shows, especially among the ordinary gardeners and nurserymen, whom she always favoured. They kept her in touch with the world of horticulture, with new developments, new plants and innovations in garden design and cultivation. Increasingly, this was where Connie felt she belonged, rather than in the pressured hothouse atmosphere of society functions. She particularly loved the camaraderie of the great marquee where nurserymen, hybridists and ordinary gardeners met on common ground, where royalty, lords and ladies, bishops and politicians could be found deep in horticultural conversation with head gardeners, city clerks, housewives and shopkeepers. It was the 'glorious mix' that Connie always thrived on, her 'freemasonry of flowers'.

During her visits to RHS shows at Chelsea and Vincent Square Connie got to know Sir William Lawrence, the Society's Treasurer. He admired her work and suggested she apply for a stand at the Chelsea Flower Show. In 1932 the first Constance Spry stand appeared, on 'Sundries Avenue'. Connie recalled the agonies of planning for Chelsea: 'To gardeners and flower arrangers, Chelsea is a compound of pleasure and pain . . . the surfeit of pleasure in so much beauty, the frustration of not being able to afford all the plants one wanted, and the special torment of putting up a stand with sleepless nights spent worrying over the fear of producing something stale or dull.' She always claimed that she never had any ideas until George Foss opened the back of the van and showed her what he had found, at which point she was inspired to create something utterly spontaneous and all her fears were forgotten:

Connie aged about five.

Connie aged about sixteen.

Connie (far left) and her father, George Fletcher,
(fourth from left) with the Phoenix Caravan in
Dublin in 1909. Lord and Lady Aberdeen can be
seen in front of the horse.

Connie's engagement photo, 1910.

James Heppell Marr standing by the donkey and cart
he bought for his children, Joan and Tony, together
with their Cook cousins in Yorkshire, 1925.

Syrie Maugham at a
luncheon party in 1936.

Shav Spry in the garden at
Ard Daraich aged about seventy.

Gluck wearing daisies in
her lapel in about 1933.

Rosemary Hume with two
classic Spry arrangements
in about 1935.

Val Pirie modelling an unusual
bridal bouquet of cabbage leaves,
sword-fern, scented geranium, red
tulips, red ranunculi, an amaryllis
lily, red and green striped parrot
tulips and striped red croton leaves.

OPPOSITE PAGE:
Above An exotic display for Atkinsons'
Perfumery window.

Below 'Chromatic' Gluck's first painting
of a Spry arrangement. Connie wrote:
'It exemplifies the delicacy and the
strength, the subtleties and the
grandeur of white flowers.'

Oliver Messel decorating the Pavilion Room at the Dorchester Hotel.

Victor Stiebel surrounded by models at his couture salon in about 1936.

Top Connie looking very sophisticated checking an arrangement of roses in a head-shaped vase for one of Victor Stiebel's shows.

Above The famous decorative kale leaves that shocked many of her clients.

Right 'Blackamoor with whitewashed leaves'. A classic Spry/Messel party decoration in the 1930s.

The shop and the Modern School of Flower Work in South Audley Street.

Staff in the flower shop.

George Foss can find beauty in unexpected places . . . He could produce a rare fruit, a common vegetable, an exotic that makes you gasp, all with an air as if to say: 'I can't think what you were worrying about.' For good measure he will add in a 'rabbit-out-of-the hat' tone that he has found some especially grand magnolia, or azalea, or pieris, or what you will, and the cup is full.

Then she fell to, and with help from Sheila and Robbo the work began. In contrast to the fun-fair effect of some of the other exhibits there, Connie kept her stand simple and uncluttered. She would use her collection of huge alabaster urns to show just a couple of arrangements with such dramatic appeal that they would stand out in the small space allotted to her. One vase was usually white and green, with lilies and anthurium or magnolia; the other was filled with the soft pinks and mauves of lilac and iris, azalea and fruit blooms. Some visitors expected to see examples of living-room displays and Connie soon tired of explaining that they would be almost invisible to the tight-packed Chelsea crowd. 'Of course the displays are large in size,' she cried, 'they have to be; of course we use interesting material when we can get it: after all, this *is* Chelsea.' Every year she dreamed up something dramatic and surprising. Once the centrepiece was an old gilt font from which cascaded a mass of maidenhair fern, a plant she usually derided, but she wanted to show how even something less than ideal could be used to good creative effect. In later years she sometimes used the cut-glass mirrors that she had rescued from Atkinsons' when it closed. For the 1936 show Connie created an enormous display in which she filled a vase with green foliage, green tomatoes, rhubarb and artichokes. The *Daily Telegraph* reported that the King and Queen visited the Constance Spry stand and were particularly impressed.

Year after year, Connie created fresh and extraordinary arrangements. 'She never looked back,' a staff member said. 'She was always looking towards the next great idea.' Preparing for Chelsea was a huge strain and extra work for everyone. More often than not, Connie would return to the shop scarcely able to describe how that year's effort had been received. Worn out and tearful with exhaustion from all their efforts, her disappointed staff would hear Connie excitedly announce, '*Next* year I know what we'll do.'

SEVEN

Made for Happiness

1932—1936

4 January 1932

Dear Gluck

Three things.

1. The camellias are marvellous.

*2. I am sending you herewith a feather of white velour, which
I think is lovely.*

*3. Edward and I are giving ourselves the pleasure of sending
you up a 'Mixed Bunch' of white flowers for your Studio. I have
commissioned my friend Mrs Spry to do it and to ring you up
when certain flowers which I have asked for are procurable. She
will probably lend you a white marble vase to put them in — she
often brings her own when she does not know people's own vases.
I think she has a genius for flowers and you have a genius for
paint, so that ought to make for happiness. Anyhow, we send them
to you with our love and very deep appreciation of your sympathy
in work.*

Bless you,

Prudence Maufe

Connie was away when the Maufe order was taken at the shop,
and it was Val who was deputed to go to the artist Gluck's house
in Hampstead in North London to carry out the commission, a
present to celebrate the new studio built for her by Edward
Maufe. Val arrived with a Warwick vase and a box of white
flowers – anthurium, amaryllis, arums and tulips. She remembered
the place as being very grand. The maid who showed her in
fetched a pedestal and a jug of water and Val got on with her
work. Gluck eventually came in from the studio wearing smock
and trousers, 'looking extremely handsome and cross at being disturbed from painting'. She stood watching as Val deftly created a
classic Spry arrangement. Suddenly she announced that she wanted

to paint it. Val, who was quite used to the eccentricities of the rich and famous, finished the job and left her to it.

Several days later a call came through to the shop from Gluck's home. The flowers were wilting and the artist had not finished painting them. Someone was required to return to Hampstead and replenish the vase. As each week passed, the whole display had to be replaced exactly as before, but even after some months the painting was still not complete. Connie grew more and more curious; she had learned that Gluck always wore men's clothes, and there seemed to be a considerable amount of discreet gossip about her, too. She decided to go to Hampstead, check the flowers and meet the artist herself.

Gluck's real name, which even family and friends were forbidden to use, was Hannah Gluckstein. 'No prefix, suffix or quotes,' she demanded, not even a 'Miss' – just Gluck (as in duck). She came from a wealthy Jewish family: the Salmons and the Gluck-steins had made their fortune in tobacco and their fame through ownership of the J. Lyons catering company with its tea shops and Corner Houses. Gluck grew up rebelling against her family as well as against the social and sexual conventions of the time. Her parents reluctantly allowed her to study at St John's Wood Art School and she later spent time with the Newlyn School, the artists' colony in Cornwall. By the age of twenty-one Gluck had cropped her hair, changed her name and begun to dress exclusively in men's clothes. Her father despaired of her, but gave her a generous allowance all the same. Her mother once described her as having 'a kink in the brain' which she hoped would pass, but did not give up on Gluck, continuing to dominate her daughter and to interfere in her life.

When Connie first met Gluck, the artist was thirty-seven, nine years younger than Connie. She had already had two successful 'one-woman' shows, one in 1924 and another at the Fine Art Society in 1926. She called this exhibition *Stage and Country* as it reflected her two worlds: the sophistication and gaiety of theatre life in London and the peace and tranquillity of the Cornish countryside. Alongside landscapes of Cornwall were numerous paintings of café society and backstage life. Gluck spent many hours sketching behind the scenes at the London Pavilion for Cochran's hit show *On with the Dance* and his cabarets at the Trocadero, which the Gluckstein family conveniently owned. Her Eton crop, breeches, man's soft hat and pipe did not look out of place in the theatre environment, where female eccentricities were tolerated so long as they were not obviously connected with sex. Gluck also executed numerous portraits of eminent figures and society names. She painted the American artist Romaine Brooks, though she was never part of the 'lesbian *haut monde*' which included Una, Lady Troubridge, and the author Radclyffe Hall (whose book *The Well of Loneliness* was published in 1928 and immediately banned).

After the success of her first exhibition Gluck's father bought her a house at the heart of Hampstead village. Bolton House was a tall redbrick building with a wide drive entered through wrought-iron gates. Gluck had been particularly pleased to discover that it had once belonged to the poet and dramatist Joanna Baillie, an esteemed member of the literary establishment of her time who was frequently visited by Wordsworth, Scott and Byron as well as by several independent women including the novelist Maria Edgeworth and the scientist Mary Somerville. Baillie herself had had a long relationship with the writer Lucy Aitkin, who lived nearby.

While only a cab drive away from the West End theatres and cafés, Hampstead in the early Thirties offered the comforts and privacy of village life plus the attractions of intellectual and artistic social circles. Among Gluck's Hampstead friends were the composer Arthur Bliss and the artist Arthur Watts. One of Watts's daughters recalled Gluck 'walking the streets of Hampstead in the thirties, with cloak, bow-tie and cane, looking like a small, well-dressed, dandyish Italianate man'. Hampstead society was more tolerant of 'deviant' sexual or other eccentric behaviour, and it was not particularly remarkable to see there a woman painter of independent means who, by Watts's daughter's account, 'looked like Ivor Novello and appeared at soirées in a dinner jacket and black tie'.

In wider society, lesbianism was neither condemned nor condoned. There was punitive legislation against homosexual men, but female homosexuality was not so proscribed. While the story that Queen Victoria refused to believe that women were capable of such behaviour, rendering pointless any legislation forbidding it, is almost certainly apocryphal, gently brought up women were largely unaware that it was possible. There had always been women who favoured men's clothing, but they were generally assumed to be merely mildly eccentric. According to Gluck's biographer Diana Souhami, 'Many a well-to-do family had one, living somewhere in the country with a "wife" in skirts, reading the financial pages of *The Times*, drinking brandy after dinner and seeming to appropriate the supposedly male domains of intelligence and activity.' However, in some quarters lesbianism was acknowledged – and with revulsion. On the publication of *The Well of Loneliness*, hardly a graphic account of lesbian sex, the leader writer of the *Daily Express* wrote: 'I would rather give a healthy boy or girl a phial of prussic acid than this book.'

On the day of her first visit, Gluck waited with some interest for Constance Spry to arrive. The Spry name epitomized refinement and respectability, glamour and high fashion – everyone ordered their flowers from Mrs Spry. Like her friend Prudence Maufe before her, she no doubt expected to receive a grand and elegant lady. But her first impression of Connie was hardly likely to have set her heart racing with desire. It was said that Gluck was attracted to sophisticated women who were glamorous and remote – nothing could have been less like Connie. And yet, despite her air of middle-aged solidity, as soon as Connie spoke and smiled and people felt the fire of her enthusiasm and her genuine interest in them, few failed to be seduced by her charm. Gluck was delighted by her honest appreciation of her painting and her home and was immediately drawn to her quiet but confident manner. The mutual attraction seems to have been immediate – they hit it off at once.

Gluck called her painting of the now many times refreshed Spry arrangement *Chromatic*. It was the first and most spectacular of all her flower paintings and it took her months of painstaking work. By the time it was finished her relationship with Connie had developed into intimacy and love. It was a true meeting of minds and a genuine collaboration of two artists, combining Gluck's 'genius for paint' and Connie's 'genius for flowers'. Connie was hugely impressed with *Chromatic*, writing in her book *Flower Decoration*: 'Gluck's painting of this group exemplifies the delicacy and the strength, the subtleties and the grandeur of white flowers. It has another point of interest to those who admire the paintings of the old Flemish masters, since here we have a modern artist painting flowers in a spacious and decorative manner, but with the same delicate precision and feeling that characterized the work of these men.'

With Gluck, Connie was able to escape from the demands of the commercial success she had unwittingly created for herself. She had found someone who was interested only in pure art, someone who understood her flower arranging as an art form that was both something to be appreciated and admired for itself and worthy of being committed to canvas. With Gluck she could discuss her two great loves, art and the natural world; for both Gluck and Connie, landscape and the plants therein were both inspiration and material for their chosen forms of expression. From Connie, Gluck learned about the nature and characteristics of flowers, while Connie learned from her about colour and composition. Many years later Gluck wrote some notes on flower painting which reflected the extent to which she had learned from and been influenced by Connie's ideas and knowledge:

Always give your flowers a setting in keeping with their essential characteristics, just as you would a portrait. If you had a queen to paint you would see that her surroundings were as regal as they could be. Flowers have these degrees of flamboyancy and simplicity and to be arbitrary about your setting is to be as stupid and unreceptive as to set a . . . coal heaver in a sitting room . . . Be very quick at first essentials of character. As much character in a flower however tiny as in a portrait. Same principle as in everything else, but always be on the extra qui vive for the special delicacy of flowers. Impermanency. Feel the direction of growth . . .

The down-to-earth style of these notes is similar to Connie's prose style, and there are phrases such as 'Feel the direction of growth' that can be found in several of her books. It is interesting to see Connie's ideas quoted from the painter's perspective.

Interior designers who were using Spry flowers to complete their room schemes were also hanging works by contemporary artists on the walls. Connie saw that Gluck's flower paintings would work wonderfully well in Syrie Maugham's all-white interiors. With her generous and enthusiastic nature, she had always taken pride and pleasure in adopting people with talent and in promoting and recommending them to others. Now she drew Gluck into her circle, ensuring that her name became known and her work highly sought after. She introduced her to Syrie and to Norman Wilkinson and Oliver Hill. Lord Vernon, whose house in Carlyle Square was designed by Hill, was one of Gluck's first clients. She did a painting of lilies set in one of her own patented frames made of weathered sycamore to complement the wood floor and sycamore-lined walls in the white and green drawing-room. Lord Vernon paid sixty guineas for it, hung it over the fireplace and described it as 'the making of the room'.

Connie's own recent experience had taught her that if one or two of her leading customers were pleased with Gluck, her work would soon be in great demand. Gluck's 'Spry' flower paintings graced the walls of numerous wealthy patrons. Soon the artist was being fêted at cocktail parties and dining with prospective clients. It was through Connie that Gluck's career really took off.

Together they visited art galleries, where they studied the Flemish and Dutch flower paintings that had influenced Connie and the French and English landscapes and portraits by Velázquez and Ingres that Gluck admired. They went to the theatre and the cinema and spent long intimate evenings discussing painting and gardening, design and the theatre. At first the relationship was very private. For Connie, the affair was an extraordinary departure. She must have known about female homosexuality and have been aware from the start that Gluck was a lesbian. But so many of her friends and clients were homosexual that this would not have shocked her. And since Gluck described their nights together as 'very peaceful and sweet', sex was probably not the predominant force in their relationship. If she wanted the fierce passion of her other affairs Gluck visited women friends such as the Austrian painter Mariette Lydis, Comtesse de Govonne, with whom she spent occasional nights in Paris hotels.

The sight of the middle-aged, bird-like Connie travelling around with a handsome woman artist dressed in male clothes must surely have raised eyebrows. Gluck's diary entries leave no doubt as to the nature of the relationship, but did anyone realize? They do not appear to have been particularly discreet or secretive about it. Connie stayed regularly at Gluck's house, they went on holiday together and travelled around the countryside visiting gardens and staying with friends such as Syrie Maugham in Le Touquet.

Val, however, certainly knew the full nature of their relationship. Later, she would tell Diana Souhami that when Connie first met Gluck in 1932 the Spry marriage had 'run into problems'. It would appear, of course, that the problem was Val herself. After Connie's death Val made considerable efforts to suppress some of Connie's letters and diaries, and there is no doubt that her version of events is in her interest, not Connie's, although she never suggested that her relationship with Gluck was anything more than friendship. However, Vita Marr, Connie's daughter-in-law, recalls a curious conversation when Val said, 'We could have left her, you know — at any time.' But they didn't and, perhaps more to the point, Shav Spry once told Tony Marr, 'Your mother was the only one, you know, the one and only. The other was just a bit on the side.'

As ever, Connie's way of handling a potentially difficult situation was to shoot off in a new direction, hoping to leave it behind her. Her new friend Sir William Lawrence, Treasurer of the Royal Horticultural Society, urged her to consider writing a book about flower decorating. Some time before, she had begun to write regular articles about flower arranging for several fashion magazines including *Vogue* and *Harper's Bazaar*. By contrast, she had written a piece for the journal *Women's Employment* that echoed her earlier belief in every woman's freedom to enjoy and express her taste in beautiful things. She enjoyed writing, and a book seemed an exciting challenge, an escape from the endless round of shop, flower market and clients' demands, not to mention any problems in her private life. Sir William promised to give Connie horticultural advice, read her manuscript and write the foreword. To her surprise and delight she soon found a publisher – J.M. Dent & Sons, whose managing director W.G. Taylor became another long-term friend and support.

It turned out to be a good time to write a flower book; in the rapidly expanding suburbs thousands were taking up gardening for the first time, and flower arranging was becoming increasingly popular. In 1932 Beverley Nichols had published *Down the Garden Path*, a witty, idiosyncratic and very personal memoir of his cottage garden at Glatton in Huntingdonshire. Compared to the theatre, he reckoned writing about gardening was astonishingly easy: 'It was more like arranging a bunch of mixed flowers, here a story, here a winding paragraph, here a purple passage, and suddenly there was a book.' It was a huge success. Of all the accolades he received, the two Nichols treasured most came from his friends Vita Sackville-West and Constance Spry, who described him as 'a pioneer in innovation for his experiment and development of winter flowers'. Nichols, in turn, encouraged Connie to write. He later also wrote a book on flower arranging, describing the art as 'pre-Spry' and 'post-Spry'.

A particularly popular element of Nichols's book was the illustrations by his friend Rex Whistler. According to him, Whistler was at first far from keen to do the job. 'It's the Tudor cottage to end all Tudor cottages. Not me at all,' he said. 'I'm only good at stately homes with long avenues and lakes in the distance and balustrades and cherubs holding heraldic arms over the roof.' He picked up a watering-can. 'What could I do with a thing like that?' he enquired. Nichols thought for a moment. 'You could give it to a cherub and by his side you could draw another cherub with a spade.' This suggestion is supposed to have unlocked Whistler's imagination and he quickly produced the picture that appeared on the first page of Chapter 1. For the endpapers he drew a plan of Nichols's garden to stimulate and guide the imagination of the reader.

This happy collaboration on *Down the Garden Path* was to continue with many sequels. Connie loved the humour and lightness of touch in Nichols's writing as well as Whistler's illustrations – he did several little drawings for her as well. It was exactly the kind of approach she planned to develop in her own book. As she got down to writing it and Gluck prepared for her next exhibition, they enjoyed a happy and fruitful period of mutual support and confiding affection. They relied on each other for guidance, suggestions and helpful criticism. Both emotionally and intellectually, theirs was a union of love and work.

Gluck's exhibition was to open in October 1932 at the Fine Art Society. She designed the exhibition room and hung her paintings with enormous care and attention to detail. Inspired by Connie's dictum that everything must be integral to the whole, Gluck created a personal and uniquely integrated composition of pictures and gallery setting that she called 'the Gluck Room'. The walls were to be panelled bays and pilasters to echo the stepped effect of her specially designed and built frames. Everything was painted white, of course, and she included two of Connie's dramatic displays of white flowers. The panelling was built by Mr Lawrence of the Display Centre in Regent Street, who always made the displays and exhibition stands for Connie, who had recommended him to Gluck. But unfortunately Mr Lawrence fell foul of Gluck's perfectionism. The panels were supposed to arrive on the Saturday afternoon to be set up in the gallery, but the lorry driver went to a football match and did not deliver them until the evening. He brought neither screws nor dust sheets, the pilasters had not been finished, the carpenter was not there and the lorry had been left open in the rain, which meant that the panels had to be dried out and needed an extra coat of paint. Mr Lawrence had given Gluck a verbal estimate of £100 for the job. When he finally sent a bill for £165, relations were strained to the limit and Gluck refused to pay. Prudence Maufe and Connie had to hurriedly intercede and find a surveyor, who inspected the work and Lawrence's accounts, and negotiated a compromise. Connie was made all too aware of the pitfalls of recommending anyone to an artist of Gluck's fiery temperament and high standards.

The private view in October was bursting with famous names from the theatre, photography, interior design, haute couture, fine art, high society, café society, aristocracy and even royalty. The guests were grander and richer than for Gluck's previous shows and also included many of Connie's friends and clients such as Syrie Maugham and the Maufes, Norman Wilkinson and Oliver Hill, the Mount Temples, Cecil Beaton, Lord Portland and Lord Vernon, Arthur Watts and the Oppenheimers. To her fury and embarrassment Gluck's irrepressible mother, whom she called the Meteor, even persuaded Queen Mary to call in briefly for a private view and Her Majesty admired a small picture of tulips. Unfortunately, it had already been sold, but the owner was pressured into giving it up and the Queen graciously accepted it.

The show was very well received in the press. *The Times* wrote that the Gluck frames solved the problem of 'how to hang pictures in the typically "modern" interior, with its severe lines and plane surfaces', a view echoed by Syrie Maugham who on 5 November wrote to Gluck saying: 'Just a line to tell you how much I loved your show . . . The pictures were lovely in themselves and superbly shown. I have never seen an exhibition so beautifully arranged.' The reviewer for *The Lady* wrote of her 'sensitive brush' and delicate sense of tone, colour and composition: 'no one who loves painting should miss this exhibition.' Another critic wrote of her 'exquisite flower pictures, her breadth of subject matter, her lifelike portraits which seemed about to step out of their frames'.

The popular press, however, could not resist commenting on Gluck's eccentric appearance. The *Portsmouth Evening News* described her as 'an artist of the Bohemian kind, [who] wears an Eton crop, affects a masculine type of dress and tells you she dislikes the prefix "Miss" and prefers plain "Gluck"'. Such comments inspired Connie to write a spoof of this kind of nonsense. It was clearly meant as a very private joke, for Gluck's eyes only, and is curiously whimsical and very different from Connie's usual style, the confident wit and authority of her published books. It is coquettish and punctuated here and there with doubles entendres:

Excerpt from the *Feathered World Society News*. November 5th 1932:

I have just returned from a delightful little chat with the petite and amusing Miss Gluck. I asked her why she had abandoned her patronymic for the delightful pseudonym to which she replied with a charming moue 'Because I prefer it to cluck or duck.' So you see she is a wit!

Miss Gluck was dressed in navy blue and wore shoes and stockings; she had had her hair cut at Truefitt's, she told me with a gay smile. I asked her to have a cigarette and she said 'I don't mind if I do'! She is evidently no tyro in the matter of interviews for I asked her to tell me the name of her dentifrice, having observed her beautiful teeth, and she archly handed me a sample tube saying 'Won't you give this a trial?'! We had a frank, not to say abandoned, chat about the weather and I then asked her what was her favourite holiday resort, and she dismissed my question with a gay little laugh and a sidelong glance which spoke volumes.

Of course you will have guessed that Miss Gluck is an artist. She has painted ever such a lot of pictures big and little and they're in ever such nice frames all in white. 'White for purity, you know,' said Miss Gluck with a deep note of reverence in her voice, so I asked her if she was a church woman and whether she sang in the choir. She replied in the fine old biblical fashion by asking another question: 'Have you come to see the pictures?' – so quaint of her I thought. And that reminds me, there is one picture which everyone is rushing to see; it is called *Hors de Combat*, because she painted it lying down. Of course I was immediately interested in the artistic aspect of Miss Gluck and asked her to tell me more about her pictures. With an odd little gesture she referred me to her Mother saying, 'My Mother knows more about my pictures than I do. Indeed if she were not so busy with her social work she would paint them for me to save my time.'

The exhibition was such a success that it was extended for a month and she was invited to prepare another. Eleven paintings were of Connie's flower arrangements, with *Chromatic* as the centrepiece; it was bought by Connie's great friend Ella Reeves. There were also curiously erotic paintings of fleshy lilies, luminous landscapes from Cornwall and quiet scenes of the Loire valley painted during summer holidays with Connie. Commissions poured in and Gluck's specially designed frames became all the rage. Macy's of New York were so keen that they wanted to take the whole exhibition to their store, but the Depression was beginning to bite and the market for art dwindled. The Gluck Room was dismantled and Mr Lawrence claimed the wood for salvage.

For four years, between 1932 and 1936, Connie and Gluck remained extremely close. Connie would stay a couple of nights a week in Hampstead and Gluck spent weekends with Connie at Colney Park. More and more of Gluck's paintings went up on the Spry walls – one depicted a girl as the essence of spring that the painter had called *Primavera* but that the staff from the shop nicknamed 'Interflora'. They toured the country in Gluck's car and stayed in her studio in Cornwall. They visited gardens, meeting the owners, who gave them cuttings and seeds. In Cornwall they stayed with George Johnstone at Trewithen near Truro, and visited Caerhays Castle and the Trebah ravine garden where Connie saw giant gunnera and echium which she decided would be marvellous for dramatic flower displays.

Even on their travels, they both worked hard, Gluck sketching and preparing paintings for her next exhibition while Connie kept detailed garden and flower notes and wrote her book. Once, when they stopped in a tea room en route to Cornwall, a fellow guest, a vicar, made disparaging remarks about Gluck's clothing. Connie leaped to defend her friend's taste for 'outré clobber' and reprimanded the vicar for his prejudice. 'And you a man of the cloth!' she said severely.

Connie and Gluck were invited to spend a weekend at Broadlands, Molly Mount Temple's Palladian mansion near Romsey in Hampshire, which as well as fabulous gardens boasted a polo practice-ground, a golf course, three tennis courts, eight hundred acres of shooting and room for over twenty guests. Gluck's mother, the interfering Meteor, anxious to keep up appearances, lent her daughter her Rolls and chauffeur so she and Connie could arrive in style.

When it came to flowers, Molly Mount Temple insisted that Broadlands be decorated with the same sure eye for colour that she used in London: each room had to have its complement of matching vases and flowers to tone. The saloon was copper and orange, one drawing-room was in the colours of old English and Dresden china, another had a plum carpet and green walls and the flowers were in yellow, purple and puce. Connie later described the flowers at Broadlands as being 'done with great imagination and skill . . . whatever flowers were used, or whatever scheme attempted, the results attained the highest degree of beauty and suitability.' Both the colour combinations and the methods of arrangement were not unlike Connie's own, and were certainly influenced by her. But on this occasion when her hostess demanded that Connie decorate the vast table for dinner she seems to have been uncharacteristically caught off guard.

> I wandered round the garden in dejection. The flowers were lovely, but I could think of nothing that I felt would be a possible contribution to a house so filled with beauty. Fortunately for me there was another guest in the house [Gluck] who was interested, an artist whose appreciation of flowers makes her paint them superbly, but who disowns any knowledge of the practical side of flower arrangement. She thus brought to the matter a technically unbiased mind, and her eye was arrested only by what she regarded as intrinsically beautiful, without any regard to the earthly limitations imposed by vases, or the necessity of fixing stems in water. So I got a lesson not only in flower decoration, but in the emphatic necessity of keeping a mind clear of prejudice or fixed ideas.

So Connie and Gluck happily spent the whole day walking around the grounds collecting material for what were to be Connie's unusually lavish table decorations, which she described in detail:

Red cabbage leaves followed by curly kale leaves, but only those which had turned slightly towards a yellowy green. These were arranged in two frills round a large shallow copper pan. Then velvety begonia leaves, again arranged formally, and a ring of white scabious. After that came a mound of every lovely colour: verbenas, *Phlox decussata*, salvia, bougainvillea, zinnias, pale flame geraniums, gloxinias, purple carnations, and dahlias, mauve, yellow and peach coloured. In the centre were yellow and orange African marigolds and arranged at intervals were the heads of the amethyst thistle . . . It was really exciting, a thrill of colour, satisfying and lovely to a degree. It took a long time to do, because it involved lengthy and pleasant discussion [with Gluck] about the shape and colour of every flower, but it was a great lesson.

In Scotland, Connie and Gluck went to stay with Winnifreda Portarlington, who always summered at the Castle of Stornaway on the Isle of Lewis overlooking the most northerly beach in Scotland. The castle was imposing, its rooms papered with Chinese landscapes and furnished with English antiques, and its entire staff brought up from London. Lady Portarlington, a woman 'with magnificent ideas and inherent good taste', anxious that her enormous dining-table should beat all records, asked Connie's advice about decorating it; she was determined to create a sensation for her guests. All morning they discussed the matter, visited the greenhouses, planned, argued and debated, until at length the hostess went off to 'hold conclave with her butler'. She returned later saying that the whole matter was settled, she had had a grand idea which was to be kept a secret, and Connie was not to give so much as a look at the table until dinner-time when she should have a 'real surprise'.

When the moment arrived, Connie found the gargantuan table, which stretched the length of the great dining-hall, heaped down its centre with moss and heather on which lay dozens of slain partridges arranged with 'a sort of artistic sentimentality'. 'What could be more suitable?' Connie wrote, her tongue firmly in her cheek. 'The guests had shot partridge all day, we were eating partridge, and the table was decorated with partridge. Uniformity of purpose, what more could be said. Unconsciously she had even gone to the length of conforming to the canons of a well-known authority on flower decoration by arranging her partridge *en zigzag*.'

It was here that Connie met the Italian fashion designer Elsa Schiaparelli, a friend of, and collaborator with, the Surrealists, who was then living in Paris. Her unique and wildly original knitwear was popular and chic; her creations included a dress with a Salvador Dali design of a large lobster printed on it and a hat that looked like a giant shoe. She designed the aviator Amy Johnson's clothes for her solo flight to Cape Town in 1936 and outraged the lawn tennis establishment with her culottes for the tennis champion Lili d'Alvarez. Schiaparelli was madder and more original than most of her contemporaries and Connie admired her individuality and artistry. Like Connie, she relied on inspiration rather than craftsmanship or business acumen.

Connie loved to dress Gluck, and got her friends to help. Victor Stiebel made her an austere long black velvet dress with a white tie and Elsa Schiaparelli designed for her a deeply pleated culotte in black chiffon – androgyny turned into high fashion. On a visit to Paris Madame Karinska, costume designer for the New York City Ballet, made Gluck a black crêpe evening suit appliquéd in gold. Connie, who had always loved good clothes and fine fabrics, seems to have lost interest in her own appearance and now preferred simple tailored suits with a string of pearls, plus her ubiquitous overall for work. Stiebel once made her an evening dress in black velvet with a small train to give her height. She went upstairs to try it on and came down kicking a flap of velvet in front of her saying, 'There's something wrong with this dress of Victor's.' Stiebel was hugely amused: she had put it on back to front.

Sometime in 1932, possibly while on a trip to Paris with Stiebel to attend Schiaparelli's show collection, Connie met Jean and Violet Henson. Jean Henson was a tall, handsome, rather louche American southerner who had gone to Paris and immersed himself in the heady world of the Dadaists, posing for Man Ray and befriending Jean Cocteau, Christian Bérard and Serge Lifar. Violet, similarly tall and striking, was a brigadier's daughter who had rebelled against her wealthy English upbringing, travelled extensively and developed a passion for art and literature. Both were bohemian, independent, and flouted social convention. When Connie met them, the Hensons had built a beautiful house in Hammamet on the Tunisian coast with an enormous garden overlooking the Mediterranean, which they filled with rare and exotic plants. The terraces and courtyards were crammed with fountains, sculptures and Roman, Greek and Islamic antiquities collected on their extensive travels around archaeological sites.

Connie's passion for all kinds of pots, vases and bric-a-brac and her wide knowledge of horticulture appealed to the Hensons, who insisted she visit them for a holiday. For Connie, who had never been further than southern Ireland and France, Tunisia was a fabulous new experience, a floral paradise. The boxes of exotic cut flowers bought on cold early-morning trips to Covent Garden were here growing naturally and in abundance. She found giant olive jars in which date palms and ancient gnarled olive trees grew, ilex, fig and pepper trees, wild cork oaks and juniper bushes interspersed with the bright colours of arums, flaming strelitzia, giant datura, bougainvillea and potted azaleas. Wild flowers growing by the roadside pungently scented the air.

The rooms in the house, with their cool high ceilings, were furnished with treasures from the Hensons' travels alongside the work of friends: drawings by Cocteau, and photographs, heavily influenced by the Surrealists, by Cecil Beaton, Horst and his lover George Hoyningen-Huene, chief photographer for *Vogue*. In an alcove in the drawing-room a Roman torso stood near a Bérard painting and on a Spanish table nearby was a lamp by Giacometti, its light falling upon carved African bowls heaped with the golden tangerines that Violet grew in her garden.

Hammamet became a playground for the smart international set who joined the avant-garde artists and built their summer homes there. The Hensons loved to entertain and a steady stream of artists and writers relaxed on the terraces, in the lush gardens and the nearby beach, among them Beaton, the Sitwells, André Gide, Paul Klee, Paul Bowles and Frank Lloyd-Wright. Beaton and Hoyningen-Huene made a trip through Tunisia, taking hundreds of photographs with their new lightweight Rolleiflex cameras, and Beaton later recalled the many English gardens at Hammamet: 'The Moroccan year passes in seasons of flowers. All the English spring blossoms are here as well as the summer ones; roses of unfamiliar species tumble over balconies in pillowy profusion.'

Gluck too was ecstatic about Violet's gardens, which seemed to her like 'Eden, with cats, dogs, birds and fishes all living together free and with no danger to one another'. Early every morning they were woken by peacocks screaming, before breakfasting on one of the terraces looking down over a marble courtyard, with a fountain playing, a lotus pool and a dovecote, while macaws, parrots and Siamese cats roamed freely around. Gluck recalled the 'languor and hysteria' of Tunisia, the stream of visitors to the Villa Hammamet who drank iced tea on the terraces and played halma, the starlit evenings, the sirocco that blew all day, the picnics in the hills.

> It is savage, lovely, bare country. Lunch – cold chicken, eggs, white wine, figs and grapes and coffee in the shade of a carouba tree, spreading with silver-grey low-growing branches and a grey-green leaf . . . Flocks of black goats and marvellous-looking shepherds passing every now and then, the shepherds shy and accepting with pleasure and eagerness empty Vittel bottles as if they were some rare gift. I rode back – and so home and an immediate plunge into a delicious sea to wash off the dust and sweat. My God I felt good after it. Then iced tea and then people to dinner.

Elsa Schiaparelli, who also stayed with the Hensons, drew inspiration from the Bedouin robes in the souks of nearby Nabul. She encouraged Gluck to wear baggy white Arab trousers (which Jean Henson described as Gluck's 'excrementals') tied with a scarlet Neapolitan sash, yellow shirt and green jacket, finished with a geranium behind the ear and a Hammamet cap. Gluck wrote in her diary, 'Jean said I looked the most vicious Arab he had ever seen.' She loved wandering round the souk dressed as an Arab and was excited by the beauty and subtlety of the Arabs' appearance, painting a portrait of a 'delicious' Arab boy which Violet Henson remarked would 'make a fortune if any old queers saw it'.

Connie, who had already begun designing and making her own vases, derived inspiration from antique pots she found in Tunisia. She searched through the museums in Tunis, asking Gluck to sketch the Roman, Greek and Phoenician pieces for her. Connie described their characteristic 'purity of outline and perfections of balance'. But she rejected the tourist pots turned out by 'native potters who, while often keeping the old classic shapes were apt to adorn their handiwork with too much ornament and embellishment'. All the same, she could never resist taking home quantities of earthenware pots, bric-a-brac from the souks and shells found along the beach. She recalled one occasion when an Arab fisherman gave her a curious piece of coral which he had 'dragged up from the deep'. It looked like a graceful miniature birch tree growing from a little mound of bleached grey rock. She packed it with great care and carried it carefully across the sea and on to Paris, but like so many souvenirs it had lost its charm long before she got it safely home. 'The journey was fraught with mysterious discomfort and haunting worry. I appeared to travel with an impalpable aura, something which stole on the air like a pale blue sensation developing during the scorching journey into, I regret to say, an ancient and fishlike smell.' In Paris she discovered the reason: 'Entrenched in the convolutions of the grey rocklike base was a dead and disintegrating mollusc.'

Connie and Gluck travelled home by boat to Marseilles and then on the train via Paris, their luggage bursting with Connie's Moroccan pots and plant cuttings and cut flowers that she could not resist and hoped would last the journey but rarely did, along with Gluck's rolls of canvas and paints and half-finished pictures. Her paintings of Tunisia were snapped up by English clients who loved the exotic colours and her renditions of the brilliant Mediterranean light.

Their happiness came at a price. Relations at home were becoming increasingly strained. Connie was not spending enough time at the shop or dealing personally with her clients. She spent long periods away from her home and beloved garden. It is likely also that she felt under pressure from Shav, and from Val who was always very jealous of Connie despite their apparently close working relationship. In January 1934 Shav wrote a letter to Val complaining about

Gluck's regular visits to their home. He found her irritating and neurotic:

> She can't settle down to any sort of normal and peaceful life and I doubt if she ever will . . . Everything with her is a complication and very restless. I am quite fond of Gluck but I do not like being with her for too long. There is something about the atmosphere of Bolton House that is disturbing to me – as she herself disturbs me. There are always problems and mysteries and tribulations and nothing seems to run smoothly for more than a short time. She is abnormal herself – a queer mixture of childishness and astuteness. The truth is I think she has no real inner peace – nothing to hold on to.

It is almost possible to imagine from this letter that he was ignorant of the true nature of his wife's relationship with Gluck. But given that he describes Gluck as 'abnormal herself', perhaps he was well aware of the situation.

Gluck was fortunate to have found a place in a smart society that made few moral judgements and was on the whole sexually tolerant. Despite this she was insecure, as her biographer Diana Souhami wrote:

> It was as if she had no point of balance, no safe hold on what was hers, no way of reconciling the contradictions in her life. She wanted to be independent, yet was tied to her family for her material needs. She extolled the virtues of the simple life, yet lived rather grandly. She thrived on excitement yet longed for peace. The smallest everyday transactions raised questions of integrity, yet she showed no moral qualms about infidelity or affairs with other men's wives.

But Gluck's relationship with Connie was calming, relatively undemanding, and safe; while her painting, which came before everything else, gave her order and direction.

By November 1933 Connie's first book *Flower Decoration* was ready to go to the publisher. As promised, Sir William Lawrence read and corrected the proofs and wrote a short foreword in which he bemoaned the monotonous standardization of flowers and veg-etables being grown in the UK and the present practice of flower arranging, which had been 'on a level with English cooking' until Mrs Spry came along. According to Lawrence, Connie's book 'pul-lulates with suggestions . . . and gives lists of flowers which run the gamut of architectural forms, and range from seakale gone to seed to the great white spider-lily of the tropics laden with the rich vanilla scent of Piver's [perfume] shop in Paris'. 'You will be grateful', he went on, 'to Mrs Spry for precipitating an aesthetic renaissance.' It was illustrated with beautiful if stylized black-and-white photographs by the famous artists' photographer Paul Laib, whose services were probably acquired through Gluck, and indeed the book included his reproduction of her painting *Chromatic*.

On publication *Flower Decoration* was reviewed by the *Journal of the Royal Horticultural Society*: 'A beauty specialist in the world of flowers, Mrs Constance Spry is unique in the lavish way in which she gives away secrets in her book.' Indeed, here she offered her professional 'secrets' to the general public, sharing her original vision and casting aside convention with a contemptuous sniff. The book distilled most of the ideas and principles for flower decora-tion that she had used for her clients and would use for the rest of her life. She never believed in professional rules, was always quick to admit her mistakes and often changed her mind, whether about a flower she once disliked or a combination of colours that at first hadn't seemed to work.

In March 1934 Connie held a party to celebrate publication. It was a glittering but warm-hearted affair, with society names sweeping in to offer their congratulations before going on to the theatre or a dance. Her family was there, too, and her father George was plainly immensely proud of her, even though he never really understood why she had abandoned education for doing the flowers for high society. Shav, Tony, Val and Gluck were all there, as were her other close friends. Tony had recently got work, possibly through Marjorie Russell, as a copywriter with J. Walter Thompson. He had ambitions to be a writer and felt particularly proud that his mother had actually published a book.

Connie was overwhelmed by the attention and the flattery, but the pleasure she took in her first publication was overshadowed by great sadness. Sir William Lawrence had died in January, just after the book had gone to press. And only a few weeks later, in February, came news of the sudden death of Connie's first and most beloved friend and mentor, Norman Wilkinson, at only fifty-one. His obituary described him thus: 'Whimsical, witty and lovable, his discrimination and taste in every form of decoration were an inspiration.' Connie, who had received so much help and encouragement from him, felt particularly bereft.

Less than six months later, tragedy struck again. Her adored father, the one man whom Connie loved unreservedly and whose praise she had always striven so hard to win, died. Sir Robert Blair wrote a fulsome appreciation of his old friend in *The Times*, though ending rather sourly: 'Mrs Fletcher, three sons and one daughter survive him. The daughter was a live principal of one of London's compulsory day continuation schools.' Shav, who was on holiday with Val in France when George died, wrote to Connie: 'I think it is hard for you to be mentioned only as a "live principal".' Connie's grief at the loss of her father was compounded by the problem of what to do with her mother. Etty had become frail and irritable, and could not live alone. Connie's relations with her were as bad as ever; though she had long since detached herself from her rule, their estrangement over her divorce had endured. A rather bizarre solution was found when James Heppell Marr, Etty's 'true son-in-law', returned from India after retiring and offered to look after her. A house was found for them in Sussex where Marr devotedly nursed the fretful old woman until she died. Whether Connie ever visited her mother and ex-husband is not known. Her ruthlessness in 'moving on' may have meant she put them both behind her and never gave time to considering their needs nor acknowledged any thought or care that she might owe them.

Of all the patrons Connie had found for Gluck, Molly Mount Temple had taken to the artist with particular enthusiasm. She commissioned her to paint both her portrait and Broadlands itself. Gluck spent considerable time there as a guest, often without Connie, and also produced several flower paintings, mostly of classic Spry displays made from material gathered in the gardens there. It was during one of these visits, in May 1936, that Gluck fell hopelessly in love. Nesta Obermeyer was the wife of a wealthy, elderly American. She was beautiful, stylish, glamorous, charismatic and lived life to the full. She seemed perfect at everything: painting, driving fast cars, yoga, skating, skiing and travelling. She enjoyed a glittering social life with her husband with whom she stayed for convenience, for his wealth and as a cover for her affair with Gluck, which 'was to be an absolute marriage outside of society's terms of a marriage'. The Obermeyers owned several homes, including the Mill House, Plumpton, Sussex, where Gluck now went for weekends of passion.

After what Gluck described as her 'fateful marriage night' with Nesta in May, she made only a couple more visits to Connie's home. On the first, according to Gluck's journal, Connie was cold and offhand and said she was 'bored with everything to do with flower pictures', and Gluck 'walked in the park alone'. It is extremely uncharacteristic for Connie to have made such a remark. More probably, she knew about Nesta and was jealous, even hurt, and was trying somehow to end the relationship on her own terms. If so, the attempt was clumsy and unconvincing. Another day, Gluck went to visit Connie for lunch and tea. She wrote: 'C very stuffy to begin with and not much better after. Relief to get home.' Then, a little later, when Connie stayed at Bolton House: 'C. dinner and night BH. Talk and say no more.* There was a

---

* A reference to sex.

final dinner in November: 'Awful evening Thursday' was all Gluck wrote.

A week later there followed a cryptic, confused exchange. Gluck's maid left her a telephone message: 'Flower Decorations rang up. Mrs Spry would like to spend Thursday and Friday evening with you.' Gluck phoned the shop to say she could not do these dates; in fact she was seeing Nesta on those evenings. But Connie's private secretary, Miss Lake, told Gluck that no one from the shop had telephoned her: 'A mistake has been made.' Connie wrote immediately:

> *Darling Gluck.*
>
> *I've just had such an extraordinary message – 'Miss Gluck sorry she can't put you up on Thursday and Friday.' It's Greek to me! I haven't dreamed of such a thing. It must be someone else. You must have thought me a perfect damned nuisance. We've tried to get you on the telephone to explain – or Miss Lake has – with no success and I've got to go off without having it explained to you.*
>
> *Love Constance.*

On the same day Gluck sent back Connie's nightdress with a letter. Miss Lake also wrote to Gluck:

> I assure you that no message was sent to you on Mrs Spry's behalf last evening. The shop was closed at 7 o'clock and Mrs Spry herself left here at least an hour earlier. Any message being sent from Mrs Spry or for her would definitely go through me and no other person here would have any knowledge of this.

This seems to suggest that while the loyal and discreet Miss Lake was in the know about Gluck, no one else in the shop was aware of the relationship. So who did telephone and leave the message, and why? Perhaps Connie, hoping to see Gluck again, had sent the message and, when rebuffed, denied that she done so? She was, after all, quite capable of drawing a veil over things she preferred not to acknowledge and walk away from unpleasantness while giving her own version of events. Yet her letter has an openness and directness that make it difficult to imagine that she was lying.

The following Monday Nesta Obermeyer called to see Connie. The tenor of their conversation can be guessed at from the letter Connie sent her the next day:

> My dear Nesta,
>
> I really cannot tell you how I value what you did yesterday. It was a very generous, a very wise and kind thing to have done. More of your spirit would help everyone.
>
> I look forward to seeing you again, and I'd like you to feel very sure of me — of my friendship, of my wish to be of use and of help if ever that were needed. I love courage and clear cut action — and anyone who has the first and behaves the last fills me with affection and respect. Excuse the grammar, the paper and the dirt!
>
> My affectionate thanks.
> Constance.

It would seem that while Gluck herself remained evasive and unclear with Connie about her relationship with Nesta, it was Nesta who took the decisive action to visit Connie and tell her the truth. Connie certainly admired her for her straightforward approach and her 'clear cut action'. Hope of any kind of relationship with Gluck was well and truly over. Immediately after Nesta's visit, she and Gluck went to a concert at the Wigmore Hall, and on 5 December — Connie's birthday, now scratched out of Gluck's diary — a Rolls-Royce arrived at Bolton House to take Gluck to Plumpton for the weekend. Gluck burned everything to do with past relationships, and thus her four-year affair with Connie was consigned to ashes. It is doubtful whether Connie ever spoke to either Gluck or Nesta again.

Gluck's new exhibition opened early in 1937. There were several new flower groups, showing Connie's continuing influence, as well as paintings from their holidays in Hammamet such as a cornucopia of pomegranates in a shell. The centrepiece of the exhibition, *Nature Morte*, which had been painted before the end of the relationship, was a typical Spry arrangement of wild plants: dead flowers, grasses and clematis seed-heads in one of Connie's alabaster vases.

The affair with Connie had given Gluck an entrée into a wider social circle and many new commissions. Connie, for her part, had found a soulmate, a fellow artist, someone sensitive and caring who needed her. Until Gluck, the people Connie really loved were her father, who she felt was disappointed in her; Shav, her beloved companion who betrayed her trust; and her son Tony, whom she certainly loved but never seemed to have felt very maternal towards. Gluck was possibly the only person in her life who awoke intense emotional and physical feelings buried deep inside her. Her unhappy childhood and vexed relationships had given Connie a tough, even selfish carapace. Her passion and her ardour had all been for her work; she had never allowed herself to stop and consider her own inner feelings and desires. But, briefly perhaps, with Gluck, she did.

EIGHT

Absolute Discretion

1934–1937

One bitterly cold day in the late winter of 1934, Connie was on her way home from her weekly visit to Swanley Horticultural College in Kent when she saw a building looming up out of the fog. She asked the driver to stop so she could explore what turned out to be a fruit farm abandoned during the slump and near-derelict. Park Gate was a beautiful redbrick Georgian farmhouse with a cluster of classic oast-houses, a weed-choked cobbled yard leading to a large overgrown garden and broken-down orchards. Shav had been complaining that Colney Park was too large and expensive to run. 'We must find a farm,' he had pronounced. This one seemed perfect to Connie, just what they had envisaged for their next home; a change of air and a fresh start, with plenty of space where they could cultivate productive cutting beds for the business.

The Sprys were on the move again. With Shav's colonial background and Connie's unsettled childhood, they seemed to share a peripatetic streak. Connie was a nomad at heart, restless and always ready to move on, to a new home or a new project. When a phase in her life was over, she did not look back. She was not sentimental about houses, possessions or even gardens, though she always took her beloved plants with her. 'It is always an unhappy experience to be turned out of a garden,' she wrote, yet she seemed to take an almost reckless satisfaction from the challenge of moving all her plants, on several occasions, to a new home. Whatever she was involved in, even with gardening, she hated getting bored or stuck in a groove. 'I hate to keep my feet on the ground,' she wrote. 'I was first, and hope last to be, a gardener; it was an unanticipated combination of circumstances that led me to do professionally something I did once only as a relaxation, but much as I love doing it, I don't like the groove to be too deep.'

Unlike Colney Park, which had a mature garden when they moved in, Park Gate was a blank canvas. 'There had to be a good garden there but we had to find it,' the loyal Walter Trower recalled. With help from students from Swanley, Connie and Trower launched themselves into a huge programme of landscaping around the farmhouse and outbuildings. The cobbled yard was turned into a lawn, the orchard of old fruit trees thinned, leaving just a few to make a dappled background to a sweep of herbaceous border and to form a grove between the lawn and the wild garden. Given its difficult soils and situation, it was not an easy garden. As Connie wrote, 'My garden in Kent is exposed to the four winds of heaven.'

The new garden had to be practical, so most of the beds and borders were devoted to growing flowers for the business. Fortunately, there was enough land for Connie to be able to indulge in all her favourites: banks of lilac, swathes of haunting majestic lilies, imperial fritillaries and all kinds of tulips and iris. They erected a pergola which was soon smothered in mountain clematis, and created a fragrant philadelphus walk leading from the rose garden to the nursery: 'The walk between those scented hedges is a pleasure which in itself would make the daily journey back from town worthwhile.' Connie planted a triangular piece of ground with small limes for their sweet-smelling flowers which she liked to use in decorations. She insisted on mature trees being planted because she wanted to enjoy them before she grew too old. The limes were underplanted with blue, white and lilac-pink *Scilla hispanica* and she trained heavily scented honeysuckle over stumps of dead cherry trees in the orchard, where she sowed the long grass with wild sorrel, dog daisies, foxgloves and drifts of sweet rocket along with oriental poppies, 'so flamingly, flaringly grand'. At the far end of the orchard, in a border dug out of the turf and backed by a rough field hedge of hawthorn, dog roses, spindleberry and open farmland, were planted Connie's untidy, tangled, space-consuming 'most favoured darlings', the plants with which above all others her name would be associated – the 'old' roses of her memories and dreams.

Connie had been passionate about roses since her childhood romance with the black rose in Derbyshire. Fifty years later she was still writing about this fabled flower, which she came to think was probably a gallica called 'Tuscany', an old velvet rose of dark crimson-purple. It might equally have been the moss rose 'Nuits de Young', which bears blooms of the darkest possible maroon with blackish tints. In those days old roses were out of fashion and largely forgotten. Compared to the modern hybrids with their elegant and perfect blooms, old roses have more subtle colouring and texture, but a laxer habit, with flatter, more cabbage-shaped flowers. They are, however, extremely free-flowering, vigorous, hardy and foolproof. Best of all, they have the most delicious perfume. Their origins lost in antiquity, Connie called them the roses of poetry and song; reminiscent of illustrations in old books, of paintings and tapestries and cottage gardens, they appealed to her deep-seated sense of romance and nostalgia.

Some years earlier, through Sidney Bernstein, Connie had visited Sissinghurst and admired Vita Sackville-West's rose gardens. But it was not until she saw the designer Norah Lindsay's garden at Sutton Courtenay in Oxfordshire that she was inspired to start her own collection. Norah's garden had, she wrote, a sense of 'flourishing ease and naturalness', an air of spontaneity in the planning which immediately appealed to her. There, all kinds of old-fashioned roses were flowering profusely and growing freely into graceful shapes along winding paths and up pillars and hedges; their perfume was 'distinct and intoxicating'. Connie was excited by such a diversity of colours, whether of the single rich-red and deep-pink roses or those that were striped and 'delicately feathered as if with a fine brush'. She described standing under a cascade of blooms, surrounded by a sea of them, almost drowning in their scent. 'This to me is what a rose garden should be,' she wrote, 'the apotheosis of the rose.'

Connie began her collection by buying plants from specialist growers in England, Ireland, Scotland and France. She searched in private gardens for 'lost' roses, such as 'Vierge de Cléry'. An American friend from Virginia wrote to tell her about slaves who used to plant roses on the graves of their relatives. There was an old slave cemetery on her property and she sent Connie some cuttings of a rare variety she had found growing there. Gradually Connie learned about the different types and varieties of old roses: the centifolias, damasks, gallicas, albas and moss roses. Her favourite varieties were 'Cardinal Richelieu', 'Charles de Mills', 'Nuits de Young', 'Tour de Malakoff' and 'Madame Isaac Pereire' – all now hugely popular but barely known in Connie's time.

The Sprys would live at Park Gate for longer than at any of their other houses, and it was to be Connie's biggest challenge. Although those who knew her and read her books regarded her as a garden expert with an encyclopaedic knowledge of plants, she continued to think of herself as an amateur with much still to learn. She sought help and advice from anyone who would give it. Always open about her mistakes, she described how she had once planted a bed in solid blocks of flowers rather than in drifts: 'The result was stiff and jerky, not the flowing, merging masses of colour I had hoped for.' She still spent considerable time, far more than one might think she could spare from her many other commitments, travelling around the country, exploring any gardens that sounded interesting, searching for unusual plants and fresh ideas for her garden and her books. The trial grounds at Wisley were a valuable source of inspiration, while the regular Royal Horticultural Society flower shows at Vincent Square continued to be a vital meeting place. There she could discuss 'curiosities' and cultivation problems with the nurserymen. She visited many of them at their nurseries – Mr Hillier at Winchester, Messrs Notcutt at Woodbridge and Mr Constable at Tunbridge Wells – and regularly described and quoted all their plants and their views in her books. Several of her London clients owned country estates, and those with a genuine interest and knowledge of gardening invited Connie to stay. She was especially keen to see places with fine collections of rhododendrons, azaleas, magnolias, camellias and rare varieties of shrubs and trees, such as those in Captain Soames's gardens at Sheffield Park in Sussex, laid out by Capability Brown. She always returned home from these visits laden with seeds, cuttings and ideas.

Connie would continue to develop her passion for gardening until she could write as knowledgeably about cultivating plants as about arranging them. Everywhere she went she jotted things down in her small notebook. The Oppenheimers, she recorded, had solved a particularly tricky problem in their garden in Wales, situated on the side of a very steep hill. They had had it terraced and the banks covered with hurdles held by wooden pegs. Sturdy-growing varieties of rambler rose had then been planted, their long canes tied to the hurdles. The banks were thus held fast and beautifully curtained with a wall of roses. She visited Gravetye Manor in Sussex, the home of the late William Robinson, whose gardener Ernest Markham still ruled. Markham was an expert on clematis. His collection clambered up among the trees, creating great bowers heavy with flowers in summer and wreathed in autumn with filmy seeds. Connie greatly admired Robinson's legacy of growing plants in the natural manner: 'When you walk through these gardens in the autumn you find some of the heavily laden apple trees also bearing bronzed leaves of vines which have climbed up through the branches, shining red apples and brilliant red leaves intermingling.'

One of her oldest gardening friends was Scrase Dickins, whose gardens at Coolhurst, also in Sussex, she especially admired: 'Mr Dickins has a way of growing flowers so that they look as though they had not been planted by the hand of man. In his woodland garden one might think that the rare lilies grew wild; strange and lovely plants seem to be naturalized by the streamside.' A new neighbour in Kent was Lord Darley of Cobham Hall, who showed Connie how in the Hall's great park he had naturalized colonies of sweet-scented bergamot, growing in clouds of crimson, pink and white in the open spaces among the trees. Connie was entranced. It never mattered to her whether she was discussing gardening with an earl, with his gardener or with a nurseryman; what was important was their passion and what she could learn from them. The plantsman Norman Haddon, a fellow iris enthusiast, had a woodland garden in Porlock, Somerset. He shared with her his secret for the successful slaughter of slugs in his delphinium beds: 'He told me that he mixed crushed meta [a chemical compound of carbide used instead of methylated spirit] with bran and strewed this about near his plants. The effect was remarkable.'

In the summer of 1934 Syrie Maugham wrote to Connie telling her that she had sold Villa Eliza in Le Touquet and made an arrangement to rent the Pavilion, a Victorian folly in the grounds of Waddesdon, the Rothschild estate near Aylesbury. Syrie, who was no gardener, begged Connie to come and see what could be done in the garden. Connie knew several members of the Rothschild family, who were great garden lovers, especially Lionel Rothschild at Exbury, and she was curious to see the place. Visiting for the weekend, Connie found Syrie's new garden a disappointment. Although there were some fine elms and chestnuts and open lawns spreading gracefully down to a lily-choked artificial lake, there were neither flower beds nor shrubs to give structure and excite the eye with colour. Connie made a few suggestions, planted up a few pots and left her friend to it.

She now decided the Burlington Gardens shop was too small and that that too should be moved, preferably to an even more fashionable part of town. She still put great faith in the West End, and new premises were found at 64 South Audley Street, just off Grosvenor Square, in fashionable Mayfair. 'It must be alright because it's farther west,' she said. It was probably no coincidence that Syrie Maugham was also moving her showrooms to Mayfair. Syrie, like Connie, needed constant stimulation. She was now bored with her all-white schemes and had moved on to strong colours, mirrored glass, shells, bamboo and polished steel. By

1934 *Vogue* was reporting a 'new direction', writing of one of Syrie's cocktail parties:

> [It was] a sort of farewell to the big white room, which has now become a white and scarlet room since she has acquired two big mural decorations by Christian Bérard which are a riot of colour. Instead of the sofas being covered in white they are now covered in Holland linen with red fringes, and cushions of different shades of scarlet. There were big bouquets by Mrs Spry of different shades of scarlet flowers mixed with white and a few white chairs touched with scarlet paint. So this must definitely be the end of white.

While waiting for the new Mayfair shop to be refurbished, Connie began to consider other ideas. As the business continued to grow she would obviously need to expand her staff, and new decorators would have to be trained in her unique style. Still hankering for some form of teaching role, Connie decided there was a need for a flower school. The only training then available was an apprenticeship in the workroom of one of the leading floristry shops. Fourteen-year-old school leavers worked on mossing wreaths, de-thorning roses, cutting flowers and putting them in water: dull, routine work with no creative challenge to make it worthwhile. Apprenticeship, which they had to pay for, was a long, hard grind and they had to love the work to survive. There were no courses in the kind of flower decorating Connie had made famous, and which she claimed was a quite different art. If she wanted girls skilled in her new art form, she would have to teach them herself. She had been observing the progress of her friend Rosemary Hume's Cordon Bleu cookery school, which had opened in London in 1931 and was proving very successful. Although the first students had mostly been debutantes, the intake had broadened to include serious-minded girls who viewed cookery either as a potential profession or as a source of satisfaction and pride in the home. In 1935 the school moved to an old tea shop in Sloane

Square and with the extra space had opened a proper restaurant. Rosemary's mentor Monsieur Pellaprat gave them permission to use the name Au Petit Cordon Bleu – a title that she and Dione Lucas also used for their popular book of recipes, published in 1936.

Early in 1935 Connie opened the Constance Spry Flower School in the basement of Sunderland House in Curzon Street. It was a rather amateurish affair, with two hours of lectures and demonstrations a day. As at Rosemary Hume's cookery school, many of the students were merely debutantes amusing themselves, or girls filling in time before going on to secretarial college or marriage. But there were a few with real talent and ambition who were allowed to help out in the shop and to lend a hand on rush orders. Those who showed sufficient promise were taken on when their course ended.

Connie was often asked by clients if she would train their daughters. 'It would just suit her, she's so dreamy and artistic' was frequently given as a qualification, and Connie would gently point out that flower decoration required someone with a tough disposition, great patience and skilful hands. 'Dreamy' was *not* required – 'Quickness and a sure hand are far more useful, for an eye can be trained more readily than a character changed.' Speed was certainly of the essence, and a good sense of humour also helped. In her book *Flowers for House and Garden* Connie laid out her requirements for a successful flower decorator:

An open and unprejudiced mind, a gift for constructive criticism and the ability to see the essential quality in what is beautiful are all valuable assets . . . Prejudice and preconceived ideas which refuse to be altered are a drag on one's progress. If one dislikes certain flowers, colours and combinations of colour, this is a personal matter; to refuse to understand them or to use them well is, however, a mistake. To see the possibilities of all colours and all subjects is a help.

She went on to stress the importance of really looking at the room that is to be decorated: seeing its positive values, sensing its atmosphere and understanding how different flowers could contribute to or complement those qualities. For example, one might plan a flower scheme round a single picture or piece of furniture, or to stress the colour of the walls or hangings. Even the most beautiful flower arrangement, if not in sympathy with its surroundings, can destroy the beauty and symmetry of a room, drown its subtleties and override its individuality. 'We have gone a long way', she wrote, recalling Irish memories, 'since the days when ivy was trailed round picture frames and fireplaces hidden by banks of flowers.' Just as important was the need to look for potential material in the garden, flower market or hedgerow; to see all kinds of possibilities and not be prejudiced by convention or fashion. 'Rules are there to be broken,' Connie would say to her students, and when they looked surprised she would laugh, 'in the most "suitable" way.'

Shav now decided that the business should become a limited company: Flower Decorations Ltd. The directors were to be Constance Spry, Val Pirie, a chartered accountant colleague of Shav's and Victor Stiebel, who said: 'I was there to be on Connie's side.' Stiebel had to a great degree filled the empty space in Connie's life left after the death of Norman Wilkinson. But he agreed to be a director of Flower Decorations only if Connie became a director of his company too, which she did. Eleanor Gielgud became company secretary. Shav, perhaps surprisingly, took no formal interest in the business. That said, he was undoubtedly a backseat driver with considerable influence over both Connie and Val. If one did not support his views, the other would be sure to agree with him.

In March 1935, after months of decorating and refurbishing, they finally moved into 64 South Audley Street. With contributions from Syrie and Oliver Messel, Connie had again used all her ingenuity to create a lavish-looking interior from bits and pieces:

these included offcuts from Victor Stiebel's couture workrooms, wrought-iron tables stripped and gilded by Syrie, plus marbled pedestals and gold-painted cherubs produced by Messel, leftovers from the set of one of his theatre productions. The flower school, too, moved to premises across the road, and was rather grandly renamed the Modern School of Flower Work. The new shop was spacious and the staff of fifty could work comfortably, spread over three floors: a big well-lit basement workshop, at street level an elegant shop overflowing with flowers and eager young staff and, upstairs, a special wedding room.

Weddings were now a major part of the business, and almost every Friday and Saturday a team of girls worked against the clock making bouquets and decorating a church – in high summer, often several churches. Connie had devoted a whole chapter to flowers for weddings in *Flower Decoration*: 'Flowers are part of the pageant and must complement both the bride and bridesmaids' dresses and the church where the service is to take place . . . with pageantry one needs uniformity, but not so everyone looks alike.' Connie had always had strong views regarding flower decorations in church, but she had not found it easy to gain the acceptance of the society churches favoured for London's grander weddings. For all her railing against the common practice of filling the nave with low pots of ferns and palms that no one could see after the congregation had gathered, or the commercial wedding florists' terrible (according to Connie) habit of turning a church into 'a bower of flowers or an herbaceous border', London's clergy were initially reluctant to give a 'backstreet florist' like Connie an entrée.

When Emily Lutyens, wife of the architect and a regular customer of Connie's, was planning her daughter Mary's wedding at St Margaret's, Westminster, in February 1930, she wanted Connie to decorate the church. The clergy at the church were particularly unwilling to allow Mrs Spry and her innovative arrangements across their portals. Lady Lutyens, however, was a forceful personality and that, allied to her husband's prestigious name, won the day. February could not be a more difficult month for flowers; Connie raided the markets and found huge branches of the beautiful *Eucalyptus globulus* with its creamy-white seed-heads. She and her team sat up half the night painting the backs of the leathery leaves blue. The branches were then arranged in urns on alabaster pedestals so that they looked like two waterfalls, cascading down on either side of the chancel steps. The effect was exquisite and quite unlike anything that had been seen at St Margaret's, or indeed any wedding, before. It was typical Connie – she was always adamant that displays in a church must never obscure the building's architectural features, nor be dotted haphazardly around. Two dramatic displays at the chancel became her classic wedding style. In the newspapers the Lutyens wedding attracted much publicity, of which the flowers received their full share. After this triumph, it was harder for the smart churches to refuse Connie entry.

When the Duchess of Norfolk was married in Brompton Oratory, a difficult interior to decorate with its cavernous space and low lighting, Connie matched the flowers in the church with those carried by the bridesmaids: the brilliant carmines and scarlets toned with their pale-blue dresses and 'the place simply glowed'. The marriage of Lady Howard de Walden's daughter in the Russian church in South Kensington presented other problems, not least that the congregation was expected to remain standing throughout the ceremony. So posts were attached to the pillars, and vases like Venetian lanterns attached to the posts, then the vases filled with large bouquets of white flowers so that the whole aisle seemed to be a floral guard of honour. For a marriage in a synagogue, Connie used the wedding canopy of white brocade embroidered with silver thread to make an arbour, then garlands of flowers crowned with a slender plume of white lilies.

The vastness of St Paul's Cathedral demanded something more dramatic, so for a wedding there she placed at the chancel steps two large formal settings of enormously tall swords of New Zealand flax with generous stabs of scarlet amaryllis. The effect was one of grandeur, austerity and beauty: 'the groups had some of the character of their surroundings and were not dwarfed or dimmed, but fell into place.' For her wedding in Southwark Cathedral Betsan Horlick carried a shower of brilliant blue gentians which *Vogue* reported as 'completely novel'. The Cathedral was decorated with twelve-foot-high stands of lilies, pampas grass, green hydrangeas and a few yellow globe-headed chrysanthemums: 'All done by Mrs Spry,' *Vogue* reported. 'We do seem to be very far from the days of Romney bridesmaids and orange-blossom!'

Young ladies and their mothers would gather in the Wedding Room to pore over examples of bouquets and headdresses, with Connie and her team in patient attendance. It called for considerable tact: 'weddings being very individual and personal affairs sometimes means the bride will carry, for sentimental reasons, flowers which neither assist the general effect nor improve the appearance of her gown,' Connie wrote somewhat wearily. Her trademark hand spray was a creamy waterfall of huge wax-like lilies flowing in a crescent from waist to hem. *Lilium regale*, white marguerites and romantic old-fashioned roses were all popular. Sheila Young remembered driving the van from Park Gate to London with buckets of warm water filled with hundreds of stems of orange blossom cut from Connie's famous walk. The church was then decorated with philadelphus and huge flowering branches of lime, their outer leaves removed. 'The soft blend of green and white colours and the warm sweet scent was sublime.'

When Cecil Beaton's sister Nancy married a Grenadier Guards officer, Connie was naturally asked to do the flowers. She almost overreached herself. It was to be a classic winter wedding and the bride 'looked like the Snow Queen'. Connie had the bridesmaids linked together 'like snowflakes' with whitewashed ropes entwined with garlands of chalk-white flowers, but in the hot, packed church, the whitewash began to flake off, leaving a chalky trail up to the chancel steps and back again, like a small snow storm. 'It was quite a time', George Foss recalled, 'before we were allowed into St Margaret's again after that.' But the Beaton family loved it, as did all the guests, and it was talked about long after.

But the wedding most often remembered for Connie's sheer daring and originality was that of Lady Violet Bonham Carter's daughter Laura to Jo Grimond in 1938. Connie filled St Margaret's, which had been forced, albeit reluctantly, to accept her, with nothing but white urns filled with great billowing sprays of cow-parsley, creating an exquisitely lacy effect – though it is possible that some guests were sneezing by the end of the service. The idea was so successful that it was repeated at a debutante ball at Claridge's Hotel, where she created a wonderful, creamy summer idyll effect with girls in their white evening dresses 'floating around the ballroom afoam with ox-eye daisies and cow-parsley'. The hotel management were apparently not amused; they did not expect controversy in the floral decorations. Fearing ridicule and consequent disaster, Connie was delighted when the society pages responded ecstatically and everyone wanted 'country weeds'. Because of her use of wild material, a popular joke at the time was to say of an inadequate vase of bedraggled-looking flowers, 'Ah, Constance Spry – no expense spared!'

Connie had by now received some royal commissions, her first client being Prince George, Duke of Kent. The Duke, a neighbour of Lady Portarlington, having admired Connie's flowers at her parties invited her to do the flowers at his private home in Belgrave Square. The Duke's wedding to Princess Marina of Greece was the highlight of the 1934 Season and Connie was to do the bride's bouquet. Prince George was a keen gardener and liked to chat to her about gardening while he watched her team at work. He was amused by their free use of pieces from the royal family's Meissen and Sèvres dinner services, though when his mother Queen Mary came for luncheon they were expected to use conventional pink carnations in more traditional receptacles. The Duchess once asked Sheila Young to remove a vase of lichen-covered branches and decorative kale before her brother arrived from Greece as she felt he would not understand it.

The following year, on the Duke's recommendation, Connie was invited to do the flowers for another royal wedding, that of his brother the Duke of Gloucester and Lady Alice Montagu-Douglas-Scott. Connie and her girls might have been allowed into St Margaret's, Westminster, but they were still not permitted to work in the Chapel Royal where the ceremony took place. They did, though, provide the bouquets for the bride and bridesmaids who included the Princesses Elizabeth and Margaret. Norman Hartnell designed the gowns and the bride carried a bouquet

> made of cream-coloured flowers in a graceful crescent shape and in order that no note of green should disturb the delicate aspect of this bouquet some of the flowers were mounted on fine wires which were bound with silver. This enabled an effect of richness to be achieved without heaviness. The bridesmaids carried the palest of flesh-pink roses and here again no green was used, but a few fragile skeletonised magnolia leaves veined with gold leaf, mounted on gold-bound stems, were introduced among the roses.

'Skeletonised' leaves veined with gold or silver-leaf were quite a novelty and became a Spry hallmark. Once again the press declared that Mrs Spry 'had set a new standard in elegance and grace'.

A further sign of royal favour came when the Prince of Wales became a regular client. On the evening of the Duke of Gloucester's wedding his father, King George V, wrote in his diary, 'Now all the children are married except David.' The Prince of Wales, known to his friends and family as David, was now forty years old but still a confirmed bachelor. To his father's huge disapproval he had become involved with a succession of married women, notably Freda Dudley Ward, the wife of a Liberal MP.

Fort Belvedere, the Prince's bachelor home, was an oddity on the edge of Windsor Great Park, a mock-Gothic folly built in

1750 by George II as a military lookout post; it still boasted a line of four-pounder guns. The Prince flew the flag of the Duchy of Cornwall to make it clear that it was his private retreat, and came to love it more than anywhere else. Connie, accompanied by either Sheila or Robbo, visited regularly to do the flowers. They were always made to feel welcome at the Fort and were well looked after by Mrs Mason, the housekeeper. There was always a jigsaw puzzle laid out in the drawing-room, music from the gramophone to listen to while they worked, and they were allowed free run of the gardens to pick whatever they wanted for their arrangements. The girls took sandwiches for lunch, but if the Prince was in residence Connie was invited to join him. A keen and knowledgeable gardener, he greatly enjoyed their horticultural discussions. He was one of the few people to show interest in her previous work as an educator and questioned her closely about her experiences in Ireland and the East End. He was at that time particularly concerned with the plight of the miners, but it is unlikely that Connie ever confided that her first husband was a mine manager and that, for several years, she had lived within sight and sound of an Irish coalmine.

The Prince had recently taken up with a new companion, an American divorcee. 'Lunched with Emerald [Cunard] to meet Mrs Simpson,' the Conservative MP and diarist Henry 'Chips' Channon wrote on 23 January 1935. 'She is a nice, quiet, well-bred mouse of a woman with large startled eyes and a huge mole. I think she is surprised and rather conscience-stricken by her present position and the limelight which consequently falls upon her.'

Wallis Simpson, who was living in London with her second husband Ernest Simpson, was also a client of Flower Decorations Ltd. She was very fastidious, hated wire-netting to show and knew nothing about flowers, but she always gave warm praise when the job was done and everyone at the shop wanted to do her flowers. Sheila Young, who usually attended her house to make up the vases and tend the exotic plants in two glass accumulator tanks, remembered Mrs Simpson saying, in her American drawl, how she would like some spring branches 'with those cute little yellow worms on them'.

Mr and Mrs Simpson were introduced to the Prince of Wales at a party in London given by Thelma, Lady Furness, then the Prince's mistress. Wallis found herself curtseying to a small fair man in very loud tweeds and recalled that their first conversation was about central heating. Some time later Lady Furness arrived late at a dinner party given by Syrie Maugham and discovered the Prince and Wallis Simpson quite alone in Syrie's intimate library. It did not take long for the news to spread, and by the following year Wallis Simpson had become a popular hostess, playing bridge and giving little dinner parties at which she served American food and entertained her guests with her fresh, unguarded transatlantic talk. One guest described her Regent's Park house as 'quite lovely, with old mirrors and new colours supplied mostly by Syrie Maugham and fresh flowers supplied by Constance Spry'. Cecil Beaton, who was a regular visitor, once rather bitchily described Connie's work for Wallis Simpson as 'arrangements of expensive flowers, mixed with bark and local weeds'.

Mr and Mrs Simpson stayed at Fort Belvedere for a weekend party, where they found the kilted Prince doing embroidery on a sofa, an art his mother had taught him. He spent the days billhooking the shrubbery and evenings dancing to the gramophone. Soon he, too, became a regular guest at the Simpsons' little dinners. 'He was lonely,' Wallis Simpson later recalled, 'and perhaps I had been one of the first to penetrate the heart of his inner loneliness, his sense of separateness.' The Prince was also 'the open sesame to a new and glittering world that excited me as nothing in my life had ever done before . . . It seemed unbelievable that I, Wallis Warfield of Baltimore, Maryland, could be part of this enchanted world . . . it was like being Wallis in Wonderland.' Not a word of their relationship appeared in the British press, and the upper classes were horrified when they realized that the Prince was intent upon marrying her. Connie, who saw only

A class in flower arranging.

Connie did the classic
crescent bouquet and
church flowers for the
wedding of Lady Alice
Montagu-Douglas-Scott
to HRH The Duke of
Gloucester in 1935.

Connie's great friend, Helen
Kirkpatrick, as a US war
correspondent.

Lesley Blanch's drawing of Connie
in her wartime kitchen garden.

Coolings Gallery, Bond Street, 1939.
The sandbags were decked out with
Connie's flowers 'to cheer people up'.

The first meeting of the first floral decoration society in Britain which took place at Dorchester Corn Exchange in June 1950.

Connie with Mrs Pope judging at the Dorchester Flower Show.

Connie adds the finishing touches – stephanotis flowers – to the table decorations for the Coronation Banquet at Lancaster House, 1953.

Connie and Ministry of Works architect, Eric Bedford, inspect huge tubs of poppies made by disabled ex-servicemen to decorate the Coronation route.

A green table decoration including rhubarb leaves, marrow flowers, green
tomatoes, seed heads, passion flower, figs, peas, poppy head, water lilies,
an agapanthus seed head and the fruit of *Pyrus japonica*.

Chrysanthemums with brown leaves and berries that
should have 'gone out with the wheelbarrow'.

Top Connie and Sheila McQueen in Brisbane in March 1959 during their lecture tour in Australia.

Above Connie and Gilbert Harding inspect early spring blossom, 1958.

Left Connie relaxing and doing her tapestry.

A very formal photograph of Connie posing in front of some of
her favourite vases and one of her rescued Atkinsons' mirrors.

An early favourite of Connie's; the old-fashioned Niphetos
'Bridal Rose' and lily of the valley.

romance and cared little for scandal or politics, was fond of both the Prince of Wales and Mrs Simpson and was determined to do all she could to protect their privacy. She summoned her staff, telling them firmly, 'These are two of our best customers, none of you have had anything but kindness from them, and I want you to be absolutely silent and loyal.' Every member of Connie's team kept silent.

On the night of 20 January 1936, King George V died. To ease the King's end and ensure the announcement could meet the morning papers, the royal physician Lord Dawson administered a lethal injection of cocaine and morphine. Two days later the Prince of Wales was proclaimed King Edward VIII. Despite his father's gloomy prognostication that 'after I am gone the boy will ruin himself within twelve months', the new King seemed determined to prove himself a successful modern monarch. Yet he also seemed intent on enjoying himself, and spent the summer on board a yacht cruising the Dalmatian coast with Wallis Simpson, Lord Mountbatten and Duff and Diana Cooper. The British press refrained from fuelling scandal by reporting on the lovers' progress, but American and other foreign newspapers covered the King's holiday keenly, publishing photographs of him sunbathing shirtless on deck. Six months later Wallis's divorce became absolute and she was free to remarry. Stanley Baldwin, the Prime Minister, urged the King not to marry her. On 30 November Harold Nicolson noted in his diary:

The Cabinet are determined that he shall abdicate. So are the Privy Council. But he imagines that the country, the great warm heart of the people, are with him. I do not think so. The upper classes mind her being an American more than they mind her being divorced. The lower classes do not mind her being an American but loathe the idea that she has had two husbands already.

Three days later, on 3 December, Nicolson wrote:

The storm breaks . . . the streets flame with posters, 'The King and Mrs Simpson' . . . I do not find people angry with Mrs Simpson. But I do find a deep enraged fury against the King himself. In eight months he has destroyed the great structure of popularity which he had raised.

Baldwin once again met with the King and told him that the country would not tolerate a marriage between the sovereign and a married woman. The crisis, which left the country divided for some time, reached its long-drawn-out conclusion when Baldwin held firm and the King abdicated on 10 December. In his now famous abdication broadcast he said: 'You must believe me when I tell you that I have found it impossible to carry the heavy burden of responsibility and discharge my duties as King as I would wish to do without the help and support of the woman I love.' The King was given the title of Duke of Windsor and sailed to France, where Wallis Simpson was waiting for him.

The King's departure was reported in women's magazines as a story of 'the king who had given up everything for his true love'. Connie was particularly saddened by the abdication and felt she had lost not only two valuable clients but two people who had been important to her. Just before Christmas 1936 she received a strange letter from Mabel Mason, the Duke's housekeeper at Fort Belvedere, with whom she had been in close correspondence over the whole 'terrible business'. Mrs Mason, who seemed to regard herself as a clairvoyant, wrote that she had seen Connie in a sort of vision, 'a week before the crisis', dressed in black, weeping, and saying: 'I am so sorry about it all. Oh dear, oh dear, what shall we do?' The wretched housekeeper, who was clearly very upset that no one had told her anything about the abdication and now felt abandoned, appeared to believe that Connie was 'communicating' with her about it. Although she had had several offers of work, Mrs Mason wrote, 'I am not inclined to go anywhere where I shall undoubtedly be besieged with questions about our little man.' She was sure he would return to the Fort: 'HM told me he hoped when he came back that I would come back in service to him!' Connie, who was far too down to earth to believe in telepathy, wrote a polite and tactful reply:

> I am greatly interested in what you tell me and certainly if thoughts could carry themselves, I should have been with you all that dreadful time as I was thinking about you and how wretched and upset you must be . . . I am sure that when HM returns, all of us will want to rally round and show our loyalty and love for him . . . I feel just as you do about questions. People have no reticence and not much decency, I think.

The coronation of George VI on 12 May 1937 brought several extra commissions for parties and festivities and everyone tried to forget the unpleasantness of the abdication. Connie, though busy, received no work from the royal family, hardly surprising since she was so closely associated with the former King. One day, soon after the coronation, she received an invitation to do the flowers for the wedding of Wallis Simpson and the Duke of Windsor which was taking place on 3 June at the Château de Candé, the home of the Duke's Franco-American friends Charles and Fern Bedaux. The chateau happened to be near Val Pirie's family home, the Château de Varennes, near Tours. Without hesitation, and without pausing to consider whether or not this was a wise step, Connie said yes. The great love between Wallis and the Duke had touched her sentimental and romantic soul. Through her own experiences of failed marriage and secret love, she could sympathize with their plight.

Connie and Val took the train to Paris where they visited the flower markets and ordered three dozen Madonna lilies and quantities of peonies. Then they hired a car and Val drove them to the Château de Varennes, where they stayed with her family and spent two days 'picking like mad' in the gardens: syringa, more peonies, and great sprays of rambler roses. With the car crammed with flowers they arrived at the Château de Candé to find the place under siege, reporters from all over the world camping at the gates. The house was in a state of turmoil as everyone prepared for the wedding. Connie was unable to do her flowers *in situ*, as she preferred, and instead set herself up in the Orangery.

Cecil Beaton, who was to do the photographs for *Vogue*, recorded the wedding preparations in his diary: 'Mrs Spry and her assistant Miss Pirie, two laden Ganymedes, calmly went about their business of decorating the whole Château with magnificent mountains of mixed flowers.' For days there was a general air of harassed comedy, with people rushing around and delivery vans breaking through the press phalanx, roaring up the drive. Dogs raced about too, among them a greyhound, a saluki and 'endless cairns'. It was the kind of make-do or make-it-up-as-you-go-along sort of event that Connie adored.

Despite Wallis's two divorces, the Duke of Windsor had wanted a short religious ceremony, and the Reverend Robert Jardine, an obscure vicar from Darlington, running the risk of his bishop's disapproval had volunteered to officiate. Beaton described him as a 'comic-looking little man with a red bun face, protruding teeth and a broad grin'. When Jardine complained there was no altar, the entire household ran from room to room looking for something that would serve. Eventually a heavily carved chest was dragged from the hall into the music room with the Duke directing things: 'Marvellous. That's marvellous, but put it farther back; put it here . . . there . . . no, a little more this way.' Everyone puffed and heaved and swore under their breath, while he continued flapping his arms in all directions. Then someone noticed that the front of the chest was decorated with fat caryatids. Wallis shrieked, 'We must have something to cover up that row of extra women', and suggested a tea cloth that they had bought in Budapest as a souvenir. Not any old tea cloth, but a rather fine one in a pale coffee colour with silver-thread leaves in it. Wallis's cockney maid was sent to unpack the linen trunk and, after much grumbling, found it. 'If it's as much trouble as this getting married,' she moaned, 'I'm sure I'll never go through with it myself.'

Meanwhile, Connie had set up two huge pedestals of flowers on either side of the improvised altar. Beaton noted in his diary: 'Mrs Spry, robin-like in a picture hat and overalls, sentimentally broke off a branch of laurel: "I'm going to make the flowers as beautiful as I can. I'm so glad they've got what they want with this religious ceremony. I'd do anything for her. I adore her."'

It took two days to complete the job and the Duke soon tired of watching preparations in the music room and instead took to hovering around the Orangery chatting to Connie while she worked. Old copies of *The Times* were spread on the floor and the flowers plunged into buckets of water. Huge pink peonies bulged over in their troughs, cascades of lilies, great trails of blossom, syringa and flowering laurel lay on sheets, and spikes of acanthus and white yucca reared up out of their buckets. The Duke noticed a buckle on Val's belt – a souvenir of his abandoned coronation. She was very embarrassed, but he seemed unmoved. Like the homesick exile that he was, he spent hours kneeling on the floor hungrily reading from the carpet of damp old English newspapers.

At noon on the day of the wedding everyone stopped. The Duke and Mrs Simpson, the vicar from Darlington, the Duke's equerry and solicitor, Cecil Beaton, Monsieur and Madame Bedaux, Connie and Val and the whole household of helpers sat down to lunch, while Wallis regaled everyone with her maid's complaints about all the fuss that was being made. 'I couldn't let the poor girl be put off matrimony for life,' she told them. 'I felt it my bounden duty to say: "Oh, it's not always as bad as this, but it just happens to be if you're marrying the ex-King of England."' The embarrassed diners were unsure whether to laugh at her American wisecracking or to murmur politely into their soup. None of the guests, except Beaton, seemed to notice how strangely matched the bridal pair was: 'The Duke, so blond and insouciant, exudes an aura of tweed, Scottie dogs and briar pipe, an essentially "out-of-door" type . . .

[while Wallis,] so polished and sophisticated with her sleek dark hair, belongs to the world of restaurants and drawing-rooms.' Beaton noted that the Duke's mood alternated from gay and witty to frowning introspection. He had been deeply hurt that some of his personal friends had not attended, but the final snub came in a letter from his brother the King: his new Duchess was not to be accorded the title of Her Royal Highness. 'This little action ruined my day,' he told his equerry Walter Monckton.

Connie was so anxious to create perfect flower arrangements that she re-did several times an enormous assemblage of mixed flowers with which she was not entirely pleased. When she had at last finished to her satisfaction, Beaton noted there was 'a welter' of flowers everywhere in the house – in the music room, in the hall and in the dining-room for the wedding breakfast. 'The flowers were out of all proportion to the scale of the house and the small numbers of people who would see them,' he recalled, though the 'overall effect was certainly gay and festive'. From this it would seem that Connie had become far too emotionally involved and had abandoned her own very strict rules about proportion and scale.

Beaton, having taken dozens of photographs of the bridal couple, raced back to Paris with them, whereupon they were published in both the American and French editions of *Vogue*. Recently Hamish Bowles, now *Vogue*'s European editor, described a picture of Wallis Simpson wearing a dress by Schiaparelli, with flower decorations by Constance Spry and photographed by Cecil Beaton: '*The* florist of the moment, *the* woman of the moment, in a dress by *the* designer of the moment, by *the* photographer of the moment . . . what more could you ask?' English *Vogue*, however, completely ignored the wedding, publishing instead a report of a royal garden party at Buckingham Palace.

Connie and Val stayed for the short service, sitting at the back of the music room with its makeshift altar, pea-green walls and crushed-strawberry-coloured chairs. Val recalled that there were only about twenty people present and that 'without the so English flowers, it might even have seemed rather forlorn'. Another guest said, 'They were married in circumstances which all the art of Constance Spry and [couturier] Mainbocher could not redeem from shabbiness.'

The two drove back to Paris, where Connie collapsed with exhaustion, her feet so swollen she could barely stand. After a night in a hotel she had recovered sufficiently to take the train home. The shop staff were in raptures when she presented them with a large wedge of wedding cake which the Duke had specially requested a footman to cut and pack 'for his girls' at the shop. Sheila Young wrote that they all slept with a slice under their pillows, except for one girl who kept hers in a box which has survived and is now at Longleat in Lord Bath's collection of the Duke of Windsor's artefacts.

The new King and Queen lacked the Duke's glamour and easy popularity. Many believed that the Duke should have been allowed to marry his mistress and keep his throne. George VI was shy and nervous, with a noticeable stutter. He relied heavily on his wife who, according to Harold Nicolson, possessed 'an astonishing gift for being sincerely interested in dull people and dull occasions'. However, women's magazines and newsreels regularly featured the King, Queen and the young princesses and their portraits were seen on numerous front covers. The couturier Norman Hartnell was summoned to help glamorize the Queen's wardrobe, which proved a great success, and one evening in July 1939, almost two years after the coronation, Cecil Beaton received a telephone call from Buckingham Palace: 'The Queen wants to know if you will photograph her tomorrow afternoon.' 'This honour came most un-expectedly,' Beaton wrote in his diary. His glamorous and roman-tic portraits of the Queen were to play an important role in the creation of the new royal image. Beaton's involvement with the Windsor wedding was quickly forgotten and he would often be called upon to photograph the Queen and the princesses.

Connie, who had previously done the flowers for the homes and weddings of several members of the royal family, was not so fortunate; she would not be invited to serve them again for several years.

NINE

Silver-Tong Manners

1937–1939

Despite losing her royal commissions, Connie was still one of society's most fashionable 'flower ladies', dominating the market in flower decorations for the upper classes. Titled mothers still made appointments with Mrs Spry at her shop in South Audley Street, bringing their daughters for advice about bouquets, head-dresses and corsages, and ordering party decorations and flowers for their luncheon and dinner tables. Connie's flowers were a crucial element of any London Season and she, chameleon-like as ever, put on her 'silver-tong manners' for her clients, who treated her as a friend, even a confidante.

The Season began with the presentation courts held at Buck-ingham Palace, at which over a thousand debutantes curtsied to the Queen, many of them carrying Spry bouquets. On the first Monday in May the opening of the Royal Academy Summer Exhibition in the morning, followed by the opera at Covent Garden in the evening, set things rolling, and there followed a round of lunches, cocktail parties, dances and coming-out balls in the marquees and ballrooms, many decorated by Connie's staff. Good manners were essential and the dress code strict: it mattered greatly how low the neckline, how long the train, how high the three white ostrich feathers. Many of the dresses were made by Connie's friends Victor Stiebel and Norman Hartnell. One debu-tante recalled: 'It would be put in the paper that one was in London for the season and then piles of advertisements would come through the door.' But Connie never advertised; she didn't need to. During the Season, her staff were in huge demand. Sheila Young recalled:

There were times when in one day we made as many as 40 bouquets for the court, and then all hands were brought in to help. We made necklaces of fresh flowers, earrings of lily-of-the-valley, and corsages. Bouquets were made of tulip tree flowers and gentians, on bound white or gold stems, and fern was replaced by delicate trails of variegated ivies. Pepperomia and tradescantia foliage, seed heads of clematis and berries were all incorporated in unusual and delicate bouquets.

Connie insisted that all the bouquets should be delivered personally, and her staff enjoyed seeing the excited girls unwrap their flowers and hold them against their gorgeous evening dresses.

It was a time of feverish activity for the shop. Most debutante parties were held either in private houses or hotels such as Claridge's and the Dorchester. There would be long formal dinner parties beforehand and, after the ball, breakfast at dawn. It was said that a young man who owned a white tie and tails could eat free for the whole Season. Sunderland House in Curzon Street was a particularly popular venue for summer balls. In one week alone, it was decorated by Connie's team on three nights in succession. They often reused the same flowers, but in different arrangements so that clients would never notice. One decorator was once heard saying to a stem of eremurus: 'Get in there, you really should know by now; you have been there three times already this week!'

When the Season wound up in early August, the exhausted debs would either retire to the country or be off to Cowes to sail or to Scotland to shoot. Many were then sent to be 'finished' in Paris, Florence, even Munich or Dresden, or to enjoy winter sports in Austria. Already in 1937 there were rumours of trouble in Germany, where the Nazi Party had been in power since 1933, and some came home with unpleasant tales of anti-Semitism and German thuggishness. But the English upper classes seemed largely unaware of any threat from Germany, and possible war was simply not discussed. In August 1938 Lady Elsie Mendl gave a lavish circus ball for seven hundred guests in the gardens of her Villa Trianon at Versailles. House and gardens were transformed into an 'enchanting setting', where guests were entertained by satin-clad circus acrobats and miniature white ponies from Finland, and danced on a specially sprung dance floor to three orchestras – an American 'Negro', a Cuban rumba and an all-woman Hungarian waltz band. Theatrical illuminations were by the great Wendel; Oliver Messel created a dance pavilion with his favourite artificial trees and Moorish statuary; Stéphane Boudin of Maison Jonsen in Paris made the candy-striped curtains and the parasol over the circular champagne bar; Mainbocher designed Lady Mendl's white organdie dress; and Constance Spry, of course, did the flowers.

Huge urns filled with cut flowers stood in the gardens, garlands of red roses were hung over the doorways and massed over the mantels, and the candelabras on the buffet table were smothered in pink roses. Vast quantities of flowers, many from Connie's own rose gardens, had been packed in cotton wool and flown to Paris in three planeloads. According to *Vogue* they were a gift from Connie, which seems extraordinary given the sheer quantity and cost involved. Despite her husband's immense wealth, Elsie Mendl, whose motto was 'only the best, nothing but the best', had taken a whole year to pay the flower bill after a previous party. Connie was often prey to the overgenerous grand gesture, and this latest extravagance must have caused great consternation to the directors of the company.

But it was the success of the Wedding Room at the shop that was causing the directors the greatest problems. The top floor at 64 South Audley Street was let to a private tenant who claimed his privacy was disturbed by the stream of clients visiting the Wedding Room on the first floor and the noise of their loud chatter. By the terms of the lease, business tenants were not permitted above ground-floor level, so he was able to bring an action against the landlord and against Flower Decorations Ltd. The case dragged on for several years, causing considerable uncertainty.

Even as the newspapers began to carry increasingly alarming news from the Continent, the lavish parties carried on regardless. For young and underpaid decorators like Sheila Young, working among such wealth and glamour must sometimes have been rather overwhelming: 'What a pleasure it was to see all the gold and silver treasures and trophies which were brought out from the vaults for these special occasions. Once when I was fetching water to fill up the vases, I was fascinated to see 60 legs of lamb slowly rotating in front of a wall of red-hot charcoal.' She remembered doing flowers for Lord Derby's Derby night banquet in Stafford House near Oxford Street. His Lordship's racing colours were echoed in the flowers. The buffet vases were filled with fruits and flowers sent up from the estate farms; peaches, nectarines and grapes, still covered in bloom from the hothouses, were piled on high compotes with camellias, orchids and stephanotis tucked in between them. For Henley Regatta, one host had a marquee erected on the bank of the Thames which Connie hung with straw hats trailing ribbon bows and filled with a profusion of summer flowers: cascading roses, sweet william, foxgloves and delphinium. Spry teams travelled all over the country decorating country mansions with fabulous displays, as well as doing the flowers for banquets at the Mansion House, the Guildhall and for the City livery companies.

Connie's position as *the* floral decorator led naturally to her becoming an arbiter of 'correct' taste. Many debutantes and young brides wanted her advice on the most tasteful ways of decorating their homes. Since the bulk of these enquiries concerned table decorations, Connie decided she would put on an exhibition of them and asked her friend the interior designer Herman Schrijver for help. Schrijver, who had already co-decorated with Connie on several projects, had great admiration for her: 'She had a marvellous eye, not only for different colours, but for spacing and placing everything perfectly,' he recalled. 'She used such unusual materials.'

Characteristically, Connie was quick to undermine the idea that she did things 'in the correct manner'. She wanted to show – as she had always done – that anyone could bring elegance, charm and gaiety to their dinner table. 'You can do it without the blessings of inheritance or wealth, [but] with a few yards of the right material, a needle and thread, some garden flowers and an absence of fear or ridicule,' she later wrote, and typically illustrated her point with a rather uncomfortable childhood memory. She described the thrill of winning a prize at a table-decorating competition at school with a pretty display of pink roses and pink ribbon bows. But her moment of triumph was short-lived when the teacher dressed her down: 'I should like to point out to you that the guests at dinner-parties are usually of more mature age than you have yet attained, and your decoration would be trying to the complexions of most of one's guests. I hope in future you will show a greater consideration for the feelings of others in this respect.' Even when Connie *had* attained a more mature age and was decorating tables professionally, it continued to amaze her that several of her grander clients still sent her swatches of the material of their gowns (though not necessarily those of their guests) so the flowers might complement their patterns or colours. 'Gowns of the hostess, gowns of the guests, complexions of the young, the middle-aged and old . . . how can anyone ever decorate a table and live?' Connie despaired.

As she was well aware, table decorating was a minefield, and the unwary or nervous hostess could easily be caught out. Since, in the early nineteenth century, dining *à la française*, where food was set out on the table and guests served themselves, had given way to *service à la russe* where they were served individually by servants, the centre of the table had been left free for floral masterpieces of ever increasing grandeur and absurdity. What began with heavy epergnes, palm trees and pyramid arrangements of fruit and flowers was later followed by snaking garlands and trails of smilax.* Smart Victorian and Edwardian dining-tables would be laden with tiered flower stands, glass or silver trumpet vases and shallow bowls filled with lily-of-the-valley, maidenhair fern, forget-me-nots, pansies, rosebuds or small bunches of grapes.

* Smilax (*Asparagus asparagoides*), native in southern Africa, introduced to other parts of the world in the 1850s and became popular in bridal bouquets and for table decorations. Now regarded as an invasive, unwanted pest.

Reckless hostesses even cut holes in the dining-table and their best damask cloths in order that palms and ferns might appear to be growing through, giving a 'tropical forest effect'. Such ghastly, if admittedly eye-catching, decorations simply afforded an opportunity for hostesses to vie with one another. For Connie, all this was anathema.

Connie owned several books on table decorating, including *Flower Decoration in the House* by Gertrude Jekyll, whom she respected for encouraging women of her day to break away from stereotyped fashions. She shared in particular Jekyll's battle with the 'tyranny of damask'. Another book, *Flowers in the Home* by Menie Watt, suggested that instead of relying on one's gardener, 'a home horticulturist' might visit daily and attend to plants and flowers in the house. 'No one', it added, 'without knowledge and taste should be permitted the privilege of attending to these small matters.' 'Small matters indeed,' Connie responded with disgust, 'and privilege be damned.'

The Encyclopaedia of Practical Cookery, published in the late nineteenth century, had illustrations of fantastic table decorations. One in particular was so outrageous and caused Connie such mirth that she later reproduced it in her own, last, book, *Favourite Flowers*. Captioned 'Artistic arrangement for the dinner table', its central feature was a 'gorgeous fountain of scented water' which cascaded into a shallow lake in which real fish such as sticklebacks, minnows and small tench swam; model pagodas, swans, boats and lilies were cunningly tethered to the rustic banks. The 'lake' was surrounded by a sinuous frieze of mosses, studded with small flowers, encircling the table. The instructions warned, 'Do not make up the aquarium effect with toads, lizards, water snails, tortoises, or any other such horrors' – which might frighten the guests and possibly eat the wretched fish. 'What time they devoted to their dinner tables,' cried Connie in mock horror. 'What fun they must have had and how exhilarating an objective for the prized but generally neglected stickleback!'

Her exhibition opened in June 1937. Tables were laid out with inspiring ideas suited to every occasion. One memorable table had a wine-red linen cloth on which black candles in low holders were surrounded and linked by garlands of the brilliant autumn leaves of Virginia creeper – 'nothing could have been simpler and nothing more vivid and exciting.' On another, delicate flowers such as mallow, phlox, violas and garden pinks were laid in wreaths on pads of wet moss; others had scented flowers – short sprays of stephanotis, syringa, jasmine and gardenias – in old wine glasses or flat dishes, massed roses in simple containers, or solid blocks of camellias and iris. For a breakfast table Connie suggested a white jar of pinks or a mixed bunch of old-fashioned cabbage roses; for a spring table, a basket with mixed polyanthus, violets and wild daffodils, or some bright anemones in an old brown casserole or a mass of red geraniums. For an autumn country lunch she showed a table with a still more adventurous display: a rich, deep-coloured arrangement of brown toadstools, red wild arum berries, small wild ferns, cone twigs and sprays of bright-red miniature tomatoes all in a basket of moss.

But not everyone favoured Connie's casting-off of accepted conventions, and some critics mocked her use of vegetables on the dining table. 'Cabbages are chic!' announced the *Evening Standard* in its report on her exhibition: 'Don't be surprised next time you go to a dinner party to find yourself looking at a cabbage, a turnip or two and some tomatoes nestling among gladioli or roses or sweet peas. This is the latest table decoration.' Soon afterwards at a public dinner, Brussels sprouts were heaped in front of her and she was invited, amid great hilarity, to arrange them for the table. She later regretted that she was too surprised at the time to come up with a suitable riposte. But had her detractors looked at the table dubbed *Le Potager* at her exhibition, they might have seen what wonderful things she could do with a pineapple, a melon, a cauliflower, green tomatoes, pea-pods, onions, a cabbage, a lettuce and mushrooms, along with yellow fennel flowers, pomegranates, passion flowers, thistles, clematis and marguerites. The much-derided Brussels sprout might yet have found its place.

When once asked about decorating tables in restaurants, Connie replied: 'Nothing short of an earthquake will bring about reformation here . . . Flowers on tables are either pushed out of the way or mangled by busy waiters – large groups strategically placed would be more effective.' She persuaded one fashionable restaurant to discard its numerous small receptacles and put flowers in wall vases, which she designed for them. But she despaired of restaurants that 'still have the old-fashioned conventional table decorations; the same old damask cloths, the same ugly table-napkins . . . one's eye comes back from the beautiful display [of flowers] to the anti-climax of an ordinary uninteresting table – the centre of the feast – the cynosure of all eyes – and it is *dull, dull, dull.*'

In 1937 Connie's second book, *Flowers in House and Garden*, was published. The foreword was written by her friend Phyllis, the wife of Sir Frederick Moore, Director of the Botanic Garden in Dublin. She dedicated the book to 'my unselfish, generous and encouraging friends Jean and Violet Henson'. Rex Whistler did some witty drawings, and she persuaded Cecil Beaton and Hoyningen-Huene to photograph the flower arrangements illustrating the book. There are also three photographs taken in Tunisia, credited to 'Gerard Auton'. Auton was in fact a pseudonym of the occultist Aleister Crowley, who lived in Tunis, not far from the Hensons.

This new book was still some way from a hands-on gardening book. She assumed her readers not only had a large garden but also employed a gardener ready to give 'the fullest co-operation' in supplying cut flowers for use in the house. She continued to outline what had always been her basic philosophy – freedom of expression, breaking with old conventions and a complete absence of rules:

I think there should be one clear and simple aim: to make flower arrangements of any colour or shape, of any flowers, vegetables, fruits or leaves which look well together, and are suitable to their background. We want to be born again with new eyes, so that we may be newly surprised with the beauty of much to which we have grown blind with custom . . . It is all bound up with the freedom to express our individual taste in our backgrounds, freedom from convention and above all freedom from a form of monetary-value snobbishness.

That Christmas *Flowers in House and Garden* reached number three in the bestseller list and several journals published admiring reviews. According to *Homes and Gardens*: 'There could hardly be a garden lover who would not derive both pleasure and profit from this book dealing with the decorative aspect of every kind of plant, annual and herbaceous, as well as shrubs, roses and water plants.' The *Daily Telegraph* declared it 'altogether a unique and delightful book by one of the most famous flower artists'.

In November that year Violet Henson wrote a review in *Harper's Bazaar*, which helped to spread Connie's fame beyond England: 'She instructs with the lavishness of a true artist. All [readers'] preconceived ideas on class-consciousness in flowers will be changed as well. One has only to look at the lovely line and form of the group of kale leaves to realize that the humble kitchen garden can hold its own with the aristocrats of the hothouses.' As a result, America clamoured for a share of the new Spry flowers and Connie accepted an invitation to go to New York to give two lectures on flower decorating. She had no doubt heard many colourful tales of American life from Syrie Maugham who at various times had shops in New York and Chicago, and her London-based American clients said they told everyone about her and her wonderful flowers when they went back home.

The tour was part of a fund-raising campaign for the Brooklyn Botanic Garden and was probably arranged through Phyllis Moore and the Botanic Gardens in Dublin. In her foreword to *Flowers in House and Garden* Lady Moore had observed that in America flower arranging had 'long reached a position of perfection', much thought and time being spent on it. The great spring shows of New York, Boston and Philadelphia held popular competitions;

details of background, lighting and containers were studied with great care. Connie amazed her audiences with her slides of common English blackberries mingling with hothouse roses, and shocked them with her combined use of cultivated and wild materials. The lectures proved so successful that she was immediately asked to do a nationwide tour under the auspices of the Garden Clubs of America.

These clubs, as Connie was soon to discover, were rather different from English garden clubs: their members were predominantly women and meetings were primarily social rather than horticultural. Few members owned sizeable gardens, most having backyards or a front lawn, and only a few undertook any real gardening activities. Unlike England, America was not a nation of gardeners. Garden club members held coffee mornings to raise funds for landscape preservation, for the greening of city streets and for the conservation of old houses. They loved gardens and flowers and made regular seasonal visits to the most famous national gardens. However, what really excited these ladies were their lavish, stylized arrangements of flowers and house-plants in the home, in which they took enormous pride. American flower shows, so praised by Lady Moore, were about the art of flower arranging mostly with the use of commercially grown material. There were a number of famous names in the field: in San Diego, Gregory Conway was taking America by storm with his luxuriant and interesting but formal arrangements, while in New York there was a famous Japanese arranger called Madame Oria. Connie had her own views on ikebana and Japanese flower arranging – beautiful but quite unsuited to English homes.

As the leading exponent of the English art of flower arranging, Connie was fêted and admired wherever she travelled. America seemed to have fallen in love with her and, for a while, the feeling was mutual.

But this first trip to the US was made in November, so she did not see any spring shows or any gardens of special merit. Nonetheless, in her travels across the eastern and southern states she made frequent notes on whatever she could see growing in the cold winter months. As well as lecturing, she appeared on radio shows and as guest of honour at social events. She was particularly interested in the food and drink and noted in Texas a *café brûlé* heavily laced with both rum and cognac — 'so warming to the vitals' — while in Kentucky she had spiced tea with cinnamon and cloves, 'perfect for a cold and frosty day'. One evening in Oregon, when she was feeling rather homesick, she attended a grand dinner party and immediately felt transported back home: the rooms were exquisitely furnished with English antiques, the women were dressed in the latest Paris fashions and the food was deliciously European. At one point a long loaf was brought in, very light in texture, 'as indeed is most American bread — hot, crisp and sliced'. Each slice had been thickly spread with garlic butter and baked for a few moments. It was her first taste of garlic bread. She thoroughly enjoyed it and was much amused when the ladies subsequently repaired to the bathroom to administer mouthwash.

Since she was a small girl, Connie had always been passion-ately keen on Christmas — all the business of the preparations and decorating the house. She was in Colonial Williamsburg as Christmas approached. Most of middle-class America had adopted Victorian traditions but Williamsburg was determined to do the festival in the grandest possible style. The previous year, the wife of the Governor of Virginia had called on Mrs Louise Fisher, an 'ardent gardener' and keen flower arranger, to help. A stickler for historical accuracy, Mrs Fisher searched the Library of Congress archives for inspiring pictures of decorations from times past. She came up with sculpted cornucopias of fruits, flowers and vegetables by sculptors such as Luca della Robbia and the English woodcarver Grinling Gibbons. The society ladies of Old Williamsburg vied with each other to create a prize-winning 'della Robbia' wreath, while the district's Christmas style was widely imitated across America's East Coast.

Mrs Fisher invited Connie to visit and admire the festive wintry scene: the streets and houses, front doors and windows, lamp posts and fences were smothered in greenery or swathed in highly wrought and often fantastic wreaths, with sprays or swags of leaves, fruits and berries all artfully wired together. Connie had never been keen on dried flowers, except naturally dried seedpods, and any form of dyeing or artificial colouring, tinsel and tawdry painted aluminium baubles – which she called 'plumbing' – were most definitely out. But she loved the use of natural locally gathered material and, though she thought it all rather excessive, she was both amused and enchanted. She politely reserved judgement and enquired whether the birds and squirrels ate the free supply of food.

Just before leaving New York for Christmas at home, Connie was invited to meet a group of wealthy society hostesses including Josephine Forrestal, whose husband was Secretary of the Navy, and Mrs Ogden Mills, wife of the Secretary of the Treasury. Both told Connie how much they admired her work and that they longed for her to have a shop in New York. It was already the in thing to have flowers arranged in the Constance Spry style, so a shop was the obvious next step. With her name, they gushed, it would be hugely successful. What this coterie of rich ladies wanted was not profit, but rather the realization of some vaguely conceived idea that with Connie's help they could revolutionize the American home and garden. Such a shop, they envisaged, would be a 'fountain whence her influence would flow'. It is not quite clear what they thought was wrong with the American home and garden as it then was, only that as leaders of genteel society they were best suited to influence such changes as might be deemed necessary.

Always susceptible to flattery and persuasion, particularly if it involved doing something new and exciting, Connie listened to the ladies' ideas with enthusiasm. Pleased with her positive response, they outlined their plans: they would fund the shop, set up the business and pay the staff wages. Connie would receive a small number of shares and a generous percentage of the profits. In return she would give her name to the shop and send her London staff to train their American counterparts. She would also be required to be in the shop personally for five months of the winter season, from October to April, returning to London for the summer.

Connie was overwhelmed. It seemed a dream offer, a fresh horizon to conquer. She threw caution to the wind and ecstatically accepted, on the spot, without consulting Shav, the other directors, or the staff who might be expected to come to New York. Like most of her big adventures, she did not think it through. It was enough that she had fallen in love with America, with wealthy Americans and with their free-and-easy warm-heartedness. She was greatly impressed by the similarities she perceived but blinkered to the differences between the culture and climate of the two countries.

Back in England for Christmas, Connie regaled everyone with her 'wonderful news'. It was not received with much enthusiasm. The directors of the business were busy with the South Audley Street lawsuit. Shav tried to warn Connie that the name was too valuable to hand to a business over which she would have no control. But she brushed all objections aside. Dazzled by her new American friends, by the generosity of their 'business offer', she thought that giving her name (even though it was not, strictly speaking, hers) was the least she could do in return.

There was no time to lose. Connie was on a roll and nothing and no one could slow her down or stop her headlong rush into this new adventure. The Americans sent over Patricia Easterbrook, a dynamic young Australian with knowledge of American floristry who spent the summer of 1938 in South Audley Street learning the Spry technique. Connie was expected to send a decorator and a florist for six months to train the American staff. There was no lack of volunteers, and Sheila McQueen (formerly Young) was disappointed not to be chosen because she was too young. Instead Margaret Watson, who had trained at Broadlands and Swanley College, was sent as decorator and Ivy Pierotti, or 'Pierrot', the 'cheerful little cockney with magical fingers and an empty head', was sent as the florist.

Meanwhile, Connie continued to fire everyone in London with her enthusiasm and pour out her impatience in daily letters to Mrs Mills in New York. The American ladies duly formed their incorporated company, appointed Josephine Forrestal as president and bought 'charming but tucked away' premises at 62 East 54th Street. An architect was commissioned to convert and decorate the shop – a pretty ground-floor showroom with an English bow-window at the front and a fresh-flower work-room and storage iceboxes at the rear. It was to be all white, with a few 'bits and pieces' from Syrie Maugham's New York shop. On the second floor were more elegantly furnished showrooms, then several more work-rooms on the third floor for painting and waxing the flowers for the artificial arrangements, for making potpourri and Christmas decorations of wreaths, sprigs and kissing-boughs.

Earlier in the summer Josephine Forrestal had brilliantly solved the need for both an experienced decorator and a source of cut flowers. Her friend Adele Lovett, passionate gardener and wife of a prominent banker, owned a 24-acre estate called Pending at Locust Valley on Long Island. Her hobby was making towering pillar and pedestal flower arrangements with a Flemish inspiration to suit her high-ceilinged rooms. They were created with a Spry-like lavishness of line and a disregard of convention and rule. She used material from her huge, partly wild garden, with its long flower borders, generous vegetable garden, flower meadows and orchard. Strangely, Adele had not heard of Connie or her ideas but Josephine Forrestal persuaded her that she was the only person in America whose approach to flower arrangement was the same as Mrs Spry's. Furthermore, Adele possessed not only a special knowledge of American horticulture but a garden that could supply most of the flowers needed for the shop. She agreed to start work immediately, without pay, and prepare and plan the shop in advance of Connie's return in late summer.

Soon after her arrival, Connie went to see Adele's gardens and was very impressed. Adele was equally charmed by Connie: 'She was a small, round cheerful person with enormous vitality, a delicious sense of humour, warmth, and exquisite manners. She was, besides, incredibly capable, imaginative, practical and talented.' They toured the big picking garden with masses of flowering and berried shrubs, the vegetable garden surrounded by four large herb borders; the orchard with peach, apple and pear trees, and the big meadow full of grasses and wild flowers. Connie was staggered by the sheer size and abundance of the plant material. She was particularly interested in so many plants not available in England; everywhere she looked she found new and unusual things.

Early in September Margaret Watson and Pierrot arrived in New York and were installed with Connie in a hotel near the shop. Every moment of the day and much of the night were busy. As soon as the paint had dried, they got down to teaching the American staff and preparing for the opening. Adele recorded:

> Mrs Spry taught us to make all the things she needed: potpourri, pomander balls, Christmas ornaments glittered with gold or silver. She showed us how to mount the skeletonized magnolia leaves which came in packages of single leaves from the wholesalers; these were wired on to twigs and branches to make lovely frail sand-colored boughs, to mix with her dried flower arrangements, or to use instead of fresh greens in her flower bouquets. We learned to paint and wax and wire the artificial paper flowers that were her specialty, and to make her giant fresh cabbage roses and enormous carnations, that became the rage, for corsages.

These last were cannibalized from a dozen flowers wired together, and would seem to have been one of several lapses from Connie's own rules. Perhaps because wiring and artificiality were so successful in American flower decorations she felt it necessary to compromise her own taste and standards.

Christmas, however, was an entirely different matter. On her return from her first visit to New York Connie had burst into Flo

Standfast's 'Arts' work-room and declared, 'I've found the most marvellous stuff, my dears, you've never seen anything like it!' It was Scotch tape, which immediately transformed the huge task the Arts team faced every Christmas. Connie was never happier than when sitting on the first floor at South Audley Street chatting to the girls in 'the Arts', twisting up bits of wire and velvet and silver tissue to produce some exquisite object no one else could have thought of, her ideas flowing inexhaustibly. She loved the new materials such as cellophanes and plastics, and tried out the decorative possibilities of everything she could lay her hands on. She painted evergreens with gum and glitter to give the delicate effect of hoarfrost, and designed her own 'baubles'.

The three months before Christmas became the most strenuous in the shop's year. Parcels of Christmas decorations were sent out to clients all over the country; the very last would be put on the night train at Euston or King's Cross on Christmas Eve. Patricia Easterbrook and Val were sent to Czechoslovakia to buy up huge quantities of handmade Christmas decorations – carved wooden angels and fruits and translucent bells – which they sent over to stock the New York shop for its opening in November 1938.

The New York storerooms were filled to bursting with all the 'fripperies and nonsense' that were becoming so fashionable. Connie had brought with her some vase moulds made by Flo Standfast from her own designs and they found a place in Brooklyn that could make them up for the shop. There were six designs, all finished inside with a high gloss and outside with a matt finish so that they could be tinted to suit the room in which they were to be used – another popular innovation. Connie was firing out ideas by the minute. She now insisted everyone wore a uniform: an unbleached muslin coat with a widely flaring skirt and wide sleeves, designed by Claire McCardle, one of the leading New York dress designers. They could be slipped on over day dresses and were both practical and smart.

Constance Spry Inc. opened its doors on 4 November with a grand cocktail party the night before, when most of chic New

York turned up. Parking was solid all along 54th Street and street musicians did a roaring trade. Reminiscent of Atkinsons', the bow-window framed a single dramatic group, exquisitely lit. The shop was a glittering sight packed with people sitting on the beautiful staircase and all around the gallery, looking down on the shop floor. 'The scent of all those flowers was like heaven – and finer than any perfume worn by the ladies,' one gentleman recalled. The staff wore their muslin coats and upswept hairdos, a novel idea among women in New York, who were still devoted to the long bob.

The press adored the 'so-English Constance' and her shop. The *New York Herald* wrote:

> When Nature doesn't produce just what she wants, Mrs Spry doesn't hesitate to create something of her own – two little trees, for instance, which stand at the entrance of the shop, made of brilliant bay leaves wired on in symmetrical rows, leaves that she brought back from Europe 'by the yard.' Of special interest are her winter flowers and vases of dried leaves, and magnolia leaves that have been turned into shadows by a special treatment. Milkweed pods are used in contrast with strange dried lotus and enormous pine cones in other arrangements. The new shop also contains a room for brides decorated in the mood of romance.

Another reporter wrote: 'No one, we venture to say, will pass the shop [without stopping] for there is practically nothing that suggests the traditional American flower shop.'

In its first few weeks 62 East 54th Street became a popular meeting place for some of the smartest people in town: the flower club ladies, curious members of the press, friends from Europe passing through, new clients enquiring about a party or a wedding to be done. One day a terrible hurricane hit New York and the shop was filled with soaked customers and staff. Connie had their wet things hung around the radiators and everyone drank hot tea

– 'it was like a party all day.' The staff always had a morning break for 'elevenses' with a cup of tea and a bun, and another at about 3 p.m. Connie was always there: full of the latest news and developments, always demanding more effort, always making it amusing with her delicious sense of humour – everyone adored her.

Launched, lauded and loved, Connie went home for Christmas well satisfied. She had left her staff in New York to face over-whelming pressure of work. It never occurred to her that she had compromised her own standards in flower decoration in order to please her American friends, nor that having the shop in a small out-of-the-way place in New York made even less sense in 1938 than it had in London ten years earlier; nor that two decorators and a florist were simply inadequate for a business that was as busy as South Audley Street where she employed up to seventy people. The indomitable Patricia Easterbrook drove her little American team hard. They learned there was no such thing as a normal working day: 'funerals, big parties, weddings – whatever . . . you started as early as necessary and worked late until the job was done.' Sometimes they surpassed themselves and produced superb Spry decorations – for all-white coming-out parties, or cream-and-gold ones with the skeletonized leaves well in evidence. For a party on the roof of the St Regis Hotel for which the host wanted pink lilies when only white could be found, white lilies were smothered in pink theatrical face powder, and no one realized.

America was still slowly emerging from the Depression, yet the numbers of people who found they could afford, even at New York prices, to have fresh flowers done regularly in their houses increased month by month. The windows of leading stores such as Bergdorf Goodman boasted Spry arrangements, too. Store flowers had to be done on Sundays, which meant that the flower staff worked a seven-day week. Some felt they were working twenty-four hours a day as well.

By the time Connie returned to the US after celebrating a

relaxing Christmas in Park Gate, the two English girls had had enough. Ivy Pierotti, who was engaged to be married, said she was going home. Margaret Watson was eventually persuaded to stay on for the summer and found herself working with Connie on flowers for the British Pavilion at the New York World's Fair, which opened on a sweltering-hot 30 April 1939. A gigantic vase of boughs and enormous leaves, in many tones of green and some of them the size of small tea-trays, reasserted Connie's love of the natural all-green group. Up on the first floor a semicircular display of heraldry had niches built in at either side for two more huge vases – so large that ladders were needed to fill them – which picked up the heraldic colours with flowers in scarlet, blue and gold. Connie stayed for King George VI and Queen Elizabeth's visit, then sailed back to England, leaving Margaret to tend the vases and battle against increasing ill-health and overwork. Finally, she collapsed with thyroid trouble and she too went home. There was now no resident English representative of the Spry style. The shop limped through the summer and the ladies waited anxiously and eagerly for Connie's return for another triumphant winter season, bringing more vases and boxloads of the popular Czechoslovakian Christmas decorations.

But Connie did not return. On 3 September 1939 Britain declared war on Germany. In the following years the lady backers of Constance Spry Inc. found that they too had other things on their minds. Josephine Forrestal and Mrs Mills now turned to their husbands' political careers and the war effort. Adele Lovett's husband was appointed special assistant secretary to the Secretary of War, so they left their garden at Long Island for Washington. The remaining backers grouped themselves under Mrs William Thayer, who did at least have some business experience. But her appeals to Connie to keep her promise and inject her vitality into the flagging concern grew more and more frantic. Connie's replies became increasingly evasive: she couldn't come because it would be dishonourable to leave England in her hour of need; she needed to remain in London during the South Audley Street lawsuit; there were royal parties and other prestigious events that she couldn't possibly drop; it was unreasonable for the American customers to complain they never saw Mrs Spry – it had never been practicable for her to see clients individually. But next month perhaps, or next year, she might see her way clear to returning . . .

Connie was certainly extremely worked up over the lawsuit, so much so that she said she could not go into the witness box. Instead, Val Pirie represented the firm and was cross-examined for two hours. Lady Violet Bonham Carter, a long-time customer, also spoke for them and confirmed that the business was a quietly conducted affair that could not possibly incommode tenants on the top floor. But the terms of the complainant's lease were specific and judgement was given against Flower Decorations Ltd and its landlord. They were ordered to confine themselves to the basement and the ground floor, so the Wedding Room had to go. The embarrassing defeat added to the general air of depression.

Meanwhile, the wretched Margaret Watson was obliged to return to New York. She had been turned down for war work on account of her poor health, and Connie somewhat forcefully convinced her that helping to keep the New York business going was an equally valuable contribution to the war effort and to the maintenance of British morale. She reminded Margaret of the important work she had achieved for the British Pavilion at the previous year's New York World's Fair.

Some of the old clients trickled back, though their spending was no longer so lavish. But Margaret was no substitute for Connie, nor could she tell the American ladies the truth – that Mrs Spry was unlikely to face the dangerous ordeal of an Atlantic crossing in wartime. Eventually the ladies did grasp the situation, and when another New York florist offered to take over the business, name and all, on advantageous terms, they accepted. They had not gone into the business for profit but, being amateurs, neither had they envisaged an actual loss. Connie had brought not only prosperity, but fun and glamour, and it was largely for the fun and glamour that they had backed her. But Connie had not entirely kept her side of the bargain, and there was no guarantee that she would ever do so. Without her there was little else but hard work and worry, which they were not prepared to take on.

The new management moved the shop to Fifth Avenue and restyled it on the lines of a conventional American flower shop, concentrating on profit – cut flowers were the order of the day, not Constance Spry's elaborate artistic creations. Americans loved high class artificial flowers far more than the English did, and the Fifth Avenue shop was one of the first flower businesses to use the new plastic materials. Margaret Watson stayed on under the new management and Connie, who seemed entirely unaware of what was happening, continued to try to involve herself from England. She badgered Margaret with suggestions and urged an all-white decor. But Margaret's flower arrangements were either altered or dispensed with and she soon realized that the Spry style was no longer wanted. The beautiful specially designed vases that had been brought from Europe or found in junk-shops on Third Avenue were sold to customers. After a few miserable months, Margaret resigned.

It is doubtful whether Connie ever fully grasped the implications of what she had done. A firm bearing her name was now at liberty to market throughout America the goods and services that bore her famous and distinctive signature. It was just as Shav had warned her – she now had no control whatsoever. All she could do, the directors decided, was to rename the London shop Constance Spry Ltd, which she did in March 1940.

Connie later wrote to an American newspaper that the New York shop had nothing to do with her, that it had been started by some friends in her honour and merely called after her. This was typical of Connie – distancing herself from the facts and reinventing history when it did not suit her. If her own version was less than truthful, at least Patricia Easterbook recalled Connie's contribution in America with generosity:

Flowers are flowers, and she opened their eyes to the beauty of form – whether it was a poppy, a seed pod, a bunch of grass or a lovely leaf. She talked with great horticultural knowledge, which they respected, and she arranged with such joy and abandon that she released them from the Garden Club panic pressure and the Ikebana stuff. Not the whole country – it was too big a job for a couple of trips – but her name is still known after all these years, and it's not because of the hats she wore.

Connie's 'fountain of influence' had flowed, if only briefly, and made a difference after all.

TEN

The Sprys' Wartime
Household

1940–1945

By the beginning of 1940 the British were slowly, anxiously, coming to terms with the idea of being at war once again. Connie, in a state of nervous exhaustion after her American experiences and the South Audley Street lawsuit, now had to face the misery and uncertainty of another war and the possible destruction of a decade of hard work.

In despair, she rushed over to see Kate Barrett at Swanley College. 'Would gardening and flowers and beauty and everything she had worked for, ever be wanted again?' Connie asked. Dr Barrett replied that of course they would – she planned to carry on herself, and she urged Connie to do the same. Fired by her friend's robust attitude, Connie returned to London. 'Come what may, I shall keep this business going and your jobs open,' she assured her staff. But they were already leaving, the men signing up for the forces and the women gradually trickling off into war work. For a while it looked as if Constance Spry Ltd would have to close. The Modern School of Flower Work had already closed and would remain so for the duration of the war. Rosemary Hume's Cordon Bleu cookery school was also suspended but the restaurant Au Petit Cordon Bleu remained open, and when her partner Dione Lucas went to America to set up on her own Rosemary was left to run the place single-handed.

But after a few months customers grew tired of the 'phoney war' and returned to buy flowers again – just a few, to cheer themselves up. The few remaining staff were kept busy with embassies and society clients who felt it necessary to keep up a decorative front, while weddings and funerals still needed flowers, though on a more modest scale. The flower markets remained open, flowers continued to be sent up from English gardens, but there were no more baskets of exotics from abroad. Although the government was urging shops and small businesses 'to keep going at all costs' as reopening would be difficult after the war, for now they could only struggle on and wait and see what might happen. Connie expressed surprise that the interest and desire for flowers still seemed to be so strong, and with renewed optimism she wrote: 'Miss Pirie and I looked at one another and said: "If we go on like this we shall soon be decorating parties again."' But the days of lavish parties and entertainments were over.

In May, just as the war was hotting up, Connie's third book *Garden Notebook* was published, and was welcomed as an antidote to the few 'austerity' books available in the bookstores. It had originally been commissioned to help 'emerging' American gardeners, but instead became a very English gardening book, full of seasonal advice and information. It was classic Connie – charming, chatty and very personal. The ubiquitous photographs of flower arrangements this time were mainly set in the home instead of against the professional lighting and backdrops of previous books. Informal photos of her house and garden invited readers to glimpse her simple all-white bedroom, flagstone floors, French armoires and indoor tubs of *Sparmannia africana*. Evocative descriptions of her life and her flowers set the daily scene, taking the reader through every month in her garden and never losing sight of the pleasures of gardening, even in the very depth of winter.

Connie's writing has a wit and freshness to it coupled with an encyclopaedic knowledge of plants, but her interest in cultivation never outstripped her enthusiasm for creating an exciting new display. She continued to search for new plants that would inspire her to do something surprising and different. Significantly, the magazine *Gardening Illustrated* noted that Mrs Spry's abilities as a flower decorator were now combined with a talent for practical gardening fostered by years of experience, observation and study.

Connie dedicated this book to 'H.E.S., who makes all things possible'. It was her first published acknowledgement of affection and debt to Shav, the man whose name she had made famous. In one or two other books she would drop occasional remarks about 'the master of the house'. But this book, and the one she was about to embark on, were her most personal in tone and imbued with a real sense of Connie at home with Shav. No one can be said to enjoy war, but for Connie these years were in many ways some of the happiest of her life. One reason was that Val Pirie, whom, quite unaccountably, Connie persisted in describing as her 'partner, warmest ally, and friend', had left Park Gate to work for the Red Cross in France, where her fluent French was invaluable. She was later appointed assistant to the Deputy Commissioner for Civilian Relief, North West Europe. Connie's son Tony was convinced that with Val away most of the time, his mother and Shav enjoyed a more companionable and peaceful time.

But Connie, now in her mid-fifties, was never a peaceful person and would not keep still for long. It could not have been easy for her suddenly to find, with the war, that her services were no longer required and that the demands of upper-class society upon which her business relied had diminished and changed. Many businesswomen in her situation might have felt shattered and unable to see any kind of life or future for themselves. For Connie it was an opportunity to move on. She began to realize that her exclusive and glamorous image was not the person she wanted to be. It was time to reinvent herself, find a fresh outlet and decide what she was going to do for the duration of the war.

At first, as the war began to grip, Connie prepared her home for tough times ahead. She was determined not to destroy her garden, as many gardeners had done in 1914 in a surge of patriotic enthusiasm to make room for growing vegetables. Instead, she turned over those parts of the garden that did not involve digging up mature lawns and shrubs or her beloved rose beds. She installed an incubator for chickens and looked forward to her own fresh eggs and delicious *petits poussins*. She bought a horse and cart to use locally instead of the car. In a frenzy of activity, she and Gladys Trower threw themselves into making jam and preserving everything they could lay their hands on in late autumn. Connie then remembered that she had forgotten to take cuttings of some of the more precious old roses, so Walter Trower hastily dug trenches against a north wall, filled them with soil well mixed with sand and inserted cuttings where they could be left in peace until the next year. But autumn was followed by the coldest winter for forty-five years: pipes seized up, cars stuck in snow-drifts, railways were blocked, milk froze in their bottles on the doorsteps, as did food on larder shelves – even the Thames froze. Shops were bare of vegetables, which could not be dug from the iron-hard earth, and then in early January food rationing began.

It was a difficult start for the Dig for Victory campaign, set up to encourage people to produce some of their own food. House-holds were bombarded with 'Growmore' and 'Food Facts' leaflets; women's magazine articles and newsreels urged people to grow food; parks and open spaces were turned over to vegetables; allotments spread along railway sidings and roundabouts; tomatoes and herbs were grown in window boxes. Collecting wild food – the field and hedgerow harvest of rosehips, nuts, berries, crab apples, mushrooms – was encouraged. Burdock could be picked as a substitute for cabbage, dandelion leaves or wild watercress for lettuce, and stinging nettles for spinach. Civilians were urged to keep pigs, chickens and rabbits and to feed them with food scraps, lawn clippings, thistles, pea-pods and the like.

In 1940 when the bombing raids began, Connie decided to join the local ARP (Air Raid Precautions), where she was remembered for wearing a blue serge uniform several sizes too big for her. Her anxious determination during practise sessions to extinguish smoke-bombs reduced her team to hysterical laughter. Fortunately, war-dens with a sense of humour were considered a good thing and Connie herself was amused by the ARP poster put up in the shelters:

> *ARP – All Right Presently.*
> *Air raid precautions can be fun*
> *If we're cheerful – everyone,*
> *Don't be dismal, wear a smile,*
> *T'will be quite OK in a while.*

But smiles began wearing thin quite quickly when the raids increased in both frequency and intensity and being a warden became much more dangerous, even in Kent. Connie and Shav found they were in 'bomb alley', where the enemy planes dumped surplus bombs over farms, villages and seaside towns in 'tip and run' raids on their return journeys. Barrage balloons filled the sky around them. ARP wardens had to patrol their area at night and if a bomb dropped, estimate the damage, alert the emergency services and help the survivors. Women were recruited for their maturity and their ability to keep calm and cope with civilians facing devastation to family and home. But Connie was not cut out for the ARP; perhaps her bloody and violent experiences of the Easter Rising might have been an asset, but her age and her nerves, which she tried to hide, were not.

When the London Blitz began in September 1940 she continued to struggle up to London on erratic trains to the shop, where a skeleton staff kept the show going. She feared people would think her crazy to keep a flower shop open during a war – was it frivolously unpatriotic? The city was heavily hit by bombs, and she arrived one morning to find a near-miss had shattered the glass and the shop floor was under water from the firemen's hoses.

> The whole place was in a dim half-light because of the broken and boarded up windows [she wrote]. A customer came in early for flowers, and because of the friendliness which was one of the features of those times, everyone gathered round to talk. As she left, we thanked her and apologized for so much confusion; she gave an indifferent glance at the mess around her and a smiling one at the flowers she carried, and she remarked that in her view flowers made one feel normal.

Once again, the 'freemasonry of flowers' had performed its miracle, and Connie began to believe that the way she could best help in the war would be to try to make people feel normal and hold on to the hope of better times. 'Whatever comes,' she wrote, 'however much destruction and devastation may be ahead of us, I am quite certain that gardens and gardening and flowers and their decoration will not decline in interest for us, but will become more and more a refuge and passionate preoccupation.'

Connie had always been interested in the healing powers of flowers and gardening. She had already written about how, during the First World War, people had found solace and the alleviation of strained nerves through working on their allotments. On her trips to New York she had particularly noted the 'relief' and 'welfare' gardens that were created in the cities during the Depression to combat food shortages and ease emotional stress. 'Growing flowers . . . and working among plants and earth [brings with them] a potent and unnameable satisfaction,' she wrote, '. . . a cure for frayed nerves.' She wanted to find a way to bring beauty and pleasure into stressed lives as she had done for the children in the East End.

One Monday morning in September 1940, shoppers were astonished to find some elaborate changes to the frontage of Coolings Art Gallery in Bond Street. For some years Connie had been doing flower arrangements for the two Coolings brothers, art dealers from Holland. The Spry decorators were expected to do flowers that were in character with the single painting displayed in each window, whether it was a Dutch interior, a marine painting or a pastoral landscape. That day, the sandbags over the basement lights in the pavement were covered in imitation grass. On the outside of the windows hung three immense bouquets – a brilliant mass of dahlias, gladioli, chrysanthemums and sunflowers – and in the upper windows floated the flags of the Allies. A reporter from *The Times* was sent to investigate:

'The decorations are to make people laugh,' one of the Coolings brothers told me, 'they have no advertising purpose as unfortunately for the artists, no one is buying pictures right now. It is all meant to draw attention to the dismal appearance of the street.' Some streets look like the firing-line with unsightly heaps of sandbags, windows boarded up or criss-crossed with paper stripping. Some other shops had also painted their sandbags green, but Mr Cooling recommends they should be covered with earth and planted with flowers and foliage. 'What a grand and cheerful idea,' agreed *The Times*.

It was, of course, Connie's idea, one which the Coolings brothers had happily agreed to. There was even a suggestion people might grow some vegetables, such as carrots, in their sandbags, an idea quickly scotched by the local authorities. But no one could deny it had cheered people up and made them laugh – exactly what Connie had intended.

Connie found her true calling for war work when she was invited early in 1941 by the Ministry of Information to do a series of lecture tours around the country, talking to women employed in military work and factories, 'to lift people's spirits'. What she found were dispirited audiences tired of rationing and make-do-and-mend. While Connie sat and waited her turn to speak she heard officials droning on about how to fill in forms for permission to keep a pig or obtain a packet of vegetable seed. When her turn came, she would stand up and exhort the assembled women to return colour and creative expression to their lives. She spoke of flowers, 'that natural, unrationed source of beauty'. The art of flower arranging in wartime, she argued, was not a frivolous idea. After the war a former WAAF wrote to Connie and reminded her of a lecture she gave at the time of Dunkirk:

> You wore navy, a white frilly jabot, a bracelet of dangling seals, you brought to all of us a sense that 'the world will still go on', in spite of the news from Belgium, particularly bad at that time. I was engaged to a gunner officer, posted missing, though he turned up next month from Dunkirk . . . You spoke of old roses in old gardens and held us spellbound, and at the end thanked us for listening to you on what seemed a trivial and unimportant matter at this grim time in our history. So,

nineteen years and three sons later, we have our own roses, and I would like you to know how long your words stayed with me.

These lectures put her back in touch with people from all walks of life, people who were frightened and tired and away from home. She brought flowers and talked to them about how to arrange them, however simply. Once, to prove her point, she created an arrangement of grasses and seed-heads with fireweed (willowherb) – 'that inspiring magenta flower that seems to spring up wherever fire has scorched the earth' – all gathered from a bombsite. She also made several new friends. Effie Barker, a dashing character who hunted and owned a pack of beagles in Berkshire, had turned her farm into a market garden staffed by Land Army girls whom Connie gave talks to. Later, Effie went to work for the Red Cross in Europe on civilian relief in Belsen. After the war she continued to supply Connie and the cookery school with vegetables.

But during these lecture tours Connie was disturbed to discover how few of the people she addressed had heard of her, and realized how much her reputation had been confined to high society. It was not what she had planned or wanted, and in her last books she was still anxiously trying to dispel this image of herself and her work.

To cope with her nerves during these strenuous tours, Connie took up tapestry. On long train journeys she worked squares for a large floral carpet which she had designed from old flower and fruit pictures. 'I began to think I had started too late in life and would never do twenty-four squares this side of the grave, and to wonder whether I should adapt my first square to an outsize pincushion.' To speed things up, she got friends to help, carrying their squares, needles and thread about in their gas-mask cases. Her interest in textile design went back to embroidery lessons from Alice Messel, Oliver's sister. Bettie Smail, the daughter of one of George Fletcher's colleagues, regularly visited Connie at

Park Gate for advice and inspiration. Bettie was a young designer for a Lancashire cotton firm employed by the government to keep up design standards in order to regain exports after the war. They would walk round the garden together, selecting and assembling groups and colour combinations for Bettie to paint.

Victor Stiebel had closed his couture house and volunteered for military duties. He and Oliver Messel were posted to the Eastern Command Camouflage School housed in the Assembly Rooms in Norwich. It was staffed by a charismatic and flamboyant group of 'arty types' that included painters, architects, theatre designers, an opera singer, a picture restorer, a cabinetmaker and a magician. Messel's official task was to disguise pill-boxes – as Gothic lodges, caravans, haystacks, wayside cafés. 'Plant some old-man's-beard here in the spring,' he would instruct his workforce, or 'Paint a pot of flowers in that window.' He always asked Connie for advice with horticultural detail.

Oliver Messel spent much of his spare time restoring the once elegant Georgian Assembly Rooms and holding lavish parties. In the summer of 1941, Messel and Stiebel wrote to Connie begging her to come and help them organize a ball in their 'stately home'. Connie, at the time visiting Kate Barrett who had been evacuated with Swanley College to the east Midlands, readily agreed to make a detour on her way home. She arrived at the Assembly Rooms to find the place semi-derelict, the panelling boarded up and ugly pieces of military furniture scattered forlornly around the great rooms. She rolled up her sleeves, found yards of scrim, a roughly woven hessian used for camouflage netting, dyed it in bright colours and got local ladies to run it up into covers for the army-issue chairs. She sent orders to her shop to put quantities of flowers on the train and wired friends with nearby gardens for help. She created enormous floral wall groups and cajoled some Sappers into setting up dramatic lighting effects for them. Everyone put on their best clothes, a band was got up from volunteers and a colourful buffet of raw-vegetable salads and spicy soups was laid out on tables covered with dyed army sheets. The ball was 'a terrific and splendid success . . . all thanks to dear Connie . . . what a lark!'

Park Gate became a popular sanctuary for old and new friends who came to stay for weekends and summer breaks. Sidney Bernstein and his first wife the American journalist Zoë Farmer had bought a farm nearby in Kent, and visited along with their friends. Charles Laughton was a popular visitor plus, of course, 'dear Komis'. One or two old friends became permanent fixtures: Marjorie Russell had retired and was now part of the household. She was becoming increasingly eccentric and dependent on Connie. Flo Standfast was another live-in friend at Park Gate towards whom Connie had always felt very protective. Rosemary Hume came often, finding rest and recuperation from running Au Petit Cordon Bleu, always returning to London laden with fresh vegetables for the restaurant. A steady round of visitors would take their place at Connie's famous kitchen suppers, and would be dragged into the garden to admire the roses or join a weeding party where gossip and laughter filled the air – and the piles of weeds barely grew, much to Walter Trower's irritation.

As well as good company and gossip, some brought welcome food rations. Connie was a keen swapper and barterer of home-produced foods, though she always vehemently denied using the black market. American friends sent food parcels and friends in the military could usually rustle up something as a contribution, especially GI rations.

One of Connie's most regular guests was the American journalist Helen Kirkpatrick. Connie's lecture agent in New York had introduced them, and when Kirkpatrick came to England to work as a journalist Connie had immediately taken to her powerful personality and invited her to Park Gate. Her marriage had been a disappointment, Kirkpatrick told Connie, so she had gone to Geneva on a summer job escorting teenage girls round Europe, which she loved – so much so that she cabled her husband: 'Not returning!' Tall, sandy-haired and blue-eyed, with 'a roguish smile and enquiring mind', Helen Kirkpatrick was known and respected for her political acumen and integrity. By 1940 she was the London war correspondent for the *Chicago Daily News*, writing graphic descriptions of life in London during the Blitz. Outspoken and tough-talking, when told by the newspaper that it did not have women on the staff, she promptly replied, 'I can't change my sex. But you can change your policy.' During the course of the war she travelled extensively, covering the campaigns in Algiers, Italy and Corsica, the liberation of France and the advance into Germany, often under dangerous conditions.

Kirkpatrick lived in a mews house in London, where Connie would visit with baskets piled with her own tomatoes, onions, baby marrows, garlic, savory, chives, lettuce and tarragon, and plant up her window boxes with herbs. Kirkpatrick, whose typically American view on English cooking was of overboiled cabbage and stale fish served in hotel dining-rooms and boat-train dining-cars, wrote that Connie had refused to be daunted by the rigours and restrictions of war. For her, rations were an incentive to discover new ways of doing things: 'No stately home of England, no smart Mayfair restaurant has presented a boiled-potato-and-cabbage-shy American with the sumptuous repasts of the Spry household.' Another popular if demanding guest was Lesley Blanch, a contemporary of Oliver Messel and Rex Whistler at the Slade. Blanch later did book illustrations and book jackets before turning to writing and journalism, and in the 1930s was feature editor of *Vogue* in London. During the war she covered various aspects of Britain at war for the Ministry of Information and documented the lives of women in the forces with her friend the photographer Lee Miller. Having been bombed out of three London flats, she sought sanctuary with Connie in Kent.

Blanch was independent-minded, glamorous and a tremendous gossip and wit. She adored patchouli, attar of roses, the clank of exotic but well-chosen jewellery and wrote books about Russia. What most appealed to Connie about her was her passion for food. She liked to travel without plans, relishing the unexpected: 'the juxtaposition of kebabs, tin plates and licked fingers along the road' or 'long days, gazing and guzzling'. Like Helen Kirkpatrick, Blanch had been married briefly in the Thirties and divorced in 1941. When John Gielgud was staying at Park Gate with his sister Eleanor, he saw Lesley under a table during an air raid 'canoodling with a Russian'. Romain Kacew was a Russian-born Lithuanian Jew, serving in London with the Free French forces. He and Blanch were married after the war, when Kacew changed his name to Romain Gary.

Connie soon found that her true wartime métier was to be pursued at home in her garden and kitchen. It was here that she embarked on an entirely new campaign: 'We need a food revolution, we need to be flung out of our old, indifferent, wasteful habits,' she wrote. 'Food is in the news, and here we are in the middle of the war, rationed and restricted as never before, with economy and belt-tightening the order of the day, and yet I want to cry out about food. The only unlimited thing about food today is talking about it.'

Which is what she did. At a time when people were writing about 'austerity' food and digging for victory, Connie was talking about growing food for taste and pleasure; sitting with friends around her kitchen table, discussing, arguing, experimenting and writing about everything and anything to do with growing and cooking delicious food. For Connie, the Wartime Kitchen Front was a warm country kitchen filled with the aromas of bubbling soups and freshly harvested vegetables. At the heart of her kitchen was a glass-fronted cupboard bursting with cookery books. She used these daily, poring over them, marking them with comments and food stains, clipping the edges together and stuffing cuttings and other bits and pieces of paper between the pages. She loved books that told her how to use country produce – 'they make me feel rich and resourceful.' Amongst her collection was Ambrose Heath's *Good Soups* in which the author claimed soup making to be a great adventure, *Good Food on the Aga*, and the great domestic goddesses of the past – Mrs Beeton and, in America, Fannie Merritt Farmer.

These were practical books for practical use but, as Connie wrote, they were also there to inspire and make the sky their limit. As noted earlier, she was less interested in wartime books of make-do and austerity. 'It was always better', she explained, 'to take an idea that started out as tantalising, even lavish – a big pattern which could be cut into a smaller shape.' War, she reckoned, was a time not of compromise but of challenge. In using the best recipes of classic cooking one could be spurred on to create *exciting* food. 'I would rather have a few high spots in the week's menus than a dead level,' she wrote. 'I'd rather have enough sugar in today's sweet and have, if necessary, no sweet tomorrow.' There was always a way to find a good substitute for unobtainable ingredients, and she had little time for Lord Woolton, the Minster of Food, with his sermons and wholesome advice about making the best of ration foods, especially his famous pie.

She liked cookery books that teemed with brilliant ideas; intriguing titles particularly attracted her: *Caviare to Candy*, *Cantaloupe to Cabbage*, the American *Tried Temptations, Old and New* and the *Picayune Creole Cook Book* with its aura of New Orleans romance. But she reserved her greatest respect for French cuisine – Madame Prunier, Marcel Boulestin – and of course, her friends Rosemary Hume and Dione Lucas's own *Au Petit Cordon Bleu*. War or no war, Connie wrote, with a few modifications, cooking guided by this book will never be commonplace, even if some of the ingredients cannot be obtained and the lack of cream and brandy 'may floor you'.

Connie's greatest concern about wartime food was the lack of interest in fresh vegetables and the English inability to cook them properly. She described sitting in her kitchen with friends one Sunday afternoon, listening to *The Brains Trust* on the radio. The panel had been asked to remember their nicest dish or meal: 'Professor Joad spoke tantalizingly of an omelette contained in a crisp French loaf eaten at a picnic luncheon in France.' Others described spaghetti and *fritto misto*, Cornish cream and even baked deer's heart. 'They had us all practically dribbling,' she wrote.

'But', she countered, 'I missed vegetables, and I'd like them to consider the merits of the first peas and new potatoes accompanying baby lamb, home-grown asparagus and young sweet corn, braised endive . . . and what about real cabbage soup done in the French way, or country teas with cos lettuce, watercress, spring onions, and white icicle radishes?'

Despite her claims to ignorance on such matters Helen Kirkpatrick, like several other friends, supported Connie's advocacy of good homegrown food. 'I knew less than nothing about cooking,' she wrote, 'and herbs were totally foreign to me.' But on her visits to Park Gate she would browse through Connie's cookery books and hang around the kitchen asking questions about sauces and dressings. She noted how Connie typically refrained from giving instructions. 'Having piqued my curiosity, she helped me as my interest in learning to cook steadily increased; her method of teaching was to allow one to discover and to inquire.' Sometimes the air-raid siren sounded and everyone would take shelter under the stairs, still talking, too absorbed to notice the bombers overhead. Later Connie would go into the kitchen and assemble a simple, delicious homegrown meal.

Living this busy, cheerful and rather wild life, she decided to write her own wartime food book. It would be a cookery-cum-gardening book that would combine ideas and recipes, including soups, meats and sweets, but the real heart of it would be vegetables, a plea to readers to grow them and eat them with imagination and enthusiasm. 'Books and talking about country life and fare, about fruits and flavours, always drive me first out of doors to grow or collect, and then into the kitchen to experiment.' In her new book Connie recalled childhood raids on free food in the countryside – nettles for beer, mushrooms, elderflowers, nuts and wild salad leaves; and how later, as an ignorant young wife, she wrote from her remote home in Kilkenny to Harrods for things she could have got at home for the asking. 'It is a dull-witted thing to live in the country and not know how country women use its produce,' she wrote. She celebrated the practical wisdom of practical people; the good salt-of-the-earth knowledge that had never been needed more than now. 'Even under the severest rationing, no one, not even the Marthas [the less bright], should be reduced to dullness.'

Instead, Connie brought the brightness of her garden into the kitchen. Whether the book was her own idea or she was talked into it by her friends is not known. Perhaps it was Lesley Blanch, who did the delightful drawings and was already writing her own food and travel book, *Round the World in 80 Dishes: The World through the Kitchen Window*, which she published after the war; or Helen Kirkpatrick, who wrote the foreword and helped Connie with her writing; or Rosemary Hume who supplied and tested the recipes – her professional contribution was considerable – or Sidney Bernstein whose persuasive powers had set Connie on her meteoric career a decade earlier. The title – *Come into the Garden, Cook* – is said to have been a 'brilliant inspiration' of Shav Spry's. However it came about, it would become Connie's best-loved book.

Everyone was consulted and recipes were begged, borrowed – though, she assures her readers, 'not stolen' – from books, correspondents and friends. She collected ideas from everyone and anyone who sat in her kitchen or wrote to her. June Platt was an American cookery writer whom Connie met in New York before the war. 'Fortunate to be beautiful, clever to wear lovely clothes, and wise to know all about food' was how Connie described her. Platt sent her several of the little 15-cent books such as the Pennsylvania Dutch, New England and Southern cookbooks compiled by groups of women who collected and published traditional recipes from their families and their community to raise money for social work – a marvellous way to record and celebrate the 'foodways' of America. Similarly, though not so widespread, the Federation of Women's Institutes in the UK published *Country Housewife's Handbooks*, and Connie made several contributions to her own branch in West Kent. Full of first-hand information, they ranged from a plan for a three-year rotation of vegetable crops, through fruit, flowers, herbs, poultry and bees, to the brewing of wines and the preserving of all kinds of home-produced foods. Another of her sources was the compilation of country-cooking called *Farmhouse Fare* published by *Farmer's Weekly* in 1935.

Connie's writing style was simple, direct and witty: 'Corned beef and cabbage has not a party sound, but it is lifted out of the prosaic by the addition of horse-radish bread sauce.' She was unalterably opposed to mediocrity in any form, had a genius for improvising and refused to accept grey compromise. She argued that out of wartime austerity might emerge positive changes that would replace the old eating habits, those interminable dinners of numerous rich dishes. She wrote about a simple summer wartime lunch that in the past would have appeared meagre but now seemed so much healthier, more delicious and 'suitable': 'A salad of grated, raw vegetables with a cream dressing well flavoured with chopped chives and chervil accompanied by hot golden fried potatoes followed by a dish of cold, creamy rice with a thin sprinkling of sugar browned under the grill, and home-bottled fruit.' She could not live without cream and she gave instructions on how to make it with four ounces of margarine and a gill of milk – 'One can make nearly ½ pint of thick cream.'

Violet Henson, who wrote articles on food from Tunisia for *Harper's Bazaar*, was a rich fund of recipes and suggestions. The Hensons were by then living under German occupation and, according to Connie, were half starved. Violet was forced to turn their exotic garden over to growing vegetables and herbs. She and Connie kept up a regular correspondence, much of it about food:

> She told me of sardines that she was salting and tomatoes being dried in the sun and pounded into purée and covered with oil to keep through the winter and then she said: 'Jerusalem artichokes grow here like weeds, and I am going to try them done like a potato salad – they might be eatable like that . . . Have you tried them cut in thin slices and fried like potatoes? Quite good and you can do them in oil if you have any – we have no fats but that now.'

Connie wrote to Violet that pigeons were one of the few free foods available in England, but people were reluctant to eat them. Violet sent her a recipe for her book for *Compôte de Pigeons* with Raisins and Onions. Connie also recalled: 'In Hammamet they often ate wild asparagus. It grows there in pure sand that runs through your fingers like a silver trickle . . . I was surprised to see Arabs bringing in baskets of wild asparagus which they picked near the sea.'

Anyone could come into the kitchen to try something out and produce a recipe. Val Pirie, home on leave, made French pâté – Connie's war version replaced some of the meat with Prem or Spam, which might have made it unrecognizable to the French palate but was a brave attempt to spice up an otherwise dreary meat substitute. On another occasion, 'Miss Pirie, who is always game to try any caprice in the kitchen, cooked savoy cabbage as she remembered having it often in her home in Angers. Small heads cooked whole, well drained and served with béchamel sauce.' Not a lumpy English white sauce but a French béchamel carefully made with margarine and vegetable water – indispensable, declared Connie, even in wartime. She was a champion of well-made sauces and despaired of the typical Englishman's 'I like to see what I'm eating, give me good, plain English food' attitude, which most likely pointed to bad sauces, badly made. '[The English] will swallow dreadful gravy, accept Gloy on cauliflower, and eat shockingly bad mint sauce,' she wrote with ill-concealed outrage. 'There are people who seem proud to proclaim their dislike of sauces. They almost imply that there is something patriotic about their point of view, with a sort of "dirty-foreigner-slosh-him-in-the-eye" touch . . . It all sounds very John Bull, solid English, and no nonsense.'

The solution for Connie was always to look to French cooking: simple traditional regional dishes such as Val's childhood *Pommes au Beurre* and *Galette de Savennières* from the village baker, her own memories of dishes eaten in Paris restaurants before the war, and Rosemary Hume's of haute cuisine learned at the Cordon Bleu.

There was also the mystery 'John, a professional cook', whose critical eye, Connie acknowledged in her book, 'saved her from many a gaffe'. Shav was regularly consulted. He had a passion for suet puddings and longed for the curries he had eaten in India. Connie despaired: 'Nothing short of molten lava would pass for a properly hot curry.' But she worked on improving her vegetable curries with piquant homemade chutneys, which were not the genuine article but Shav enjoyed them anyway.

Sidney Bernstein, who was running the Films division at the Ministry of Information producing propaganda films, confided to Connie that he was looking for a good American voice to narrate *London Can Take It* – a short film about Londoners' valiant response to the Blitz – for showing in the US. Connie immediately suggested Helen Kirkpatrick, who was infuriated to be rejected on the grounds that she was a woman. When commissioned by Lord Woolton to produce films about home food production, Bernstein consulted Connie about vegetables. In 1941 there was a bumper crop of carrots and a film was needed to encourage their consumption. Bernstein appealed to Walt Disney for cartoon characters such as Doctor Carrot, Clara Carrot and Carrotty George. In *Come into the Garden, Cook* Connie made a dig at these propaganda films, particularly the Disneyfied carrots: 'The unfortunate carrot is suffering, like certain film stars, from too much publicity. Really it is a tortuous path from fresh, crisp raw carrot to carrot flan, and I, for one, don't want to travel it. I'd rather eat them raw, though this is by no means the only excellent alternative. It's no use allowing a certain wartime carrot impatience to put you off when it comes to the garden.'

It was in her garden that Connie always found the greatest pleasure; there she could retreat and find satisfaction in making things grow while letting her imagination run free. 'Giving up flowers to make room for vegetables is not all wartime sacrifice, unless you do it reluctantly,' she wrote. Indeed, for her the aesthetic pleasure of a vegetable garden was as important as the culinary rewards in the kitchen, and she argued that a vegetable garden, particularly the French *potager* of her dreams, was as beautiful and colourful, in any season, as the flowerbed. In describing her imaginary *potager* Connie saw symmetry and formality, colour and texture:

There is a splash of bright green like a rug thrown over the brown earth lying next to rows of grey flags, with common or garden parsley and leeks and edgings of herbs . . . Overall a grey-green bloom jewelled at intervals with rubied fruits, with here and there embroidery of strawberries. There's a breadth of what might be tropical ferns, but is in fact *chou de Russie*; the bloom and curl of its leaves giving an illusion of softest velvet . . . sweet corn looks like tropical bedding and globe artichokes are as fine in form as the classic acanthus. There's grandeur and colour in rows of red cabbages and purple, decorative kale.

She dreamed of alleys of old pleached fruit trees, iron hoops like great croquet hoops on which soft fruits would be closely trained. In summer there would be unusual vegetables such as calabrese, aubergines and all kinds of salad such as lamb's lettuce, and sorrel growing between hedges of common fennel: 'thick soft feather-green in summer with shapely and stately yellow flowers flung up' in autumn. In January there would be a fine crop of creamy-headed chicory and good seakale to be kept in the cellar. On the walls with their old-fashioned thatched eaves would be espaliered fruits, melons and gourds growing in the hothouse, and the cool fruit shed smothered in clematis 'Virgin's Bower'.

Come into the Garden, Cook was published in 1942 using paper and binding that conformed to strict war-economy standards. Connie dedicated it to her friend Ella Reeves, 'with affection and gratitude'. With Helen Kirkpatrick's foreword and Lesley Blanch's delightful comic drawings, it felt like a warm-hearted group effort. Everyone had contributed something – recipes, garden advice, encouragement, good humour – or had just enjoyed the good food. The book was an instant success and went into several editions before the war had ended.

Meanwhile, Constance Spry Ltd was doing surprisingly well. Despite the austerity and the bombs, wealthy London society still clung to as much of its extravagant lifestyle as it could, managing without armies of servants by dining out, dancing until dawn to make the most of the blackout, and indulging in country pursuits at weekends when they might bag a rabbit or two to fill out the meat ration. The Dorchester kept its contract with Connie's shop throughout the war and several of her patrons continued to request her skills with flower decorations, even if they expected her to use material grown in their own gardens. Another source of business was the GIs who turned nearby Grosvenor Square into a 'Little America' where they hung about, 'bunching' their girls in South Audley Street and impressing them with expensive bouquets and corsages of flowers bought from the shop. Most of the remaining staff held other part-time jobs such as night shifts at a precision-tool factory in Clapham, where their floristry-trained fingers were especially valued. Sheila McQueen, now married with a baby, was the most senior decorator and did most of the flowers for quiet weddings and parties for soldiers on leave:

> I found that I had acquired great speed doing three or four arrangements in a matter of a few hours between visits to the air-raid shelter. My undying memory of those war days, when the blitz was at its height, was to go to work in the morning to the sound of the sweeping up of broken glass and the sight of torn buildings – a bath or a fireplace the only things hanging on the wall of what was once a home . . . It is a miracle that people in those circumstances still thought about and indeed wanted their homes and small celebrations decorated with flowers – but they did.

In May 1944 Helen Kirkpatrick and her young GI brother Kirk, went to Park Gate for the weekend. As usual they arrived with ration-busting goodies including 'a most wonderful packet of brown sugar like gold dust'. Their mother, who lived in America, sent Connie regular food parcels including boxes of luscious candied fruits. Connie, who was struggling to learn to type, sent a typed thank-you letter in which she wrote of her admiration and affection for Helen and Kirk, who had shown her photographs of his new baby. Connie, who was never a great baby fan, seemed to be feeling some hankering for a grandchild, and she wrote to Mrs Kirkpatrick about her 'ridiculous pleasure in a baby belonging to a maid', who 'lays siege to any heart she fancies and I can well imagine what pleasure the real authentic grandchild can give'. Connie's son Tony was serving as a captain in Supply Training, where he clearly felt undervalued. He had applied to work with Information Service Control, stating his experience with radio scriptwriting and programme production, but for some reason he was refused. He and his first wife Maggie sometimes visited Connie. She was always pleased to see them and was perhaps sad that they apparently showed little sign of wanting a family.

In July 1944, everyone was shocked to hear that Rex Whistler had been killed in the Normandy campaign. In August Helen Kirkpatrick wrote with news of entering Paris riding in a tank of the Free French forces, then had nearly been killed by snipers at a thanksgiving service in Notre Dame Cathedral attended by General de Gaulle. She later described a visit to the Eagle's Nest, Hitler's mountain retreat where, Connie was delighted to hear, she had swiped a frying pan from the Führer's kitchen to cook field rations. By the following summer the war was finally over, but it would be several years before life could return to normal.

ELEVEN

A Beginning School

1945–1950

The end of the war brought a tremendous sense of relief and celebration. In the cities there were scenes of wild excitement in the streets, people dancing, jumping in fountains and climbing lamp posts. In the country they lit bonfires and sang 'Land of Hope and Glory' and 'Auld Lang Syne' and went home late to Spam and chips. In the weeks following VE day, Connie noted, everyone wanted flowers: 'lots of them – for parties to celebrate, to wear in their hair or a buttonhole, or a bunch to give to mother, the wife or some friends who had helped out in the past. Flowers are for everyone . . . we're going to have peace now, it will all be different, you'll see.'

But for the first few years after the war, things were not all that different. Austerity Britain lasted into the early 1950s, with high prices, worsening shortages, continued rationing, plus a fuel crisis and terrible weather. Life for the average housewife was still one of drudgery, with no servants and either no husband or one who was struggling to recover from his war experiences, not always with much success. Women just out of uniform or who had gone out to work to help the war effort were forced back into domestic life, losing their independence and once again becoming the 'voiceless, submerged half of the population'. They were fed up; the war was over, but life was still shabby and stale. They longed for colour and a bit of cheerfulness, not more shortages and make-do-and-mend.

Connie, who had spent her war trying to cheer people up, decided it was time to educate them as well. Rather than doing flowers for other people, she felt, it was now time they learned to do them for themselves – and it need not be just about flowers. If young women could regain a sense of satisfaction and pleasure in making a beautiful and successful home, surely that in itself would bring purpose and colour back into their lives. Connie recognized that social and economic changes brought about by war would change people's prospects. But her natural get-up-and-go approach allowed little patience with people who let themselves become frustrated or depressed. 'Because we have to adopt a different way of life, it need not be unattractive,' she wrote. On the outbreak of war a student who had just completed the course at Connie's flower school had said to her, 'After the war, could you not add cookery lessons to our flower programme? I think we shall need it.'

With this suggestion in mind Connie and Rosemary Hume decided in the autumn of 1945 to reopen and combine their two schools into the Cordon Bleu Cookery and Flower School. During the war Connie had often dropped in for lunch at Rosemary's restaurant when she was in London and they had mulled over ideas. Rosemary asked an old friend, Muriel Downes, to replace Dione Lucas as her partner at the restaurant, and they set up in new premises in Marylebone Lane where it could once again be run as a training 'kitchen restaurant' for the students while remaining open to the public. Until they could find suitable premises for the cookery school Rosemary and Connie arranged with the Central London Electricity Company to use their Model Kitchen in Victoria Street for pupils to study classic bourgeois French cookery – 'elegant but not extravagant' – as taught at the École du Petit Cordon Bleu in Paris. Connie's flower school, meanwhile, found temporary premises in Belgrave Road, where students received training in table decoration, arranging flowers for the house, florist's work and some practical gardening, plus shopkeeping and business management. Students were asked to bring green overalls or aprons and a card index for filing recipes. Connie, always alert to rival flower businesses, stipulated that students sign an undertaking that they would not engage in professional work during their period of training; if a student proved any good, she would take her on herself. At around forty guineas, fees for the full year's combined cookery and flower courses were not cheap. The day courses were quickly booked up, with a waiting list mostly of women wishing to work as professional cooks or run their own flower business.

Connie now began to think about a far more ambitious project, one that would return her to full-time education. Why not open a residential school where women from all over the country could come and live for a year while they trained? Connie had lectured to hundreds of women during the war and shown them how to decorate their Nissen huts with flowers, grow their own vegetables and cook delicious meals with rationed food. She knew that they responded, like the children at Homerton had, to any element of pleasure and beauty introduced into their lives. She and Rosemary agreed that young women leaving the armed forces and girls just leaving school could benefit from a year spent in beautiful surroundings learning to cook excellent food despite the all-pervasive rationing, as well as mastering the art of creating a cheerful, elegant home. These young women all faced a very different future from their pre-war sisters – they could not expect to have servants to run their homes and some would have jobs as well as a husband and children. Life was altogether more demanding than it once had been.

Connie's scheme was certainly not what Parliament had had in mind when it passed the new Education Act in 1944 and raised the school leaving age to fifteen, granting full access to free secondary schooling. It had also introduced the 11-plus examination, intended as a means of assessing pupils for the school best suited to their 'abilities and aptitudes'. In practice the exam was divisive and widely loathed, since it meant that most children went to a secondary modern school while the 'cream' attended grammar school. Private education, the preserve of the upper classes, was unchanged: boys were generally sent to the public school their fathers had attended, while their sisters went to genteel non-academic establishments in the country. Although day-continuation schools had long since disappeared, the idea of training the non-academic in 'vocational' skills to fit them for work endured with colleges, as did apprenticeships for working people. In most kinds of further education, men outnumbered women by four to one; little consideration had been given to the women.

Connie's views on education were rarely bedded in reality and usually stemmed from her own memories. She continued to believe that, even in 1945, girls were divided into two camps: the Marthas and the Marys – or 'the butterfly and the blue stocking'. The Marthas were encouraged to 'look pretty, dress well, dance divinely, in short, to be attractive, even glamorous'. The Marys, on the other hand, belonged in the 'be clever and you will be happy' camp where scholastic attainment was encouraged. Connie had moved well beyond her old muse Mrs Earle's belief that for most girls their highest vocation was marriage and motherhood, and was not against them being educated for a profession. She and Rosemary had after all been through it themselves, despite both having been thought of as duffers, and had thereby gained their own independence. They could hold themselves up as models of successful businesswomen.

Connie and Rosemary's new school was to be, in effect, a middle-class continuation school. It would be neither a domestic science school nor a finishing school like the 'French' schools which turned out fully polished young ladies with what Connie called 'a touch of the *mademoiselle à la cuisine qui fait des pâtisseries*'. Rather, it would be a 'beginning' school for a new generation of wives, mothers and professional women. They would learn serious cookery, housekeeping, home decoration, flower arrangement, gardening, bookbinding and fine needlework. Connie persisted with the idea that whether clever or not, every girl should be given confidence 'in charm, gaiety and elegance'. It was the kind of old-fashioned approach that liberated girls just a generation later would deride, but in postwar years when class and social conventions had changed very little, the idea seemed eminently sensible.

They found the premises for the school advertised in *Country Life*. Winkfield Place was a rambling Georgian house with a large stable block, midway between Windsor and Ascot, perfect for the home counties families who were their target market. There was a large, dull-looking garden bisected by a rectangular lake, the remains of an eighteenth-century canal. But there was plenty of space for flowerbeds for commercial picking, and the price was low as the house had been used as a military orthopaedic hospital during the war and was in a poor state of repair. The walls were pitted with holes where patients had played darts, from the ceiling hung orthopaedic hooks used to support legs in plaster. Everything had been reduced to institutional paint and dark linoleum. The whole place had an air of 'grey, brown and black'. It was a daunting prospect.

But with characteristic enthusiasm and energy Connie launched herself into gathering together yet another team and transforming Winkfield into a 'place of beauty and inspiration'. It meant, of course, that she and Shav would have to leave Park Gate. Although it was the home she had loved most and lived in the longest, she had grown tired of it; perhaps it was too grand, too perfect and she was restless. Connie was never sentimental about houses, gardens or objects – her peripatetic childhood had encouraged the nomad in her. But Shav was quite the opposite: he loved Park Gate and the garden, he loathed moving and had no wish to live in suburban Windsor. He had reached retirement age and was hoping for a peaceful end to his days in rural Kent. But Connie had always been the breadwinner, and though Shav probably had his own pension he had also become director of the company after the war and had little choice but to go with her. Val, without whose malign presence life had been relatively peaceful and happy for Connie and Shav, had returned from her war work. Perhaps Connie thought the move would keep Shav and Val apart, or perhaps she had simply ceased to care.

So Park Gate was sold, the removal vans came and went, and yet again Walter Trower was told to move all the plants, including Connie's precious collection of old roses, to another garden.

The preparations for the new school turned out to be Connie's greatest feat of improvisation. Much of the furnishing was war surplus. She was adamant that the girls should not sleep in dormitories but in bedrooms, where they would have curtains made of butter muslin, parachute fabric, rolls of braid stitched together and any unrationed textiles that they could find. As always, there were also the offcuts from Victor Stiebel's work-rooms, which were sewn into wild and flamboyant patchwork quilts and curtains. Connie's needlework carpet, laboriously made during her wartime travels, was laid on the drawing-room floor. Carpet in the other rooms was made from bomber felt. Bettie Smail, who came to help, suggested it should all be dyed yellow, and the resulting carpets shone 'like sunshine on the floor'. Connie and Shav had a modest flat above the stable block: a small dining-room and above it, reached by a steep little staircase, two sitting-rooms and a bedroom. Connie filled them with all kinds of en-chanting objects and in one of the sitting-rooms she hung the mirror glass from Atkinsons' shop. Rosemary commuted between London and Winkfield where she too had her own flat in the stable block, her elderly mother living with her as part of the family. Val, who had her flat in London, seemed to have no place at Winkfield and was entirely occupied in running the office at the London shop. Tony, meanwhile, had managed to get a job with the British Forces Network in Germany. Later he joined the BBC in London producing programmes for Radio Newsreel, where he could develop his talents as a writer. His wife Maggie by now was ill with muscular sclerosis, and it has been suggested that the couple had a drink problem. One Winkfield student remembers Connie locking the drinks cabinet whenever her son and daughter-in-law came to visit.

Helen Kirkpatrick, helping out while on leave from Paris, was horrified to discover that much of Connie and Shav's large collec-tion of antiques and ornaments was put into the school, where it would surely be 'unappreciated, ruined, kicked to death by a set of grubby little schoolgirls'. Connie argued that young women who had endured wartime schoolrooms or hideous barracks or offices should be able to enjoy surroundings that were elegant and of beautiful quality. If things got a bit damaged or scruffy, well so be it. She was never possessive or overprotective about precious objects. Their value was in their aesthetic appeal, not their resale price. She often gave away vases that had gone stale on her or no longer inspired her.

Connie started to pick up school staff in her usual ad hoc way, rarely checking their qualifications or background, preferring to rely on her own instincts. Christine Dickie – Mrs Dickie, as she was always known – was working as a cook in an army hospital at which Connie gave a lecture when she spotted her and promptly offered her the job of warden of the new school. Connie was to be the headmistress, but since she would not actually have the time for all that entailed Mrs Dickie would be expected to take on most of the day-to-day administration and the discipline. Mrs Dickie was not at all sure about the proposition, but as usual Connie laughed her fears away, and when her job at the hospital was finished she joined the staff. There she found Connie's new secretary Daphne Holden and Barbara Oakley, a young designer who would teach interior decorating. Several of the shop decorators, among them Evelyn Russell and Sheila McQueen, and veteran florists such as 'Whitey', occasionally came to teach. Tony, home on leave, and a motley crew of friends with help from Carl, a German ex-POW who had chosen to stay on in England, raced to get the huge kitchen decorated in time. Then they discovered dry rot under the drawing-room floor and had to start all over again. In the evening Connie would produce a huge meal and regale everyone with her plans. The ex-military members of the staff urged her to ensure that discipline was strictly enforced. She waved them aside: 'It will be alright, you'll see,' she told them. 'It always is if you're nice to people.'

At the end of June 1946 they finally moved into the house, even though it was barely ready; some bedrooms had a grand four-poster bed but only a muslin-draped orange-box for a bedside table. Connie never seemed to be satisfied and was constantly suggesting improvements – a new classroom to be added on or a new greenhouse put up or the veranda glassed in to make a conservatory. In the end the place sprouted so many wings, annexes and outbuildings that Beverley Nichols complained one could never be sure which was the front door. Connie was driving herself too hard. She was now sixty but despite her age she seemed to be firing on all cylinders. Helen Kirkpatrick, though, noticed she wasn't looking well. Connie, who feared doctors and ill-health, at last admitted that she had a swelling in her stomach. It turned out to be a benign tumour 'as big as a football' and was surgically removed. 'I'll be back in time for the opening of the school,' she told her team, and sure enough, despite looking pale and tottery, she was there in September when her first girls arrived.

Nancy Ritchie was the very first student at the school. She had wanted to do a course at the London flower school but as there were no vacancies she was instead offered a place at Winkfield. She arrived a day early on the overnight train from Edinburgh and was immediately put to work making lampshades. The twenty-seven students in that year, a mix of ex-service girls and a few debs, were more mature and appreciative of their surroundings than the girls in subsequent years. Nancy remembered sharing a room with four others, three Scots and a girl from Ireland: 'It was all so attractive, the dressing table had organdie and muslin flounces, all so feminine and lovely. Mrs Spry taught us to make something out of nothing. We made evening handbags out of Victor Stiebel's off-cuts of materials, parachute silk and sequins.'

Connie got to know this small group better than later intakes. She even did some teaching, including flower work and a salad-making class. She tried to teach the girls to plan meals and created a menu-making game where each member of the group suggested an occasion, the guests, and the food she would choose to serve. She asked them to imagine themselves being entertained by a rich host at a grand restaurant – what food would they choose? None of them could get further than chicken with peas, and ice-cream – heaven after postwar rationing, but hardly haute cuisine. One girl suggested a birthday dinner for a grandmother which included corn-on-the-cob, fried fish and potato chips, toffee pudding and ice-cream — 'crediting the old lady with the teeth and digestion of Red Riding Hood's wolf'. Connie told them about an indigestible lunch eaten in America that she had never forgotten: rich cream of mushroom soup, boiled turkey in cream sauce, creamed sweet potatoes, and finishing with an even creamier zabaglione.

Nancy recalled: 'She never imposed herself . . . always used enthusiasm to get her way . . . She made things fun.' Another girl remembered: 'Her energy and bustle and ideas of all kinds constantly flowed from her; she fired the imagination of even the slowest of us.' Connie had time and sympathy for every girl, particularly those who seemed to have problems. Gill Inchbald, who had failed to impress her teachers at school, still has a lovely letter Connie wrote to reassure her mother how well she was doing at Winkfield. 'She was so kind to us,' Gill recalled, 'a terribly warm person — always called you darling — and so sensitive to people's feelings.' Students like Nancy who lived far away stayed on in the holidays, too. There would be shopping trips into Windsor and they were sent to London to visit art galleries and then on to Gunter's tea rooms. Sometimes Connie would suddenly jump up and say, 'Let's go into the kitchen and have some fun.' Nancy remembered baking a Victoria sponge with the tin lined with scented geranium leaves.

That winter was marred by appalling freak weather; they were snowed in and could not even get as far as Windsor. The gardening lessons floundered in the March floods that followed, and fuel shortages and food rationing made it all even grimmer. But nothing could dampen their spirits, and Connie's first-year girls remembered the cheerful, lively atmosphere. At the end of the course Nancy and her fellow students gave Connie an apron on which they had embroidered their names. It had been a supremely happy and successful year. Connie had fulfilled her long-held dream of establishing her own school; she had been close to her students and really made a difference in their lives, and she looked forward to many more similar years.

But as the school roll increased to a hundred and twenty

students and twenty staff, the intimacy and fun enjoyed by those early groups inevitably gave way to daily concerns about administration, budget, discipline and curriculum. Not all the girls behaved well, but Connie seemed not to mind and even encouraged their freedom. 'You could have boyfriends from Sandhurst and cook them meals – there was always a relaxed atmosphere with a wind-up gramophone to play records and dance,' recalled Gill Inchbald. 'When we were invited to a party, Mrs Spry would come and say, "Make yourself a spray of flowers for your hair."'

But Ros Gould, a flower decorator employed in the shop, recalls going down to Winkfield to teach and seeing 'some awful behaviour . . . silly stuff really, but lots of them just fooled around, didn't really want to learn anything. Many younger girls, the debs, just treated it as a finishing school – which I suppose it was really.' Helen Kirkpatrick described them as a 'charming bunch, but hopelessly unworldly . . . They hung on Connie's every word.' One gardening instructor suggested that no matter how much training they got, many would never do anything of an artistic nature. But the rare gifted ones were taken on by Connie in the business or found work with her enormous range of influential friends.

The students had their own ideas about what they wished to learn and some complained that some of the classes were out of tune with modern life. They loved the cooking and flower arranging, but were not so keen on gardening, unlike the Swanley students who had chosen it as a career. They wanted to be taught skills that would help them find employment, so a secretarial course was added. Few were interested in fine needlework, and the class was quickly replaced by dressmaking and fashion. Miss Oakley's home decorating classes were popular, and worked well as long as there were rooms in need of decoration where they could learn to paint or hang wallpaper.

The only thing Connie was surprised by – and reluctant to accept – was the students' wish for end-of-year examinations, complete with a certificate of achievement. They wanted to compete, for there to be winners and losers, something Connie had always feared and loathed. But perhaps she was being naive, since competition is such a basic human instinct. Nevertheless, what students remembered later was not the satisfaction of gaining a diploma but the fun and stimulation Connie dispensed as they discovered how to do creative things for their own sake and learned to satisfy their individual taste and judgement – and, as Connie would say, 'let the opinion of others go hang'.

The principal aim in those early years was that the girls should learn to run civilized homes. To this end they planned menus, marketed, cooked and served the resulting meal to Mr and Mrs Spry and their guests. As Connie loved to entertain, there was always a flow of appreciative guests to whom the girls could show off their skills. Beverley Nichols, who dined there regularly, regarded Connie's students as 'rather tiresome debutantes who could not boil an egg, but who left at the end of their year having learned to make omelettes, how to arrange flowers and how to poke a cod in the stomach to see if it is fresh.' They had become 'brisk, efficient young women, thrilled with the romance of domesticity'. He described how guests were greeted in the hall with a breathtaking panorama of flowers and branches and twigs. In a drawing-room of 'sparkling prettiness':

> One was seduced by an unexpected cocktail tasting of iced black-currants accompanied by equally unexpected hors d'oeuvres. Finally one dined in the kitchen, on a scrubbed bare table glowing with arrangements of leaves and fruit, with debutantes hovering around in the guise of waitresses, offering dishes which were not only exquisite but, to most of us, unknown.

There were also several big parties through the year: a harvest festival party when the vast scrubbed kitchen table was heaped with autumn fruits and glowing red flowers; an elegant party for Ascot Gold Cup Day in the dining-room with its gold walls and yellow carpet and vases overflowing with syringa, *Lilium regale*, delphinium, roses and pinks; and the enormous end-of-year passing-out party attended by all the parents, with Victor Stiebel's mannequins putting on a dress show. Connie always insisted the several hundred guests sat down to a proper meal prepared by Rosemary's students.

Stiebel continued to support Connie as her friend and as a director of the flower business, and Oliver Messel often swanned in, threw out a few wild suggestions, made Connie laugh and was off again. 'He was queer as a coot – total whimsy,' one student recalled. But he was as brilliant and imaginative as ever and was always in huge demand, 'frightfully busy' doing sets and costumes at the London theatres. He gave lavish parties with his companion Vagn Riis-Hansen in their house in South Kensington, and it was always 'Darling Connie, do send up something really lovely, won't you.' They still worked together on luxury parties and prestigious public occasions.

For the school's passing-out party in 1952 Connie and Rosemary decided to do something very original and ambitious. They thought it would be interesting for the students of the postwar era to prepare a buffet supper in the fashion of a century earlier and set it beside an 'austerity table'. They pored over their collection of old cookery books and came up with a lavish menu for 1852 including consommé flecked with gold-leaf and a huge *langouste rampante* decorated with truffles and glazed with aspic. Unable to find a boar for stuffed boar's head, they used a pig's and blacked it with lard and soot, giving it wax tusks wreathed in bay leaves and filled with pâté. There were raised pies and mousses of veal and salmon. The *coup de grâce* was a tall pyramidal *croquenbouche*, which in Rosemary's recipe was made of tiny meringues stuck together with spun sugar, surrounded with *bavaroises*; plus jellies, trifles and two fine swans made from painted cellophane and holding sweetmeats. In the centre of the table was a gigantic epergne spouting a fountain of asparagus fern, with the inevitable garlands of smilax clustered around the edge of the buffet – exactly the kind of decoration that Connie had fought against for so long.

The 1952 'austerity table' was composed of many kinds of

homemade bread, homemade cream cheeses and a huge dish of *crudités* all arranged on a warm yellow hessian tablecloth. Although they clearly had a brilliant time preparing the nineteenth-century table, Connie, not surprisingly, favoured the simple homespun look of the contemporary fare. It was a small lesson in culinary and social history, a reminder that things had changed radically in a hundred years. Connie and Rosemary were attempting to show their students that the days of lavish and spacious living when kitchens teemed with cooks and scullions sweating over the roasting pits were a bygone age. The war had changed the way people cooked, ate and made their homes for ever.

Winkfield was now the real hub of Connie's interest and energies. She had ceased doing much teaching, though she lectured to the London school two or three times a term and gave out the end-of-course certificates. She preferred to spend most of her day in the garden at Winkfield, writing her books in her office and walking around the school keeping an eye on everything. Neither Winkfield nor the flower and cookery school in London made money – both were subsidized by the shop. Despite the tough postwar period, business had picked up quickly and Constance Spry Ltd was once again a huge concern, with a large staff carrying out a wide variety of commissions for a demanding and varied clientele. There were once again regular flower contracts for private houses, government offices and embassies, parties, weddings and debutante balls. Clients now ranged from No. 10 Downing Street where the Churchills had been back in residence since the 1951 general election, to the ICI headquarters and big commercial showrooms such as Elizabeth Arden and Cyclax.

The shop's charges were now high, but the Constance Spry brand had retained its pre-war cachet and their many customers were happy to pay premium prices for sophisticated Spry arrangements. Their chief competitors were Moyses Stevens. 'But', Connie said, 'they had a different way of doings things . . . more cheap and cheerful.'

In 1947 Connie had at last been rewarded with a new royal

commission. She was invited to do the flowers for the wedding of Princess Elizabeth and Prince Philip in Westminster Abbey. Thrilled and flattered, she dropped everything and summoned her best decorators for the prestigious challenge. The government, hoping that a royal wedding would cheer people up with a bit of colour and spectacle, agreed a generous but not enormous budget. Even Princess Elizabeth herself was not entirely immune from postwar regulations, but she was given a special extra allowance of one hundred clothing coupons for her wedding dress while her bridesmaids got twenty-three and the pages ten. 'It was considered not proper to spend large sums of money on the wedding when we are asking the workers themselves to economise in the necessities of life.'

Connie was instructed to do two large arrangements on either side of the altar. The colour scheme, chosen by Buckingham Palace, was white and pale pink. They used camellia foliage, lilies and roses with variegated dracaena leaves. Sheila McQueen remembered being driven in a large Rolls-Royce, first to Buckingham Palace to decorate the wedding cakes with garlands of white roses and then down the Mall, which was closed to traffic, and being cheered all the way to Westminster Abbey by the waiting crowds. Suddenly Connie and her flowers were back in the limelight, and prestigious commissions poured in.

In March 1950 Vincent Auriol, the President of France, and his wife came to London on a state visit. The highlight of the week was a gala ballet performance at the Royal Opera House, Covent Garden. Oliver Messel designed the costumes for Beryl Grey, Margot Fonteyn and Nadia Nerina, and collaborated with Connie on decorating the auditorium and the royal box. Messel ordered the walls to be painted pale blue and white, while the marbled pilasters had their capitals picked out in gilt. The magnificent Opera House chandelier was cleaned so that it glittered for the first time in years, and the wall brackets, black with discoloration, were regilded and fitted with burnished-steel mirror backings. For the auditorium Connie made garlands of leaves, sprayed lightly with colour to resemble fine carving. Below the wide span of the royal box and the adjoining grand tier she hung hundreds of camellias – 'formal, sweeping and massive'. Unable to obtain sufficient flowers, she sought the help of Royal Horticultural Society gardeners, and eventually had so many that she used them to frame the mirrors inside the royal box, made circles of them to catch up the folds of the muslin ceiling draperies, as well as constructing tall artificial trees of foliage and camellias on the staircase leading to the box. 'I confess that never in my life did I think to see the camellia used to such abandon,' she recalled. The effect was breathtaking. And there were enough left over for her own table at home.

When Connie made one of her regular visits to the shop in South Audley Street, her arrival always caused excitement. If any arrangement particularly pleased her, she would ask who had done it and give much cherished praise. For big important commissions she continued to head the design teams, but left the day-to-day running of the shop to her trusted old staff. Her long-serving stalwart George Foss was now Managing Director; 'Fossey' was greatly loved and respected by everyone. Many of the pre-war decorators also remained: Sheila McQueen and Joyce Robinson, who supervised the younger decorators such as Jill Waring, Evelyn Russell and Amanda Williams who was taken on after coming out top of her class at the flower school. 'We had to be punctual,' Amanda remembered, 'you'd be sacked if you were late. We weren't allowed to go out on a contract without wearing a hat and pink overalls.'

Life in the shop was now a disciplined, well-run affair, and much of the party spirit that had once made it all so worthwhile seemed to have been lost. The girls in the work-room were quietly diligent, working their fingers off wiring and twisting and making bouquets and wreaths. 'They were so clever but had to concentrate. One didn't just walk into the work-room in case you disturbed them,' Amanda recalled. The shop itself, however, was still pretty lively, with people coming and going all the time while

Fossey went round doling out encouragement and praise and occasionally commenting on the choice of material or the costing of a bouquet. Connie was never averse to new ideas, even sales gimmicks: hers was one of the first shops to produce pre-arranged bunches that could be dispatched ready for slipping into vases. Sheila described how: 'The snip of a securing string loosened the stalks to their predetermined "freedom", with exquisite grading of colours and variations in form.'

But the bulk of the shop's work was still in commissions for private clients, and Amanda Williams remembered going out to meet them at their homes:

> Some were fabulous with wonderful furniture – gosh, it made you think . . . We would price up the job, you know, three vases at £3 each say, and we would decide on the flowers and vases, unless the client chose the flowers or had a special preference. When we knew what was needed, we made a list and gave it to the Head of Decorators and the plant buyer Mr Price would go to the market; some flowers came from the Winkfield gardens as well.

For country jobs they took the van filled with material but they never stayed the night. 'We made jolly sure we got home, though it was often terribly late.' Clients rarely fed them or even gave them a cup of tea. Tips were often a source of dispute; some decorators frowned on accepting them, but as the pay was only £5 a week they were keen for any little extras, even if it was just the pairs of nylons that one client always handed out. Some clients were rather eccentric, and the decorators had to cope with all sorts of strange situations: 'You never knew what you would find.' Once, called in to do the flowers at the Persian Embassy for a visit by the Shah, two decorators were locked in and only let out when they had finished the job. Amanda Williams remembered a debutante party given by three 'witches' in a house in Knightsbridge:

They only wanted poisonous plants, Giant Hogweed for example, which is illegal to pick. Someone said there was some growing in a bomb-site nearby, so we had to get permission from the Council to pick it. There were great big vases of flowers going up the stairs filled with hogweed, foxgloves, laburnum, delphinium, oleander and trailing deadly nightshade – so bizarre. They really were witches you know.

On another occasion Amanda was told to grab a taxi and take some lilies to Abbey Road studios, where Connie was decorating the set for a Cadbury's chocolate commercial. After handing over the flowers, Amanda was told to sit in a chair and pretend to read a book while she was filmed. 'I was wearing a blue top and pink skirt . . . of course, I wasn't paid,' she remembered, 'but I don't think I was in the final film.'

The decorators were still overworked and conditions at the shop were surprisingly bad. The staff lavatory was disgusting and the little corner where they could make tea or coffee was horribly dirty and cramped. 'We had to put up with such a lot, but no one dared complain.' But on the whole the atmosphere was cheerful and many women recall their time there as marvellously happy and great fun. 'Of course we were worked into the ground,' recalled Daphne Holden, 'but goodness, how we laughed. We've never laughed like that since she died.' They always looked forward to Mrs Spry's visits with a mix of fear and excitement. They all remembered her as a great artist and a wonderfully inspiring, though also sometimes a rather frightening, even hard, presence. Connie had aged and, perhaps inevitably, had lost some of her *joie de vivre*. 'She didn't like any girl being ill, she could be very unsympathetic.' But they all still loved it when she noticed and approved of something they had done or if she selected them to do a special job. There were days when it was like old times, when inventive ideas would seem to come bursting out of Connie, and her staff could spot the signs:

She would grow abstracted, and her thick, springy hair would literally stand on end. Then she would need all her 'black boys' to help her carry out [her ideas], to draw and paint and gum and glitter, and twist wire, and fabric, perhaps till two in the morning. 'Oh, why haven't you got a third hand?' she would wail, or with compunction: 'You don't mind, darling, do you?' One was not supposed, ever, to say no when Mrs Spry had a creative fit, and it took a good while to be forgiven if one did.

Connie might still have reigned supreme, but Val Pirie ran the London office with an iron hand. Miss Pirie was, it appears, loathed by all. As one woman recalled, Val was not at all artistic and this stuck out among so many who were: 'Miss Pirie terrified the daylights out of me. Like a hard schoolmistress, always neat and tidy in a black suit and very bossy.' Another recalled: 'She was mostly in the office, stuck to the business side of things, but caused a bit of an atmosphere, you know.' 'She was an absolute bitch,' was the uncompromising view of another. Sometimes the tall, lean shadowy figure of Mr Spry would quietly appear in the shop or work-room, like a ghost. 'He never said "Hello" or "How are you?"' The staff remembered him as arrogant and distant. 'You know, the "we are up here and you are down there" sort of thing.'

'We all knew about them, but never spoke about it, never indulged in gossip or anything, just knew,' one of the decorators recalled. 'It took me ages to realize what was going on, no one said, but then when you did, you wondered how anyone could have wanted to be involved with a woman like Miss Pirie. Mrs Spry just seemed to ignore it all. I think most of us were too young to take it in or understand.' As another one-time decorator suggested, with sixty years' hindsight, 'Perhaps [Connie] was rather a damaged person, after so much in her private life. She never confided in anyone that I know of, but then she wouldn't to us, would she?' But she must occasionally have let down her guard a little. One of her greatest admirers, Dora Buckingham, once angrily demanded to know why Connie didn't 'just chuck the pair of them out'. The answer remains a mystery.

Life at Winkfield was always noisy, chaotic and almost entirely lacking in privacy. Beverley Nichols found 'quite indescribable chaos and almost hysterical confusion', with Connie presiding as a sort of amiable queen bee while her young ladies swarmed over the place. Connie's 'daughters', as she called them, and visitors too, were welcomed at all hours in the Sprys' tiny flat. Her old friend Charles Laughton once came to visit and after dinner read some passages from *A Midsummer Night's Dream*; the students could hear his sonorous rendering of Bottom in loud, bucolic overtones throughout the building, which caused great amusement.

But Shav was now seventy, and he hated the lack of privacy and peace more with every year that passed; he disliked Winkfield and missed the Kent countryside. For several years the Sprys had been visiting Scotland and Shav had fallen in love with the wild scenery and the peaceful retreat it offered. He had found an old white-washed cobbler's cottage called Ard Daraich on the shores of Loch Linnhe, which he bought and over the years extended and rebuilt. It was here that he now spent all but the winter months, with Val looking after him when she wasn't running the London office. Connie came for the summer holidays in a blaze of energy, often bringing guests, to write her books and spend some time with Shav. They enjoyed walks together along the loch or boating on its smooth waters; sometimes they drove to Inverness to indulge their passion for antique buying, or they spent time together in the garden.

Behind the cottage was a steep hill of heather and bracken and bare grey rockfaces topped with a high wire deer fence. Val tried to take in hand the little bluff of land that sloped sharply down to the house. Without Connie around to interfere, she indulged her own ideas and created a garden she and Shav could enjoy together. But the task was fraught with difficulty, and Connie was full of admiration for Val, 'the real labourer in the vineyard', as she battled with the inhospitable environment – the torrential and unceasing rainfall, the violent gales, dark boggy ground and huge rocks. Yet, as Connie recalled, it was not all bad and some plants flourished beyond expectations: 'The moist clean-washed air intensified the scents of garden and countryside. An impalpable essence of sweetness pervades the place, giving the colours of the flowers a depth and richness we do not know in the south.'

Val installed drainage channels and pipes to prevent the plants being washed out of the ground every time it rained. It was effective, but provided open doors for the local rabbits to enter the garden and eat the plants. She created 'sleeves' of ship's canvas weighted with stones and wired to the drainpipes so that the edges lay firmly together, only opening to the pressure of water above but not to the rabbits below. In pockets of enriched soil made among the huge outcrops of rock they planted silver birch and silver-leafed cytisus and large clumps of *Hosta sieboldiana*, their grey-green leaves covered in pearls of water after the rain. In spring there were camellia, erythroniums, delicate Japanese woodland plants and sulphur-yellow *Anemone alpina*. Lower down was a thick border of blue and white agapanthus.

At first Connie respected Val's way of doing things: 'she has confounded me too often, knows the way of this garden,' she wrote, generous as ever. But however tactfully she tried to let this be Val's garden, Connie could not resist the challenge of growing plants in these difficult but gloriously beautiful conditions. She was soon experimenting with many of her favourites: *Lilium regale*, which looked very happy in the wet, warm summer; astilbes, *Alchemilla mollis*, even the supreme challenge of the deep blue *Meconopsis grandis*. 'If a plant decides it will grow here, it will do so with full heart and grandeur', and none more so than their favourite *Lilium giganteum* which grew in the shelter of some shrubs. 'No matter how often you may climb the narrow mossy path to look at them, you feel a little shock of surprise at the nobility of their stature and at the fine form of the great glossy leaves.'

Connie wrote, with real love and depth of feeling for Shav, that these lilies were his particular pride and joy: 'the real fount and source of all that we enjoy in this garden . . . I think in imagination he sees the garden given over to them.' Shav does seem to have found peace and happiness in the Scottish wilds and in his garden. He was always a keen and knowledgeable gardener, but perhaps too often sidelined by Connie's assertive ways in the garden. At Ard Daraich he could retain some control, as Connie herself conceded:

> Beyond his position of generous provider the master might be described as more of an overseer than a working head. Every once in a while he disproves this and, disappearing somewhat privily from our midst, becomes dynamic. On one occasion he saved the life of a eucryphia: prodding about with a garden fork, he had discovered a nice deep island of soil in a sheltered spot; to this, with firmness of purpose, he moved the tired-looking shrub, and in this place it now flourishes.

Val appears to have been content to look after Shav in Scotland, but there seems little doubt that the relationship between Shav and Connie, whatever its problems, was still as important and mutually enriching as ever. Connie had tolerated Val's presence in a long and loving life with Shav which, despite the hurt, clearly still meant so much to her. Unsurprising then, perhaps, as Vita Marr later asserted, that Val was terribly jealous of Connie.

Connie devoted a lyrical chapter in her last book *Favourite Flowers* to the glories of the garden at Ard Daraich. She described looking from her window in late summer and autumn onto a 'Chinese scene' of mountain ash, magenta and lilac astilbes, small scarlet berries of *Sambucus racemosa*, the blues and purples of heather and hydrangea and the deep cerulean of gentians. 'What with mountains and mists, benign and lovely colours, the smell of peat smoke, an autumn day here is filled with pleasure.'

Apart from Ard Daraich, Connie's other favoured sanctuary was

Ireland. Whenever time allowed she took the steamer to Dun Laoghaire and travelled around the country giving talks and demonstrations or judging decorative classes at RHS shows. The moment she arrived in Dublin, all her worries and tensions fell away. She always stayed with her old friend Lady Phyllis Moore at her home at Rathfarnham. Lectures would be interspersed with lively lunch parties, visits to friends' gardens, the renewing of old friendships and revisiting old childhood haunts. Connie never forgot Ireland, where she was always welcomed home.

TWELVE

Never Be Funny with Flowers

1950–1953

Early one glorious Saturday morning in June 1950, hundreds of people were queuing at the entrance to the Corn Exchange in Dorchester where floral history was about to be made. For over a century country people had held flower, fruit and vegetable shows there, displaying their giant marrows and lavishly coloured dahlias, and sometimes there would be a table with a selection of amateur-looking vases of flowers. But here was the first ever show exclusively dedicated to flower arranging. Similar to the shows Connie had visited on her pre-war trips to the United States and organized by the newly created Dorchester Floral Decoration Society, over three hundred exhibits were imaginatively displayed along benches, separated into individual niches of corrugated cardboard painted in pearly apple-green.

The great hall was overflowing with flowers arranged in every imaginable way by every kind of participant: simple groupings and glorious ones, miniature and massive, ranging from grand pieces that would grace a Dorset manor house to jugs and bowls holding cottage-garden bunches. There were children's flowers, individual and classroom efforts; dish gardens, teacup posies, miniature gardens made on plates and trays and a doll's house with flowers in perfect proportion in each room. There were arrangements from countrywomen living on remote farms and from townswomen with tiny gardens or window boxes. One farmer's wife had arranged woodland moss, leaves and fungi together. All her work went into the farm, she explained; she had no garden but found inspiration in everything growing in the countryside. Mrs Steele, wife of a house-painter, had travelled twenty miles from her village bringing her own homegrown anemones arranged in a small brown pie-dish. Everyone was eager to look, admire and offer criticism and advice. But the real excitement, the star of the show, though she would prefer not

273

to have been a distraction, was the great flower arranger herself: Mrs Constance Spry.

Just before Christmas the previous year, Connie had been lecturing at Yeovil when she was approached by Mary Pope, a member of the wealthy Eldridge Pope brewing family, who owned a large and beautiful garden. Mrs Pope was a dynamic young woman, passionate about gardening and flower arranging and a keen member of the panel of judges who toured county flower and produce shows. It had been her idea to create a society devoted wholly to flower decoration, and when she described it to her, Connie expressed interest, but some doubt: 'I admired the grand idea, but wondered if it might be fraught with peril.' She was concerned that members would not really enjoy having their arrangements judged. 'Criticism and advice, even of the most constructive kind, no matter from whom, is not always a soothing affair,' she told Mrs Pope. 'I don't think it will work, but I'll give you a year, and I'll be your patron if you're still going at the end of it.'

Six months later, on that hot June day, Connie kept her promise and attended the show as its patron. Her response was one of amazement and pleasure; for here was exactly the spontaneous expression of delight in flowers, shared by all social classes, that she had longed to see. 'I saw wild flowers arranged with almost lyric beauty and found myself, on seeing the children's exhibits, envious in retrospect that such clubs did not exist when I was a child.' The event was entirely non-competitive, which to Connie was its greatest attribute. There were no prizes, no medals or ribbons, no descending order of merit. 'This', she wrote, was 'something new, something good, and something democratic. No one is shut out because she (or he, for why shouldn't men enjoy this too?) has no garden or can't grow flowers, or doesn't quite know how to start, or is shy.'

Dorchester's success fired others, and three more societies rapidly started up: one in London, one in Colchester and a third in Leicester, where Connie was guest of honour at the inaugural meeting and met its president, Isobel Barnett, who became a close friend. Two years after the Dorchester show, these four societies staged the first Floral Academy Show in the New Hall of the Royal Horticultural Society, whose president, Lord Aberconway, opened the event. Again, there were no prizes. Mary Pope explained to the press:

It will not be in any way like an orthodox flower show, nor will it be competitive. It is felt that where flower decoration is competitive, the full beauty of the individual arrangements is often lost to the public by the unavoidable comparison with other exhibits. In such events, people tend eagerly to seek out the first, second and third prize exhibits, and in their enthusiasm for competition, are moved to judge the class themselves – thereby very often missing the individual beauty and grace of any particular exhibit or even missing the whole purpose of its design.

This press notice so entirely reflected Connie's own passionately held views about competition generally that it is very likely that she either wrote it herself or suggested its content to Mary Pope. It is also possible that she threatened to remove her support if the shows did become competitive – which, of course, they soon did.

Clubs sprang up all over the country, many of them founded by former Spry trainees such as Dora Buckingham, who had taken a course at the London Flower School in its early days. Connie opened new clubs, lectured with untiring enthusiasm and without charge, attended shows and wrote careful little notes of praise and comment for each arrangement. The first tent devoted solely to flower arrangement at the Chelsea Flower Show was in 1956, and the flower-arranging tent continues to be one of the most popular features every year. In January 1959 the National Association of Flower Arrangement Societies (NAFAS) of Great Britain was formed, with Mary Pope as its first president. It was a triumphant mass movement with Connie as its inspiration and figurehead, a position she held with enormous pride but also sometimes with embarrassment. Her initial fears, expressed to Mary Pope nine years earlier, had been realized. In a long, carefully diplomatic chapter in *Favourite Flowers* Connie outlined where she felt things had gone wrong in the flower-arrangement movement. The strong feelings, tempered with polite tact, that she expressed were almost identical to those in her *Garden Notebook* written back in 1939 when she had criticized the competitive American shows. In twenty years, Connie had not changed her views: 'I feel so strongly that the art of flower arrangement should be a means of self-expression for everyone and that nobody should be afraid to express their feelings for colour and line through this medium.'

But it was inevitable that people would want to pit their skills competitively and show something outstanding, special and differ-ent. What Connie called the pitfalls of exhibiting were all too common – exhibitors straining after effect to ensure that their arrangement stood out, thus ending up with over-extravagant use of materials, too many flowers and far too much ornament. She was not alone in her concerns. One lady wrote to the *Gardener's Chronicle*:

There seems to be a growing tendency to over-arrange flowers. The pendulum has swung too far from the dreary carnation-and-maidenhair-in-narrow-glass-vase effect of pre-war years to the over-lush, unspontaneous effect exemplified, for example, in the floral arrangement tent at the Chelsea show, where to my mind, the impression was of laboured and unspontaneous effort and the effect, though truly gorgeous from the point of view of colour, was stiff and stereotyped.

Of course there had to be some rules for the show bench, but rules seem to beget more rules, and yet more regulations regarding size, style and so on were introduced. Soon there was a plethora of carefully stratified classifications under which increasingly com-plex arrangements could be submitted.

Will Ingwersen, the great plantsman and horticultural journalist, joined the debate by denouncing the 'silliness of flower arrangement'. He wrote in the *Gardener's Chronicle* of being driven to frenzies of rage and despair by 'the raids of demented female flower arrangers, to whom nothing in the garden is sacred'. One Brigadier Lucas Phillips agreed that the proper place for flowers was in the garden, unless arranged in the simple, natural manner. He loathed the current trend for 'artificial, precious arrangements which reek of self-consciousness'. He continued:

> This craze for flower 'arrangement' has gone altogether too far. It has passed from the hands of the really few people engaged in it who really understood flowers to those who have no sense or feeling for them whatever and who regard everything in the garden as mere 'material'. Many do not even know the names of the flowers they use and frequently 'arrange' them in a manner that completely destroys the flowers' character. To a gardener they are mere vandals.

Lady Ramsay-Fairfax-Lucy concurred that many arrangements were becoming stiff and unreal. She too wrote to the *Gardener's Chronicle*: 'Perhaps we are all guilty of creating a too carefully built-up arrangement for exhibition or competition, but is not the true venue of these arrangements our homes, where we want lovely colour, shape and charm of texture?'

This, for Connie, was the nub of the problem: were flower decorations intended to beautify the home or were they designed solely to win prizes as exhibits in a show? When in America before the war, she wrote, she had at first misunderstood their flower shows and was bemused with the shadow boxes, the lighting and the exotic accessories as well as the considerable influence of the Japanese style. It was only later that she came to appreciate that there was a distinction to be made between arrangements for show and arrangements for the home. In America not everyone possessed a garden in which to grow flowers for cutting, which she seemed to assume was the case in England. Somehow she still nurtured a hope that English flower arrangement would preserve its 'suitability' to our home background.

As the debate raged on, Connie travelled all over the country, lecturing and appearing on radio programmes. Sometimes there would be difficult questions or a bit of heckling, largely because of the excesses of the flower-club movement, for which she was held responsible. But she had always enjoyed a good argument and dealt with all comers as cheerfully as she had handled the obstreperous parents of Homerton. 'You shall have your turn later,' she would tell an objector, and when the lecture ended she would stand on the platform with a cheerful grin and say, 'Now then, you, let battle commence.'

Connie had wanted flower arranging to become popular, 'democratized' and open to all. But she had found the whole NAFAS fracas upsetting. The debate had opened up her own methods and style to public scrutiny and she herself was attracting plenty of criticism. But with age Connie seemed to have found a feisty ability to defend and explain herself. Her old adversary Will Ingwersen wrote an article in *Gardener's Chronicle* expressing disapproval of her method of defoliating flowers: 'I hate to see plants taken out of character and maltreated to conform to the arbitrary demands of "line", "colour" and "composition".' This stung Connie, who cared little for the opinions of people in high society, but those of her horticultural peers were important to her.

In reply she conceded that in the past she had occasionally been guilty of overdoing defoliation to the degree of making flowers 'look like plucked chickens'. But, she pointed out, many flowers cannot be used in arrangements if their leaves are left on; lilac, for example, has too much weight of foliage, while lime flowers are hidden under their cloak of leaves. She agreed that the character of the plant was important when selecting them for an arrangement: 'Most of us certainly deplore the sight of flowers used badly, used with no feeling for their personality, particularly when they are chopped about and distorted to follow a forced and arbitrary line.'

But, she argued, for the flower decorator plant material is the artist's palette of colours and textures, and must be used as though it were paints.

Connie's lectures were usually attended by the armies of ladies who 'did the church flowers' and never failed to ask, 'How do you decorate a church?' – to which Connie would reply, 'What church, for what occasion, and with what flowers?' These women took enormous pride in doing the flowers for their parish on a voluntary roster, and inevitably some element of competition and snobbery crept in; many felt their efforts were being picked to pieces during the sermon. Churchwomen who used flowers mostly grown by themselves were enthused by Connie's free and easy approach to arranging produce from their gardens, including the vegetable patch, and from the hedgerows and woods. They went home with the watchwords 'simplicity', 'dignity' and 'suitability' ringing in their ears. But church decoration generally continued to be heavy and formal, and there were always the die-hards for whom carnations, chrysanthemums and gypsophila remained the bedrock of church vases. Harvest Festival, in particular, was still celebrated with great vigour in the traditional way: festoons of flowers would be draped over pulpits and galleries, along the bases of screens and at the tops and bottoms of fonts, and garlanded round pillars; copious sheaves of corn would fill every available corner.

Connie had always regarded the decoration of churches as a particularly interesting challenge. In 1950 the Dean of Westminster asked her to help members of the London Flower Guild to decorate Westminster Abbey. He hoped she might inspire them with some new ideas that would filter down to the armies of lady volunteers up and down the country. On this occasion the ladies of the Guild were asked to bring flowers from their gardens, and Connie, with Sheila and Robbo, were to give advice on how best to arrange them. Two large lead garden urns were brought from the shop and placed ready for the arrival of the flowers. But the few dozen stems of delphiniums, lilies and pink pyrethrums that arrived were such a disappointment that Connie realized the Abbey could never be adequately supplied by small private gardens. She offered to provide flowers for the Abbey at cost price, which her staff would arrange on a voluntary basis. This arrangement continued until the National Association of Flower Arrangement Societies took over the prestigious task. How the ladies of the London Flower Guild felt about the snub is not recorded.

Meanwhile, Connie kept up her personal appearances at shows; she was terribly anxious that the flower-arrangement movement should succeed and, though reluctantly, began judging as well. She tried to ameliorate some of the worst extravagances by suggesting prizes for newcomers, and did concede the necessity for a few rules – for judges, for categories, for themes, for size, style and colour; and there would also be increasingly complex rules concerning measurements and geometry. But when members of a judging panel pointed out that a piece she favoured broke some rule, Connie would firmly answer, 'I could live with it.'

The competitive fire in some shows was too much even for Connie's reserves of tact and patience. George Foss recalled how at one show she was expected to judge a class called 'Interpreting Swan Lake'. One competitor, with infinite care, had plucked a hundred white carnations to create a large swan and set it on a piece of mirror. Connie did not give it an award and the disappointed woman pursued her across the showroom shouting furiously, 'Why didn't you give me the prize?' Connie was terrified; the experience summed up all that she had most feared would happen. Vulgar artificiality and mean-spirited competitiveness had overtaken any wish to create something beautiful for its own sake. Shortly after this alarming incident, Connie wrote to Ingwersen: 'You will hardly believe that only last week, I saw a rose dressed up with a blue crinoline of heads of delphinium, with pins stuck in to represent eyes, and labelled 'My Fair Lady'. I do so dislike these interpretative classes, and I cannot see any charm or any beauty in them.'

She tried to persuade clubs to ease up on competition and

regulations – for example, to offer a class where people could do what they liked without feeling the need for 'stunts' or 'whimsies'. She would cry with great vehemence: 'Never, never, be funny with flowers! . . . Just be natural and let the rules go hell . . . Is there true grace and charm in a triangle of tulips, in an L of gladioli, the flowers cut off by their ears? . . . Does the disposition of flowers stated in terms of geometry really charm the eye and delight the heart?'

Nevertheless, Connie continued to care about the growing popularity of flower arranging and she was happy to see it spreading into all kinds of flower clubs and shows, charity events, church decorating and the Women's Institutes and Townswomen's Guilds. Flower arranging was even offered in further education courses and evening classes – the kind she would have loved to have attended as a child. The important thing, as ever, was that everyone could do it – and if perhaps some wanted to win prizes, did it matter so very much? 'I expect by now I have irritated many whom I have no wish to annoy,' Connie wrote in *Favourite Flowers*. She certainly did not wish to alienate herself from the great popular movement that she had striven for for so long, even if its members, like wayward children, chose to go in directions she had not foreseen and could not agree with. 'I certainly have offered myself as a very perfect sacrifice to the winners of medals and trophies, who might fairly point out that I have never won anything and am hardly qualified therefore to talk about competition.'

Back at Winkfield, Connie enjoyed meeting the more mature students who came for day courses in cookery and flower decoration. Yet she found the flower-arranging controversy had penetrated even this sanctuary. One woman exclaimed at Connie's great bowls of roses, dripping onto a satin tablecloth, 'Oh, but we wouldn't be allowed to do anything like that.' 'Why on earth not?' Connie asked. 'Because table flowers must be low and they mustn't touch the table.' 'Who said so?' Connie demanded to know. 'Oh, it says so in the rules.' Another young wife told Connie how she had been taken to task over her flower arrangement by a dinner guest who proceeded to tell her how she had 'gone wrong', then demonstrated in front of the other guests how it should have been done. The hostess and her husband both decided the 'properly done' arrangement was not nearly so nice. But the damage had been done and, she told Connie, 'It'll be a long time before I do my flowers for a party again. I'll be too nervous.' Connie despaired. Rules, competition and criticism, just as she had feared, had killed the art and lost all its spontaneity.

Connie had for too long been set on a pedestal, where she had shone brilliantly but where she now felt isolated and misunderstood. In the 1989 official history of NAFAS Pamela McNicol wrote about the birth of the flower-arranging movement in the Thirties and the postwar years: 'Constance Spry brought her skills to grand occasions in palaces and stately homes, and Julia Clements [the flower arranger and writer] crusaded to open horizons to everyone. Groups of women up and down the country welcomed the new art of flower arranging.'

Connie had always thought of herself as 'Everywoman', someone who could mix and work with all kinds of people. But she had become a high-class brand name, associated with wealth and snobbery. Perhaps it was now too late to rehabilitate her image. Perhaps, as some of those who still remember her have suggested, she had become something of a snob, enjoyed being a bit grand and hobnobbing with royalty and the 'cream' of society. Perhaps there was a streak of Etty Fletcher in her. Recordings of her BBC radio performances demonstrate the classic clipped tones of the time. But her writing was always witty, irreverent and had the common touch.

One day in the late 1940s Connie had lunch with Mr Taylor, her publisher at J.M. Dent. She was feeling rather bruised from her recent experiences and did not readily agree to his proposal for a new book. 'It is an awful mistake to commit oneself to print,' she told him. 'Why?' he asked.

Because it isn't until you've been greeted, or should I say accosted, with 'Aren't you the woman who says you should take all the leaves off flowers?' or until you have been asked to admire an arrangement of daffodils with bunches of grapes because you 'like fruit and flowers', or until you have been reminded of your innumerable omissions, that you begin to see yourself as others see you and to realize that far from having advanced your simple views with lucent simplicity, you have in fact so expressed yourself that for your meaning to be clear your readers would need the gift of second sight.

Connie was being far too hard on herself; her books were wonderful examples of clarity, intelligence and inclusiveness. But it is not hard to imagine the kind of gardening ladies (and gentlemen) who were quick to find fault or omission in someone whose knowledge and experience far exceeded their own. Mr Taylor, though, managed to persuade her to embark on an ambitious new book, in two volumes and with colour photography. Armed with her publisher's confidence in her, Connie launched herself happily into this new challenge, and in 1951 her *Summer and Autumn Flowers* and *Winter and Spring Flowers* were published to great acclaim. She was now an acknowledged expert on horticulture as well as flower arranging.

Roy Hay, editor of *Gardener's Chronicle*, invited her to contribute regular articles on flower arrangement. She was already writing for several magazines, including *Vogue*, *Harper's Bazaar*, *Woman's Own*, *Housewife Magazine* and *Country Fair*. With her son Tony's assistance she wrote a correspondence course in flower arrangement, which sold all over the world and made a considerable profit. She continued to design vases with Flo Standfast and even designed 'floral' carpets, which were made up by a company in Worcestershire. Her youngest brother Lynton, a sound engineer who ran his own recording studios where many of Winston Churchill's speeches were recorded, made several gramophone records of Connie giving lectures. She regularly appeared on radio and on the television series *What's My Line?* with her great friend Isobel Barnett and Gilbert Harding. On one programme they had been discussing the return of the unfashionable house-plant. As they left the BBC's Lime Grove studios, Connie noticed an ancient aspidistra growing up the reception wall; she tapped Harding on the arm and said, '*Plus ça change, plus c'est la même chose.*'

The Chelsea Flower Show, cancelled during the war, was resumed in 1947. In 1953 the BBC invited Connie to join Roy Hay and other gardening experts to tour the exhibits and make observations. Asked what most appealed to her, she replied that although her eye was attracted to the glorious, glimmering exhibits of flag irises, her imagination was ensnared by the more restrained varieties with their 'shy beauty, slender grace, bearing flowers of muted tones, bronze tinged with violet, misted purples and cloudy pinks'. She told listeners that if she could have some of these irises, plus some of the shell-pink peonies she had seen on a nearby stand, and be allowed to arrange them together, then her day would be made. She fell into nostalgic memories over plants, 'the flowers we flower decorators made so free of in those far-off and apparently halcyon days'. She talked of past glories: of the superabundance of flowers available before the war, of the lavish blooms that arrived daily from the Continent and from Africa, and of the exotics sent up from the hothouses of English stately homes, so many of which were now empty or gone. But she was always optimistic, and saw at Chelsea the energy and promise of an exciting future: 'The times do sometimes seem out of joint,' she said. 'I want the flowers of yesteryear with this year's opportunity.'

Although she had loved the stark severity of Thirties modernism – the steel and glass furniture and uncluttered rooms – Connie mourned the lost beauties of craft-made things, even more, now, in the postwar mass-produced age. It seemed so difficult to furnish a room in an individual way unless you were very rich. The only way left to express individuality in this bland world was, she thought, through flowers: 'The repetitive patterns and designs one sees in the shops today make me yawn with an incurable exhausting boredom, everything looks alike, so impersonal, banal, a welter of ordinariness.' Even in flowers there was the commercial search for brighter colour, outstanding size, brashness; the subtler shades and graces of old flowers were in danger of neglect.

Connie had great respect for any gardener who grew purely for personal pleasure. And she would have been in complete sympathy with organic and ecologically friendly gardening – early on, she had chosen to follow the renowned William Robinson's example of wild gardening. She always disliked regimented flowerbeds and over-tidy gardens. She rarely dead-headed if the seedpods might be useful later, or if the flowers, such as hydrangeas, dried into interesting material; and she much preferred to leave the daisies to 'decorate a not too closely cut lawn'. Most of all she loved her floppy, unruly roses, so greedy for space but still possible to grow well even in the smallest garden if its owner had sufficient love, understanding and energy. She recalled seeing on the busy main road up to London a 'covey of wartime prefabs', one of which had been transformed into a little miracle of beauty: the front garden was filled with roses, in a confusion of colour that seemed to encircle and almost swallow up the little home. They had clearly been well fed with the 'good stuff' of manure, which had probably entailed great sacrifice to afford. It reminded Connie of her own attempts as a child to gather horse manure from the road with a shovel; but those days were long gone, and 'now there is nothing there but petrol fumes'.

Rex Murfitt, a New Zealander, was only twenty-six when Connie took him on at Winkfield to replace Walter Trower, who was finally due to retire in 1950. Murfitt was amazed by Connie, recalling, 'I do not know how she found the time to accomplish her enormous daily workload. Small, always impeccably dressed, her hair stylish and tidy.' He was also surprised to be told that as the head gardener he was expected to give gardening classes. He was flattered at the large number of 'young ladies' who joined his classes 'until I found out that the alternative class was in laundry skills'. He also liked Rosemary Hume and found her to be a kind, gentle person and quite unassuming. He particularly enjoyed being asked to join her cookery class to test the results of a meal cooked on the vast Aga in the teaching kitchen. 'It was a tough job, I admit, but someone had to do it!'

Murfitt recalled: 'When I first joined the staff, the layout and garden work had already begun and some of the planting was under way.' The garden was still struggling to recover from wartime neglect. Because of the heavy demand for cut flowers, the beds where vegetables were once cultivated were now full of annuals, dahlias, bulbs and the now famous kale. The students would go round cutting their own flowers, while the rest were sent to the shop in London. The main paths, made from old flagstones that Connie had dug up from the kitchen, were bordered by boxwood hedges and decorated with roses trained along swags of rope strung between wooden posts. A massive wistaria was pulled out away from the wall and draped over poles to make a bower. An ancient walled garden built of weathered terracotta brick was covered with espaliers and cordons of peaches, apricots and choice French pears. A substantial number of cuttings of Connie's old-fashioned roses occupied one of the quadrants within the old garden, planted nursery-like in rows, waiting for permanent homes.

When they had moved from Kent to Winkfield Place and Trower had been instructed yet again to move the garden, he had been very worried about Connie's precious old roses and was not hopeful that the older specimens would survive the move. Connie wrote to Graham Stuart Thomas, then the leading authority on roses – particularly the old-fashioned and French varieties – to ask if he would propagate some to ensure their perpetuity. Curious to meet Mrs Spry the great flower arranger, Stuart Thomas invited her to visit his rose nursery at Cobham, Surrey. He was surprised to meet someone who knew as much if not more than he did about these unfashionable and often rare plants. 'The long French names flowed from her, enthusiasm was at bursting point; a few glances at the little lot we had collected drew forth some remarks, that, while they were not disparaging, made me realize I had little to show. There were no half-measures with Mrs Spry – a long and growing friendship proved this over and over again.'

When Stuart Thomas first saw Connie's roses he was convinced that there was 'nothing like them today in horticulture; they had been sadly neglected by just that generation that could make best use of them.' He was overwhelmed by the extent and wealth of her collection: 'She had assiduously collected her roses from French and American nurseries and from gardens here and there, in days before the war. She had many sumptuous varieties.' Many of the rarest varieties lost on the Continent during the war, he noted, were safely growing in Connie's garden. The only other comparable collections, though they were far less comprehensive, were those of Vita Sackville-West at Sissinghurst, Norah Lindsay at Sutton Courtenay and Leonard Messel (Oliver Messel's uncle) at Nymans.

He would never forget his first visit to Park Gate, Stuart Thomas wrote. Before being allowed into the garden he was taken inside the house, where on an oval marble table a satin cloth of palest green was spread. In the centre was an almost overwhelming bowl of exotic violet, lilac, purple and maroon roses spilling over the edges on to the cloth. 'An indescribably rich contrast was given by the dusky tones of the velvety petals, and the shining satin cloth.'

After the move to Winkfield, Stuart Thomas continued to visit and check on his propagated cuttings and talk roses with Connie. When Rex Murfitt first met him, he had assumed he was instrumental in obtaining the collection for Mrs Spry: 'He knew these roses so well he could identify many by the leaf, and others by the habit of the branches – he did not need to see the flowers.' Murfitt was surprised to be told that Mrs Spry was totally responsible for creating the collection herself, over many years in her previous gardens.

Like Park Gate, Winkfield had an orchard of old apple trees. Unfortunately, many had died from neglect during the war, but in their place Connie planted old-fashioned and climbing roses. She had often grown climbers to sprawl over living fruit trees, having seen how effective it could look in Norah Lindsay's rose garden. But disaster struck in the spring when caterpillars started devouring the apple-tree leaves and then moved swiftly on to wreak havoc among the roses. In despair, Connie summoned Stuart Thomas to see the destruction and offer advice. His verdict was that she must choose between roses and apple trees. The trees produced few apples, but without them the already dull garden would look empty and flat. So it was decided to prune them into a good shape, then kill them by bark-ringing and use them as supports for various climbing and rambling roses and clematis.

For Connie, who always loathed to kill a plant or cut down trees, it seemed a drastic action. But she took courage and got Murfitt to ring them, cutting a neat little band a few inches wide and a foot or two from the base of the tree. But, Stuart Thomas pointed out, this would result in a glorious and ever-recurring crop of suckers, so they had to start again, this time taking a ring of bark a few inches below ground level. The following spring, Connie wrote: 'Like a last swan-song or death rattle, the apple trees put out a flush of leaves and blossom, a ruffle of fresh young growth which seemed to have tempered our sense of guilt.' She had planted sixteen roses to cover the eight dead trees, including 'New Dawn', 'Albertine', 'Violette', 'Adelaide d'Orléans', 'La Perle' and 'Amethyst'. By the next summer, the trees were clothed in great swathes of these roses and she could almost forgive herself for her 'reckless and murderous' action.

Much of Connie's day was now spent in her office doing 'admin' and writing her books and lectures. One student remembered that she always had a small glass containing just one flower on her desk, not for ornament, but as a botanical specimen to study. But her happiest hours were still spent in her garden: 'She did not do much hands-on gardening,' recalled Murfitt, 'but it was not unusual to find her half buried in a hedge or coppice, gathering huge branches for her wonderful arrangements.' She remained as ruthless as ever in her demands on the gardens for material; it had always been a bone of contention between her and her gardeners, as Murfitt recalled: 'She was fully prepared to raid the entire garden for her fruit and flower creations. Nothing was overlooked.' But he admired her skills and determination:

> There was no limit to her imagination. I grew lots of dwarf, brightly coloured gourds which she would pile to overflowing in large bowls. She often used them for what she called her kitchen parties and, on several occasions, businessmen's lunches. When there were no vegetables available in her own garden, she would buy exotic fruits, grapes, oranges, lemons, and even edible mushrooms. Once I saw her use the two halves of a coconut.

Occasionally there would be a flurry of activity when she worked for hours making one of her huge arrangements in the drawing-room. Her friend the designer Herman Schrijver recalled: 'When doing an arrangement she was such a perfectionist. She would tear them to pieces and do them, again and then again and then again. I loved to watch her hands, covered in rings, and she had a bracelet which must have had a hundred pieces making jangling sounds whenever she moved.' When these mammoth sessions were finished, a photographer would then busy himself with taking pictures for the books. 'She shared all the fetching and carrying with her assistants, to watch her work left no doubt she knew the business from beginning to end. It was impossible not to be influenced by what was happening all around.' These photography sessions were important, and Connie spent hours poring over the negative plates and prints before she was satisfied with her choice. Gradually she experimented with colour, but was never happy with the fish-paste pinks and lurid greens of the early hand-tinted black-and-white photographs.

Beverley Nichols, who continued to be a great support and friend, shared Connie's passion for regale lilies and was so proud of his own summer displays that on the first Sunday in July he held an annual 'lily party' to celebrate their beauty. 'What a good idea to give a party for your best and loveliest flowers,' Connie wrote, though for her it would have been the old roses, 'or the philadelphus mantled in blossom and the white delphiniums' pale spires in the half dark. White flowers in the evening light are excuse enough for any party, especially if there are lilies and tobacco plants, a cascading lace of white wistaria and white globes of light which are peonies.'

Like her past mentor Norman Wilkinson, Nichols was someone with whom Connie could share ideas and discuss flower arranging and gardening. She copied his scheme for arranging sweet peas in blocks of colour. He also enjoyed exploring junk-shops with her, and recalled how one day when they were prowling around a shop in Windsor Connie found an old Italian tazza on a dusty shelf, carved from a marble that was almost black and veined with streaks of violet. 'She picked it up, held it to the light and asked, "What would you put in this?" At random I replied, "Purple grapes." She nodded. "Of course. But what else?" I suggested deep red roses, terracotta tobacco flowers and Black Prince dianthus, which is white, flecked with dark violet.' Connie took the tazza home and made a design of precisely these plant materials but, with a touch of her own genius, she added a long spray of tiny brilliant-scarlet currant tomatoes. She had this arrangement photographed in hand-painted colour and included it in *Summer and Autumn Flowers*.

Connie was meanwhile writing another flower-decoration book, *How to Do the Flowers*, published in 1953. It was one of a series of small books that she hoped would appeal to less well-off readers, though they were still generously illustrated. In fact, this book was paid for by a firm of metal-polishers who wanted a booklet on flower arrangements in metal containers and were prepared to pay

£1,000. Many of the containers photographed in it are of well-buffed silver, brass, pewter, tin or copper. Connie distilled all that she had learned, and all that she felt was important about flower decorations, in this small publication. After twenty years of writing about flower arranging, she still stuck pretty much to her original principles. Its chief interest here, though, is in the foreword written by Beverley Nichols who, in characteristically over-ripe language, extolled the many virtues of his dear friend.

> Time and again I have heard people say: 'It makes me want to do a Constance Spry' – which means standing before a bed of hydrangeas, when summer has fled, and seeing beauty in their pallid, parchment blossoms. It means suddenly stopping in a country lane, and noting for the first time a scarlet cadenza of berries, and fitting it, in one's mind's eye, into a pewter vase against a white wall. It means bouts with brambles, flirtations with ferns, and carnival with cabbages.

It was Connie, he continued, who broke down the prejudices between the flower garden and the kitchen garden. She was 'the first floral artist who ever walked straight from the herbaceous border to the cabbage patch'. But there was nothing 'airy' or grand about her:

> She may have gold in her heart but she has mud on her hands, and scratches too. And to her ardent labours a grey and troubled world is most deeply in debt.

THIRTEEN

Lights Up — Lights Out

1952—1960

King George VI died suddenly on 6 February 1952. On the 15th, a cold grey day, a sombre funeral procession bore his coffin to Paddington Station, where a steam train took it to Windsor, for burial in St George's Chapel. At the Winkfield school and at the shop in South Audley Street students and staff had worked for days making up many of the wreaths and other floral tributes that were now massed on the ground outside the Chapel.

Princess Elizabeth, newly returned from Kenya where she had learned of her father's death, had been proclaimed Queen on 8 February. Winston Churchill, now Prime Minister again, quickly overcame his reservations about the new Queen's youth and lack of experience, realizing that her accession gave his government an opportunity. The coronation of this 'fair and youthful figure, Princess, wife, and mother', would herald the dawn of a new Elizabethan Age. It would also help the British people out of the post-imperial hangover they were still suffering and enable them to look with renewed hope and optimism to the future. It would strengthen the monarchy, improve the country's international standing and, in particular, galvanize the Commonwealth, a new-fangled term which so far had meant very little to the British people.

However, in order to realize this ambition several obstacles had to be overcome. First, there was the Duke of Windsor's wish to attend, to which Churchill responded bluntly that it would be 'quite inappropriate for a king who had abdicated to be present as an official guest at the coronation of one of his successors'. There was the Queen Mother, bereft and grieving, unsure of what her role was now that her daughter was her sovereign, but determined that the coronation should follow exactly that of King George VI. There was the wounded male pride of the Queen's husband, the Duke of Edinburgh, whose role was now utterly secondary. To placate him, the Duke was appointed chairman of the committee organizing the coronation. In practice, however, he was to play second fiddle to the vice-chairman, the Duke of Norfolk, Earl Marshall of England, a bluff, hearty figure who had overseen the coronation of George VI, was very conservative, and determined to maintain tradition and continuity.

While His Grace was in overall charge, much of the planning and stage management of the coronation fell to the Minister of Works David Eccles, a rising member of the Cabinet, if distrusted by some Conservatives for his apparent self-regard. 'Smarty Boots' Eccles had initially been given a comparatively lowly job to keep him out of trouble. Now he was delighted with the chance to make his mark. He did not impress officialdom by describing the coronation as 'show-business' and the Queen as the 'perfect leading lady'. But that was exactly what it was. It was a huge undertaking with less than a year in which to plan it all. Eccles, who described himself as the Earl Marshall's 'handyman', said at his first press conference: 'My job is to set the stage and to build a theatre inside Westminster Abbey. It is also to provide seats, standing room and decorations along the processional route; to arrange flowers, flood-lighting, fireworks and other expressions of public rejoicing; and to take care of newspapermen, broadcasters and cameramen.'

After setting up his planning committee, one of Eccles's first acts was to invite Constance Spry to decorate the processional route with flowers and to join the committee as honorary consultant on floral decoration. Eccles and his wife Sybil had been close friends of Connie's for many years; Sybil's mother, Lady Dawson of Penn, had been a Spry client since the early Thirties. According to Sheila McQueen, Eccles and Connie were known to be 'really hand in glove; very, very close friends, both artistic, with much in common'. Having done the flowers for the wedding of Princess Elizabeth and Prince Philip, Connie had clearly been forgiven for the Windsor wedding, so there was no problem in gaining royal approval for her appointment. Eccles wrote to Connie that when he told the press that he expected a major contribution from Mrs

Spry, 'they murmured (this is equal to cheers in the House of Commons) their approval.'

But neither she nor Eccles had reckoned with opposition from the mandarins at the Ministry of Works — Sir Eric de Norman, the Permanent Secretary, Major Hobkirk, the Bailiff of the Royal Parks, the architect Sir Charles Mole and Eric Bedford, the Ministry's chief architect. 'Over our dead bodies,' they told Eccles. But he held firm. 'I wasn't going to have them just wheel out the geraniums,' he wrote to Connie.

Before attending the first planning meeting in April 1952 Eccles warned Connie that the going might initially be rather sticky. To her surprise she found herself patronized, cold-shouldered and barely spoken to by the kind of men she would normally have felt comfortable with; she was not used to this kind of treatment. 'But she soon seduced them,' Eccles recalled, and stunned them with her professionalism, knowledge and flair. She turned on the old Connie Fletcher charm. A team player herself, she told them, she would have no problem in working with Eric Bedford, who was to be the chief designer, and Mr Hepburn, the Superintendent of Parks responsible for cultivating most of the flowers required. She could show them all she knew about flowers and how they could be effectively used — though of course, she added tactfully, she had much to learn from them about the techniques of decorating on a vast processional scale.

Connie soon won them round and in no time had persuaded the committee that the flowers should be banked in blocks and drifts of colour rather than dots or straight lines, and that however patriotic red, white and blue might be, the heraldic colours of scarlet, pale blue and gold were preferable; that white flowers, always difficult, were most effective when blocked together; that a blue scheme enlivened with white would be appropriate outside the Admiralty; that the parterres outside the Abbey annexe might show the soft pinks and mauves of an English country garden in high summer; and that the ubiquitous scarlet geraniums around the Queen Victoria Memorial outside Buckingham Palace would stay – indeed, would be reinforced with more red flowers such as verbena, salvia and *Phlox drummondii*.

By the time an agreement had been reached and Connie was deemed acceptable, her remit had increased substantially: she was required not only to decorate the processional route, including the Commonwealth stand in Parliament Square, but also to organize a luncheon for visiting dignitaries immediately after the coronation ceremony. Now that she was a fully accepted member of the team, her ideas, not just about flowers, were listened to. At one planning meeting they argued over the colour of the banners that would hang on each side of Eric Bedford's four graceful tubular-steel triumphal arches, surmounted by gold and silver lions, white unicorns and a coronet, which would rise seventy feet high and span the Mall. The banners had to stand out against the pale yellow-green of the plane trees. When Connie suggested two vertical panels in clashing reds, a ripple of consternation went around the planning table. She picked out two roses, in vermilion and crimson, from a bowl of flowers on the table and showed them how it could work.

David Eccles had been told that there was the potential for over twenty million television viewers to watch the coronation. There was initial opposition from both Church and Churchill, but the Queen insisted on allowing the cameras in, which added to the problems inside the Abbey. Over the following months, as the plans evolved, David Eccles and Connie kept up a constant and often comic correspondence.

Minister of Works to Constance Spry, 16th August 1952:

You are quite right about plenty of gold. When I had the 1937 films [of George VI's coronation] run over I saw that white is a cuckoo of a colour and the enemy of good pictures. So I told my people to cut it out and put in gold whenever they could.

Arrangements had to be put in hand for ten acres of flowers to be grown to bloom on exactly the right day. While gardeners in the Royal Parks greenhouses were busy growing vast quantities of Connie's chosen flowers, the Ministry's workshops were making the golden crown-shaped baskets that she and Bedford had designed to hold the masses of flowering plants to be hung high on standards along the route. Connie was adamant about keeping the flowers high up, so they could be clearly visible, as for a party. These were days of shortages and profiteering, and the small practical problems seemed limitless: for instance, timber and building supplies were in short supply, and some things seemed unobtainable. 'The Department is in the dumps about gold ropes,' Eccles wrote. 'It seems that for the thickness we want they cost 6s. 6d. a yard and we need 7000 yards (for the Mall principally). They want therefore to give up ropes, but I am not yet satisfied that we need be beaten.' Connie was never beaten, and in this case tracked down surplus rope from navy supplies and treated it with gold paint.

Eric Bedford, who believed in functional design and technical innovation such as pre-stressed concrete and lightweight tubular steel, designed a temporary annexe outside Westminster Abbey which was to be an assembly point for the processions and a retiring room for the Queen and other members of the royal family. Eccles wrote:

The design and decoration of the annexe to the Abbey are coming on well. I will try and do you a sketch, however badly. The colours will be red and gold with a blue lining to the top canopy. The roof of the lower canopy will be glass to help the cameras, and we must not put too much drapery as they want to get angle shots of the Queen alighting, etc.

Running round the base of the annexe we can have a hedge of flowers. Of course they want hydrangeas but I hanker for yellows. Anyway you can do a design and we'll put our heads

together over it . . . I am very pleased with my notion to put a
file of the Queen's Beasts – lions or unicorns – on the skyline
of the west end of the annexe.*

Meanwhile Connie also had to organize the post-coronation
luncheon. After the service three hundred and fifty dignitaries
from all over the world would need to be fed. Government
hospitality had been the responsibility of the Minister of Works
since the days of George III, who, it is said, considered that the
then holder of the office was the only man he could trust not to
put the funds allocated into his own pocket. David Eccles had
assumed that the meal would be provided by one of the top hotels
or restaurants such as the Dorchester, but by the time the team
had got round to considering the problem, they found they had
underestimated the massive public interest in attending the first
really exciting postwar event – every good hotel, caterer and
waiter was fully booked. Eccles wrote frantically to Connie that
he was at his wits' end.

'But let me and Rosemary Hume do it,' she replied. 'Our
students from Winkfield and the cookery school will do the
cooking and waiting. You find us a room somewhere near the
Abbey, and we'll do the rest.' Eccles had complete faith in
Connie's powers, but the mandarins were horrified yet again, as
was the hospitality committee: 'You are entrusting the lunch to a
set of amateurs and a cookery school?' they gasped in horror.
'What else do you suggest?' was Eccles's riposte. Since no one
offered an alternative, Connie and Rosemary took on yet another
huge challenge.

David Eccles found a venue, the great hall of nearby Westminster School, originally the Abbey dormitory. It would have been
the ideal setting of medieval splendour – vast hammer-beam roof
and oak panelling – except that most of it had been destroyed in

---

* In end the Queen's Beasts were placed around the base of the annexe and there
was no hedge of flowers.

the Blitz. What Connie and Eccles found on their first visit was an ugly temporary ceiling, bare, pitted and scarred walls, an atmosphere of sombre austerity with little warmth, and absolutely no splendour. This was not the empty canvas, the whitewashed walls that Connie yearned to work with; it would require an enormous leap of imagination to conceive of any scheme sufficiently grand or impressive to entertain visiting potentates, royals, presidents and dignitaries for luncheon.

'Well?' said Eccles, looking around the hall and hoping that Connie would come up with some suitable and reassuring scheme in the face of such desolation. She tried to imagine how her friends Oliver Messel and Norman Wilkinson would have designed a period play in this empty stage. How would they have done it? What theme could she evoke, what colours and lighting, what materials could she use? After a 'terrible fit of nerves', Connie recalled, she found herself thinking of those monks reading their illuminated missals. She 'muttered an incoherent reply about scarlet and blue and gold', and prayed for time to think.

Connie and Rosemary, who had been busy planning the menu, put their heads together to hammer out the problem. Realizing that the effect they were after could not be achieved with flowers alone, they came up with a scheme in which the long serving-tables down the sides of the hall would be draped in gleaming gold, while the dining-table cloths would be of rich blue, and the flowers of glowing scarlet – now the official coronation colours. Alternating between elation, terror and depression, they considered, argued, and developed the details.

Mindful of postwar austerity and the tight budget, Connie drew on her skills of improvisation. She wanted the gold draperies down the lengths of the serving-tables to look like gilded leather and got the effect by painting thin plastic curtain material in graduated shades of gold – which, recalled Evelyn Russell, took wearisome hours – then draping it in heavy, classic folds. They found a cheap furnishing taffeta with exactly the right soft texture and in the desired rich blue – 'brighter than powder [blue], deeper than ice'.

To give Rosemary and her students sufficient serving space, the table flowers would be in specially made tin stands, to be concealed with painted gold crowns and raised on curving metal legs, the base of each stand encircled with a garland of modelled leaves in different shades of gold. Medieval tapestries would be borrowed from the Victoria and Albert Museum to add warmth and colour to the bleak walls, and generous arrangements of flowers in rich glowing reds would be set around the hall to distract the eye from the temporary roof.

Connie's plans seemed to be shaping up and she was ready to report back to the committee. But her fear of disappointing authority – the 'cold douche of snubs and rejections' which always threatened to derail her confidence – was never far beneath the surface: 'Suppose those in authority thought we were going too far, suppose they thought we might produce something not sufficiently dignified, suppose, suppose – serving tables draped in gold! Blue cloths! They could sound tawdry – better be careful.' But Eccles wrote to reassure her: 'If, in all this, there is no cause for dismay, that must chiefly be because you are enlisted in our handful of "metteurs en scène". I believe in our team success.'

That Christmas Connie sent Sybil and David Eccles a coronation flower tableau made by Flo Standfast. Eccles immediately replied:

Minister of Works to Constance Spry, Christmas Eve 1952:

You have a special genius for pageant in miniature – the gift of perishable splendour.

> *But oh! The very reason why*
> *I clasp them is because they die.*

There's a flower-seller's song for you. Strange that England, who used to be in love with 'fantaisie', with poets and processions, has been now so long content to live on bread and rations. Our immediate fathers seem to have forgotten that the imagination is as powerful as the stomach. Our fantasy has been sleeping, but now it yawns and stretches, and if you and I pull the clothes off next June, it will get right out of bed. Only we have to navigate a new sort of imagination, a popular imagination flooding round the single lighthouse of the Throne, an imagination Commonwealth in extent and far simpler in quality than the Edwardian and Georgian mixture of peers, courtiers, and money-bags.

Eccles was reflecting on the government's wish for the new Queen to be a beacon of hope for a future of optimism and post-imperial unity. The Queen herself has always attached considerable importance to this role and at the time of her accession said:

The Commonwealth bears no resemblance to the empires of the past. It is an entirely new conception built on the highest qualities of the spirit of man: friendship, loyalty, and the desire for freedom and peace. To that new conception of an equal partnership of nations and races I shall give myself heart and soul every day of my life.

Determined that the symbolism of her coronation should include references to the Commonwealth, she asked Norman Hartnell to embroider her gown with emblems of the Commonwealth countries (eight at that time) — the lotus flower for Ceylon and India, mimosa (what Australians call wattle) for Australia, wheat and jute for Pakistan, the protea for South Africa, fern for New Zealand, shamrock for Ireland, thistle for Scotland, leek for Wales — and the rose for England.

Connie wanted to create a similar symbolic floral effect at the Commonwealth stand on the processional route, but live flowers were much more difficult to obtain than jewels for embroidery. The kind of pageant that Eccles and his team were struggling to create was not going to be easy to achieve against so much bureaucracy and postwar ennui. Eccles again wrote to Connie:

Our duty is to give her blossoming renown an outward and visible form significant to the popular imagination. If we made a mess of it, we should disappoint the hearts of millions. We might even be guilty of splintering the Commonwealth at the one and only moment allowed us to reverse the process of separation which has gone so far. And this chance must be taken with nothing better than the passive support of the Cabinet, whose thoughts are on the House of Commons and the daily conduct of State affairs, e.g. in all these months not one small suggestion for the Coronation preparations has come from either the Colonial or the Commonwealth Relations Office. As far as I know, they may be quite indifferent to the influence of the pageant upon the lives and loyalties of those for whom they are responsible, or with whom they are the link with HMG.

Despite his conservatism the Duke of Norfolk, the Earl Marshall, had a very down-to-earth attitude to the preparations: 'Solve the problem of what they call the toilets and you will have made a very good start indeed.' Unfortunately, by the following spring they were still arguing about just that. Perhaps with their war experience, Oliver Messel or Victor Stiebel could come up with a colourful way to camouflage them. Eccles wrote to Connie on 6 April 1953:

You know those corrugated tank-like structures which are lavatories, and are going up in the Parks. I won't have them blocks of Government green, and I have suggested stripes, blue and white (MEN) and pink and white (WOMEN).* Then the public would quickly grasp the colour signal and we need not have such huge notices 'Gents' 'Ladies' etc. But I fear this is too frivolous for the Parks Director of MOW [the Ministry of Works].

The stands started to go up along the processional route and the memos became more frequent and more frantic. Eccles and his

* Bedford did in fact create striped 'kiosks' in Hyde Park.

team made regular tours of inspection. By May, tensions had risen and there was concern about costs and flower supplies. Eccles wrote again to Connie: 'I am going over the route all day on Thursday with Sir Charles Mole, to see about the timetable. It will give me an opportunity to have a look at the flower positions. Next week I will try to get from the Parks just how many flowers we are going to have. I have sent for a breakdown of their Coronation budget (£15,000) which is a means of seeing what they are doing.'

The problem was that Mr Hepburn and his team of gardeners in Parks could not provide anything like the prodigious quantities of flowers in the kind of exotic and brilliant colours that Connie now required. Fortunately, the mayor and citizens of San Remo in Italy promised a coronation gift of red flowers: roses, carnations, gladioli and strelitzias. David Eccles had finally persuaded the Commonwealth countries to contribute huge quantities of their indigenous flowers. And as well as planning special supplies in her own gardens, Connie called in help from friends with large private gardens and her regular nurserymen to prepare sufficient planting for cut flowers the following June. The RHS offered branches of late-flowering rhododendrons, azaleas and lilac from Wisley.

In the last few months the shop's routine work had more than doubled. Regular clients wanted special effects for their private coronation parties and to brighten their London window boxes. 'All hands to the pump' was Connie's battle cry. Tony, still happily working at the BBC, was persuaded, initially very reluctantly, to join the business permanently. Shav, by now too old to have any serious involvement, remained for the most part in Scotland. George Foss, Robbo, Sheila McQueen, Flo Standfast, Whitey and their team in 'Arts' kept up their unceasing labour — modelling, painting, wiring, stripping, painting and sewing. The pace hotted up through May, but the Chelsea Flower Show could not be ignored and Connie insisted on her usual displays.

She could now visualize more clearly where the coronation

flowers would go and how many would be wanted. The three-deep line of scarlet geraniums at the Victoria Memorial was too thin – there must be an addition to the shelf to widen the bank of flowers; the baskets swinging above the Duke of York's Steps were insufficiently lavish, and more ivy-leaved geraniums must be found; the drifts of blue and white hydrangeas interspersed with white stocks on the Colonial Office stand were liable to block the view of those sitting immediately behind. Eric Bedford wanted these last taken out of their pots and laid on their sides in peat, but Mr Hepburn was unhappy about the watering problem this would cause. Doubts were expressed about the stability of the huge container that was to hold the flowers at Hyde Park Corner. Mr Hepburn became increasingly worried that if the weather was hot, plants would open before their time, and his stock of blue cinerarias would be much reduced. Connie suggested that any deficiencies could be filled in with common *Rhododendron ponticum*, which would look beautiful if stripped of its leaves and massed. And so it went on.

Rosemary, meanwhile, was dealing with the huge responsibility of providing the luncheon for guests from all over the world, some of whom would not eat meat, or at least certain kinds of meat. There were no cooking facilities near Westminster School hall, and only the soup and the coffee could be served hot. On 18 May she gave a lunch party at the cookery school, to which the Minister and his team were invited, to sample the menu proposed:

E II R

Potage de Tomate à l'Estragon
Truite de Rivière

~

Poulet Reine Élizabeth

ou

Cornets de Jambon Lucullus

~

Salades
Galettes aux Fraises
Roulade. Mousse au Citron
Café. Friandises.
Moselle Brauneberger '43
Champagne Krug '45

Faced with the logistical challenge of coming up with a dish that was special enough to grace such an important event but that could also be prepared in advance and served cold, Rosemary created *Poulet Reine Élizabeth* (Chicken Queen Elizabeth), or Coronation Chicken, made with strips of cold chicken in a delicate curry-flavoured sauce. Her main source of inspiration came from a nineteenth-century recipe book called *Savouries à la mode* by Harriet Anne de Salis. According to Griselda Barton, Rosemary's niece, 'The recipe was for Queen Adelaide's [wife of William IV] favourite sandwich — chicken with a curry and apricot butter. My aunt liked the combination of flavours, with the zing of the dried apricot.'

The Winkfield students, acting as waitresses, wore outfits designed for them by Victor Stiebel: grey-sprigged overall dresses tied with a blue sash and adorned with a jewelled crown on blue moiré ribbon around the neck. Connie's friend Effie Barker, who was still sending her vegetables, was to supply the lettuces for the luncheon from her farm. When told that she would be put in charge of the waiting, Effie protested that she could not possibly take this on. 'Nonsense!' — Connie brushed aside her excuses — 'You've been served by waiters all your life, and of course you must know how it's done.'

David Eccles reported back that the gentlemen found the food delicious and the service impeccable. All doubts about amateurish students were allayed.

By Whit weekend London was already bursting with people who had poured into the city to see the decorations. Souvenir sellers began doing a roaring trade with coronation mugs, programmes, coins and tiny replicas of the royal coach and white horses. The hotels were choked, trains, planes and ships continued to bring people from around the world. Thousands of soldiers, police, firemen, Red Cross and St John Ambulance nurses and doctors stood by. The coronation was the occasion for a huge national party in which everybody participated, from village carnivals to London's East End street parties. Churchill was determined that people should enjoy themselves. Food rationing had not completely ended, but he insisted that a bonus of an extra pound on the sugar ration should be issued to everyone, despite the Ministry of Food's dire warnings that this would lead to a shortage. For coronation week, caterers too would be allowed additional sugar, and extra fat to make potato crisps.

On the Friday night before the coronation, Connie and her team waited anxiously in the Hyde Park Frame Ground for news that the BOAC planes had arrived bearing the promised gifts of flowers. When by midnight they had not landed, Connie started to panic and to wonder where they might find suitable last-minute alternatives. Eventually the special liaison officer telephoned to inform them that some of the planes had landed, and he would rush the flowers through customs for immediate collection. Late on Saturday the San Remo gift finally arrived and with relief they began unpacking case after case of marvellous flowers. Seeing that the rosebuds had begun to show signs of distress, they prepared dozens of pails of warm water, took off the lowest leaves, hammered the ends of the stems and set them all in a cool place to recover.

As Saturday night turned into Sunday morning they were still tirelessly preparing the flowers, cutting stems, trimming and splitting the ends of the gladioli, which were stood in deep pails of even warmer water to induce them to open their still-folded buds. There was more panic on Sunday when the roses recovered too well and the buds began expanding; they had visions of overblown roses and fallen petals, but the cool stone-walled rooms prevented this. On Monday they started decorating the hall. But the lighting was too subdued and the brilliance of the huge rich-red arrangements seemed dimmed. In order to increase the colour range and intensify the effect Connie added azaleas and rhododendrons in pink and orange. The final flaming torches of colour that warmed the hall's cold walls were achieved by adding yet more rich reds and oranges, including jazzy strelitzias.

By now, yet more flowers had arrived at Heathrow. Case upon case was brought in, gifts from all the countries of the Commonwealth including forty huge boxes from Australia and three dozen bundles and bamboo cases from India. Amanda Williams remembers consternation at the late arrival, and rather sad appearance, of the proteas from South Africa. After treatment they were sent to Parliament Square where they were used to decorate the stand where the Commonwealth VIPs would sit to watch the procession.

A sense of unreality pervaded the nervous and exhausted flower decorators who worked flat out through that night with Connie. As they unpacked, the light of the arc-lamps revealed time and again flowers of extraordinary strangeness and exotic beauty, which filled the chill night air with their sweet tropical smells. The scene behind the Commonwealth stand was turned into a little Covent Garden. Throughout, Connie supervised and her helpers toiled away. Sheila McQueen recalled:

I can still hear her excited cry as the lids of the boxes were lifted. And then she would straighten up and decide in a split second, as only she could decide, how to make each kind of flower look its best. Her imagination told her what to do and slowly harmony grew out of confusion and Parliament Square became an exotic garden. That night's work is one of my most vivid memories of Connie.

Tension, excitement and anticipation seemed to mount as the crowds watched them work. There were the exotic orchids, the richly perfumed frangipani, huge golden flowers that looked like many-beaked birds of paradise, and Indian umbrellas composed of wax-like jasmine. A whole raft of wild flowers came from Australia, blossoms of strange trees and lotus blooms. More cases finally arrived from South Africa, from which they unpacked proteas of a size and magnificence that none of them had seen before. They found one particularly extraordinary item: something that resembled an elephant's tusk, which they puzzled over until they found written in indelible pencil the legend 'King Coconut from Ceylon'. Ignorant of what it was, they decided to split the hard shell and out tumbled a great ivory tassel bearing a number of weird fruits. 'That was how we came by material sufficiently grand and spectacular for our unusual purpose,' Amanda Williams recalled – and so much of it, indeed, that they were able to set some aside for elsewhere – cases of lotus flowers for the banquet at Lancaster House and gold and orange blooms of another tropical plant for the Abbey annexe. As the contents of the cases were set out in the places prepared for them the crowd milled around, looking, admiring and asking the names of the strange foreign flowers. Fortunately, most were carefully labelled, but even those that had not been labelled were identified, their names shouted out by people among the crowd who recognized them from their homelands, expressing pride and perhaps homesickness too. 'It was all incredibly moving,' said Sheila, 'and emotional . . . for us all.'

The Queen and her court attended a brilliant all-night pre-coronation ball at Hampton Court. The palace was floodlit, the fountains were surrounded by massed flowers, the gentlemen wore tails and the ladies ballgowns and tiaras. 'We danced in the Great Hall and supped in the Orangery,' 'Jock' Colville, Sir Winston Churchill's Principal Private Secretary, wrote in his diary. 'A world that vanished in 1939 lived again for the night.' Meanwhile, the streets were filling with expectant crowds and already the parks and pavements were impassable, thick with half a million people settling down with blankets and thermoses of tea, hip flasks of brandy, sandwiches and radios, knitting, sleeping bags, even tents improvised from raincoats and rugs. Some had champagne, chicken and asparagus. There was only one problem: it was freezing cold and pouring with rain — in fact, the coldest, wettest June day of the century. Undeterred, people sat or lay chatting in the downpour until every inch of space in the Mall, and from Marble Arch to Hyde Park Corner and Trafalgar Square, was a mass of cheerful, cold, wet humanity. The rain lashed, the temperature fell to forty-five degrees Fahrenheit. A crowd lit a bonfire in Green Park to keep warm. Throughout the night catering tents and voluntary services kept up the supply of hot tea.

But then came terrible news: William Hepburn, Superintendent of Parks, who for months had struggled with nervous exhaustion, collapsed with a heart attack and died. He was only sixty-four, but the strain had been too much. Just a few hours later his name would appear on the Coronation Honours list — he had been appointed a member of the Royal Victorian Order for personal services to the Queen. His tragic death threw everyone into confusion and distress, but his assistant Mr Barham stepped into the fray and kept the teams of gardeners cutting and gathering all the blooms that Mr Hepburn had nurtured and watched over with so much nervous anxiety for so long.

David and Sybil Eccles stayed up the whole night, helping unpack in the flower-strewn Square, giving advice, answering the questions flung at them by the people all around them; and finally, in the early hours of the morning, they conjured up food that Connie's team ravenously devoured, undeterred by the proximity of the curious hordes.

Eccles's and Connie's dream of a 'united and living' Commonwealth was embodied in this unprecedented spectacle. As Connie expresed it:

The historic occasion of the Coronation of Elizabeth II made flower history too. Because of resources undreamed of in the past, its pageantry was enhanced by a gift, a token of love and loyalty from country to country, which would have seemed, not so very many years ago, a fantastic impossibility. The eve

of that momentous occasion seemed then, and seems in retrospect, a fabulous moment.

It was the culmination of a lifetime's work, and her proudest
achievement.

At dawn the crowds woke to hear the first news broadcast of
coronation day: Everest had been conquered by the New Zealander
Edmund Hilary and Sherpa Tenzing, and there was particular
cheering in the 'Great Australia and New Zealand' sections of the
Commonwealth stand in Parliament Square. Connie and her
workers had had no opportunity for sleep, nor would they for
several hours yet. They now had one final task – to put flowers in
the retiring and luncheon rooms for the royal family. For the
Queen's room Connie chose a simple basket filled to overflowing
with the old white rose 'Blanc Double de Coubert'. 'We hoped
that the sweetness, the simplicity, of this lovely white rose might
be found appropriate.'

After the coronation service the hungry guests began to stream
out of the Abbey and into Westminster School hall, where the
beauty and vivid colour of Connie's scheme far exceeded her
expectations and was further enriched by the lavish attire of the
guests:

> Jewels scintillated everywhere among cloth of gold, tissues of
> scarlet, of gold, of blue, and of silver; a wonderful touch of
> Chinese yellow came from a soft-folded oriental head-dress;
> there were gorgeous uniforms, and a shimmer of satin and
> brocade. The room gleamed and glimmered like a jewel-
> encrusted tapestry, the whole effect heightened by the presence
> of a small group of Arabs in cream woollen robes with black
> cords round their traditional head-dresses.

Rosemary's Cordon Bleu students had to carry great trays of
cucumber rice salad and Coronation Chicken from the school
kitchen some distance away. One girl tripped and the entire

contents of her platter slipped onto the floor. Rosemary, with great aplomb, just swept it back on with a dustpan and brush. As she said afterwards, 'The pan and brush were scrupulously clean!'

During the weeks before and after the coronation Connie's team lost count of the parties, balls, receptions, banquets and gala performances that were got up in celebration. They raced from one venue to another in taxis loaded with flowers, vases and all the necessary equipment. It was exhausting but fun, and sometimes comical. Connie recalled one grand coronation buffet luncheon given for 'important visiting dignitaries', among whom was a very young 'eastern potentate' arrayed in magnificent colourful robes and accompanied by his watchful tutor. Connie observed the boy slip away from his guard and, taking in one hand his silver-headed cane and in the other his umbrella, proceed to clear a passage for himself through the assembly until he reached the buffet table. Here he collected onto one plate a heap of food: finger savouries of anchovy, sardine and cheese, sandwiches, salads, meringues, fruit salad and chocolate ice-cream. Having filled his plate, the child stirred the whole ill-assorted conglomeration together and ate it rapidly with a spoon. He then retreated to the edge of the banqueting room, curled up, and fell into a sound sleep. 'Forthright, adequate and extraordinarily satisfactory,' Connie noted with approval.

The Coronation Banquet, traditionally given to the monarch by the Secretary of State for Foreign Affairs on the occasion of the coronation and held at Lancaster House, was particularly special. Connie and her team were well known at Lancaster House, an important venue for government entertaining, where over the years they had decorated numerous important events. During the planning Connie was again juggling with several official bodies and high-ranking civil servants. She worked closely with Clarissa Eden, wife of Anthony Eden the Foreign Secretary, who had decided views on the flower decorations. But that May her husband had undergone a botched operation for gallstones and was seriously ill.

Eden was persuaded to go to America for another operation and Clarissa Eden had to withdraw from the planning. She wrote to Connie: 'I would like to tell you how very sad I am about Lancaster House, so sad in fact that, although Lady Churchill asked me to continue the arrangements, I felt I couldn't bear to do so.' With her unfailing good manners and magnanimity, Connie immediately sent Lady Eden a lavish and gorgeous arrangement of flowers. At this very late stage, Clementine Churchill took over; fortunately for Connie, she already had a very good relationship with the Churchills.

In contrast to the make-do approach to the war-damaged hall at Westminster School, Lancaster House was richly decorated and boasted many rooms of opulent magnificence. The banqueting room, the anterooms and drawing-rooms, resplendent with fine gilt mirrors and ormolu furniture, were a marvellous challenge to Connie. Preparing for this banquet was like being a child in an Aladdin's cave of treasures from which she was given the freedom to choose, she said.

Museums, stately homes, private and public gardens vied to provide myriad items for her to use. She could have gold and silver from the Wellington and Ormonde Collections at Apsley House, the residence of the Duke of Wellington, and anything that took her fancy at the Victoria and Albert Museum. For the Queen's table she borrowed the Deccan set of gold and silver tureens and a slender, graceful candelabrum in which, instead of candles, she placed tiny posies of jasmine, myrtle and miniature rosebuds. To complement the gilded plaster ornamentation on the walls she took inspiration from Grinling Gibbons's carved panels of fruit, flowers and trailing vines and made long wall drops of garlands, fashioned with extraordinary delicacy and precision from seed-heads, fruits, ears of corn and grasses, all entwined with ribbon. Her colour scheme was creams, yellows, greens and 'softest shell pinks with a touch of blue'. A lavish cornucopia of flowers poured in as gifts from private homes and from Covent Garden: dozens of stems of several varieties of lilies, roses, carnations, stocks, sweet peas, arums, gladioli, peonies, delphiniums, rhododendrons and tropical leaves.

Connie was enjoying every minute; when she had written to Sir Brian Mountain of the Covent Garden Property Company with her wish-list of flowers, she had confessed that 'it looks on paper a particularly greedy compilation'. David Eccles came up with a pair of giant malachite urns from the Victoria and Albert that were set at the head of the grand staircase and proved quite a challenge to fill. Kew produced giant leaves up to fifteen feet high from the Palm House, plus some bright hippeastrums and eremurus. Proteas left over from the Africa section of the Commonwealth stand were used along with cases of lotus flowers, still looking surprisingly fresh. Fossey had to stand on a ladder to fix them, and the completed urns stood seventeen feet high. 'We ought to have borrowed a couple of Guardsmen,' he said camply, 'to give a real sense of scale.'

Amanda Williams, one of Connie's decorators at Lancaster House, remembered her walking round to inspect the work. She nodded with approval at the garlands, which had been exquisitely made up by the inveterate Whitey. Then she stood back and looked for a moment at the low vases of roses and blue-black muscat grapes set in mounds on gold-leaf plates. ' "I know what that needs," Mrs Spry said, and with her unerring sense of what she called "suitable", took a bunch of stephanotis and lightly scattered the pink flowers like stars among the grapes; the effect was perfect. God, she was artistic.' After the banquet Lady Churchill wrote to Connie: 'I do want to congratulate you upon the lovely flower arrangements at Lancaster House. Everybody admired them. Really it was a fairylike and yet dignified scene. I know what infinite time and trouble you must have taken.'

In the Coronation Honours Connie was awarded an OBE and David Eccles received a knighthood. Later in the year she went to Buckingham Palace for the investiture accompanied by her son Tony and her secretary Daphne Holden. She was in a nervous and emotional state, and when they looked for her after the ceremony she was nowhere to be found. Overwhelmed by the occasion, she had jumped into a taxi and gone straight back to the shop.

Once the excitement had died down it was business as usual, and in September Connie went to Norway to lecture to groups of NATO wives. She was now sixty-seven and found lecturing more of a strain and Sheila, who often accompanied and usually did the actual demonstration while Connie sat and watched, remembered that she would sometimes clutch the demonstrator's hand or demand an arm to help her up onto the platform. But once she had stood to speak, she seemed to find all her old fire again. Connie also produced a new book after the coronation, *Party Flowers*, in which she described some of the work she had done for the great state occasion. She dedicated it to Sir David and Lady Eccles 'with all my love and in appreciation of a never-to-be-forgotten experience'.

Connie might have thought then that the coronation was the pinnacle of her achievements, but her work was far from over and the next few years were spent producing what, surprisingly, would turn out to be her most lasting memorial. The names Constance Spry and Rosemary Hume were now synonymous in the public mind with their school and with the coronation. The dish that Rosemary had invented for the occasion was inexpensive and easy to prepare. Coronation Chicken quickly became a popular dish at buffets and parties – and not just in England. Several women's magazines, sent out to Commonwealth countries, printed the recipe and it was proudly served up in homes in Australia, South Africa, Canada and India. Rosemary, though, was not entirely happy about the attention her dish was receiving. This was less because she was by nature a very modest person, though she was, but because it was not Cordon Bleu, not French, not really professional cooking as she knew it. Connie, who was always happy to see something made popular and accessible, was at first bemused by her friend's view. 'If I can make flower arranging accessible to all, then surely first-class cookery can similarly be made attractive to ordinary housewives.'

Having successfully collaborated in setting up the school at Winkfield Place and in producing the coronation luncheon, Connie and Rosemary decided to take on an even more ambitious project together. They had been friends for nearly thirty years and had a very warm and mutually respectful working relationship. Rosemary was a very private woman; she was over twenty years younger than Connie and it is unlikely that they exchanged personal confidences. But they understood each other and spent a considerable amount of their lives working together. According to Rosemary's niece, she was probably dyslexic – 'her spelling was a family joke' – and her first book was almost certainly written by her business partner and co-author Dione Lucas.

Now Connie suggested to Rosemary that they could join forces to produce a cookery book. They would combine their skills: Rosemary would provide clear and foolproof recipes and techniques and Connie would write them down, interspersed with some good stories – usually from her own past – which would help make the book less starchy. Connie was careful to explain in her Introduction that she should be regarded as 'Rosemary's stooge'; had watched, copied and queried, demanding fuller explanations of processes that an expert might take for granted.

In the new book Connie recalled childhood delights and her struggles as a young wife in Ireland. In the bread-making chapter she exhorted readers to bake their own. She drew on her memories of the childish pleasures of baking day: the smells that greeted their arrival home from school on a frosty afternoon, and munching on warm crusts and melting butter. She understood the reader's reluctance to prepare something that seemed fraught with effort and difficulty. She described her own first housekeeping days in Ireland when she lived miles from the shops, except for the ubiquitous public house, and even those shops were inadequate – 'the butcher who killed at very long intervals', the grocer with his limited stock and, worst of all, the bread baked in the local pub:

> Very dubious stuff it was, both in colour and content: one never quite knew what one might find in the way of odds and ends in a loaf; their presence there was always ascribed to some unaccountable malignancy by the ingenuously surprised publican. New at the game, unlearned in the domestic arts, I was taken aback and really did not know what to do, unless to abstain from eating bread at all.

But the gift of a bread-making machine and a simple recipe was a revelation, ensuring a ready supply of fresh homemade bread and a new confidence. Those isolated days of her unhappy marriage in Ireland seem to have been formative, making her self-reliant, and looking back she was keen to share the pleasure of growing fresh food and the satisfaction of providing a healthy if frugal diet.

Connie liked to poke fun at the more esoteric cooking parlance, particularly the French, though she respected it and defended it against accusations of snobbery: 'I have found myself instructing you to stand in a *bain-marie* till dinner-time, to cook the saucepan, and to pour the pudding over the sauce.' The ideas she propounded – not to waste food, to teach children early on to appreciate good food, the importance to good health of fresh food and a balanced diet, even the iniquitous food miles – are all familiar today. She was rarely dogmatic when a telling story or witticism would do the job better: 'The distribution of fish in our country has its oddities. I am sure there are adequate though not good reasons for the fact that if one eats fish at the seaside, more often than not it has had a look at London before being served up in its own home town – misguided travel which may have broadened its mind but has not improved its quality as food.'

In the Introduction to *The Constance Spry Cookery Book*, as the new book was called, Connie revealed that it was originally envisaged as a supplement for students at the cookery schools. But it became far more than a teaching aid: it was a massive undertaking, and took three years to produce. In it, Connie turned cookery into a pleasurable, fallible, human activity, something to be done with love and enjoyment without fear of failure — at least, not if you followed Rosemary Hume's admirable, straightforward recipes: 'All you have to do is begin at the beginning, continue until you reach the end, and then stop.' There was never compromise, always clarity.

Here she is on eggs:

As though one imbibed knowledge of cookery with a mother's milk the scornful say, 'My dear, she can't even boil an egg', the implication being that all you have to do is to put it in boiling water for four minutes and there you are. Well yes, so you are, but did you by chance bring the egg from a cold place and put it straight into boiling water and wonder why it cracked? Or have you ever turned a nice little aluminium saucepan black by boiling eggs in it? Or have you ever found your hard eggs soft in the middle, although you thought your timing had been right? Well, these things have happened to me, and now I'm glad to know the reasons why, and if the next few paragraphs sound like lessons in a kindergarten you must forgive them.

The Constance Spry Cookery Book was not initially intended to run to its weighty twelve hundred pages, nor indeed to become a bestseller. Published in 1956, it was an instant success and the first definitive cookery book to appear since the war. It challenged the place — and the bulk — of Mrs Beeton's *Book of Household Management* on British kitchen shelves. But Connie was embarrassed by the title because it carried her name only. One can only presume that Rosemary did not protest or mind that her enormous task had gone unrecorded, except as the co-author. Constance Spry was a famous name and Rosemary Hume was not, the publisher had insisted.

The reviews were all very good. According to the *Sunday Times*: 'This fat, full, delectable opus could easily prove the favourite wedding present', while the *Daily Telegraph* commented: 'The recipes take you from a boiled egg to a dinner party'; and the *Listener*: 'This book has everything. It explains how to make the homely things – for instance, a successful rice pudding, and how to make the exotic things – for instance, lobster *américaine*.' *The Lady*, at least, acknowledged Hume as an author: 'The authors' names are household words, their Cordon Bleu restaurant and school well-known.' The *Illustrated London News* correctly prophesied: '[Here is] a book, which, without a shadow of doubt, may be classed at once as a classic, and which is destined to remain a classic and a household god for the next hundred years or more.'

In 1957 Connie produced her tenth book, *Simple Flowers – A Millionaire for a Few Pence*. One of her short, brisk little publications, its subtitle is a quote from a poem by Vita Sackville-West and was intended to encourage readers to find flowers for decoration at little cost. Unfortunately it was widely misunderstood, many readers assuming that it would tell you how to make a fortune by becoming a florist. However hard she tried to distance herself from it, Connie still seemed to be saddled with the image of the society flower lady rather than the Everywoman she believed herself to be.

Early in 1959 she went on a lecture tour of Australia. She had been invited by the Women's Day Association of Australia and sponsored by two department stores, David Jones Ltd and George's of Melbourne. Now in her seventies, Connie again persuaded Sheila McQueen to leave her husband and children behind and accompany her as both her support and her demonstrator. On a grey cold day in February they embarked on the P&O *Himalaya* with huge quantities of luggage including vases, tablecloths and other props, plus a mirrored trough and two urns in a new kind of glass that was thick enough to hide the stems of flowers. On board Connie wrote articles and prepared the forthcoming lectures on flower arranging and cookery. They stopped off for one day at Colombo in Sri Lanka, where Connie gave a talk and did a round of sightseeing. 'We found ourselves ensnared in a wealth of richness and colours,' Sheila recalled, 'flowers we'd never seen before: orchids galore, gardenias, amaryllis, anthuriums and tropical leaves.' They dined on a beach on subtle curries and mangosteens under a velvet starlit sky. But Connie then became alarmingly exhausted. 'I shall have to be more firm,' Sheila wrote home.

This would prove far from easy. Illness and doctors were taboo, and Connie resented any attempts to check her activities or hold her back in any way. Back on board, she quickly recovered and seemed in excellent health and spirits for the rest of the tour. At Perth they gave a talk and attended a welcoming reception given by the mayor, then sailed on to Adelaide for several more lectures and demonstrations. Everywhere they went was sold out, and the press reported that 'no overseas celebrity has had a more spontaneous welcome from Australians than Mrs Spry'. Connie was overwhelmed. At each city — Perth, Adelaide, Melbourne, Canberra, Sydney, Brisbane — the cream of Australian society organized garden parties in her honour, the ladies vying with each other to wear the most eye-catching flower-bedecked hats. Connie usually outdid them; she had brought with her one of her favourites, decorated with yellow mimosa. 'I thought it would be a gesture Australian women would appreciate,' she wrote.

Connie, who disliked travelling great distances and steadfastly refused to fly anywhere, took the train to Sydney and spent a happy journey chatting with the conductor about orchids, which he and his wife grew as a hobby in their 'backyard'. In every city she appeared on television and radio programmes and, assisted by Sheila, gave two lectures a day to packed audiences. 'She went to town more than I ever heard her,' Sheila wrote home. Sometimes their hosts were disappointed to find Connie flagging as she toured their gardens, preferring to sit swapping stories in the cool of the house. But she never lost her sense of humour and at one event, amid the popping of flash-bulbs, when a photographer admitted he wouldn't notice a flower arrangement at home and just ate the food put in front of him, Connie sighed and said, 'What would one do with a man like that?'

The press loved her. 'A short, twinkling and decided person' was how one journalist described her. 'The internationally famous "Flower Girl",' wrote another. They reported on the enthusiasm of her reception wherever she went and on her many outspoken views:

> Beware of stylizing. Accept no rules. Let the flowers remind you of how they looked when growing. You are not human unless you have a way of expressing yourself. Flowers are the contemporary woman's paint-box. I detest set arrangements such as a triangle of roses or a crescent moon of chrysanthemums. Don't make lovely flowers into statements of geometry.

This was wild talk indeed, and no doubt some stalwarts were unmoved by it. It was all highly revolutionary for Australian ladies, who had become used to the American fashions in flower arrangement. But the younger women were ecstatic. They loved the 'Cordon Fleur' lady.

At the end of April Connie and Sheila were back on the *Himalaya* loaded with souvenirs, exotic plants and cuttings of eucalyptus, sweet-scented frangipani, outsize gardenias, dahlias and zinnias, some of which she used to decorate the captain's table. They arrived home in time to prepare for Chelsea Flower Show, for which Connie created a dramatic 'souvenir of Australia' display using flowers and exotics that she had had specially flown in. The president of the Australian Garden Society thanked her for the tour, informing her that new flower-arranging societies were being started every day across the country and members were exchanging flowers by air. It was at Chelsea that year that Roy Hay approached Connie to ask if she would join the committee of the Royal Gardeners' Orphan Fund. She readily agreed, and offered to lecture without fee to any flower or garden club that was willing to pass round the hat for the Fund. She raised more than a thousand pounds in one year.

Connie continued to spend long summers at Ard Daraich, where she worked on her last book, *Favourite Flowers*. Despite some perhaps inevitable repetition, it is one of her most lyrical pieces of writing, full of snatches of poetry, bubbling with life and her passion for flowers; and vivid as ever, with individual plants always observed with a fresh eye: 'Look and never let the eye grow stale,' she advised her readers. She thanked Shav, from whom 'I have the great good fortune to be accorded generous, unswerving encouragement together with solace when needed, in all things I do and have done.' Her most autobiographical book, it is suffused with childhood memories, humour, personal anecdote, self-criticism, jokes and perceptive wisdom. It also reveals her as widely read, a keen Scrabble player, and staggeringly knowledgeable in all things horticultural.

In the summer of 1959 her American friend the journalist Helen Kirkpatrick, now Mrs Robbins Milbank, came over with her husband to visit Connie. They stayed at Winkfield and enjoyed a wonderful reunion. When Helen confessed to Connie that she had been going to an ikebana class, Connie shook her head and said, 'If I catch you doing any of those affected designs, my girl, I'll cut you off without a farthing!' They all then headed to Scotland to see Shav and enjoy a few weeks' holiday at Ard Daraich. The weather was glorious and Connie was in great spirits. But Helen noted: 'Connie seemed to be very much preoccupied with tidying things up.' Her son Tony now headed the business, which had expanded into three shops, two in London and one in Guildford in Surrey. The Winkfield school continued to thrive under the joint headship of Christine Dickie and Rosemary Hume; Harold Piercy, 'a brilliant young Spry-trained decorator' who had joined the business during the coronation, became head of the flower school. George Foss and Sheila McQueen continued as the principal lecturers. 'But then,' Helen wrote, 'she was nearly seventy, and retirement of some degree seemed eminently sensible, albeit unlike her.' In fact, Connie was seventy-three; as with so many things in her life, she was never quite truthful about her age.

After the Milbanks had returned to America Connie went home to Winkfield, where the beautiful weather continued and produced an astonishing display of flowers in her garden. Her beloved roses excelled themselves, their great arching branches wreathed from end to end with sumptuous, prolific blooms. In *Favourite Flowers*, she wrote:

> My long-held dream really did materialize . . . there were a few weeks of this summer when in one part of the garden the roses flung their flowering branches about in an abandon of sweetness, when they fell in waterfalls from the old trees that supported them, when they were intoxication to the senses . . . this year they seemed to hold an element of the miraculous . . . There were moments when the glory of every flowering tree and shrub from the magnolias down to the privets seemed almost to be saying 'Look thy last on all things lovely, every hour.'

The quotation is from one of Connie's favourite verses by Walter de la Mare.

As summer turned to autumn, *Favourite Flowers* was published and Connie and Rosemary immediately embarked on a new book, to be called *Hostess* and to be illustrated with specially commissioned sketches by Lesley Blanch.

At Christmas Connie was as buoyantly inventive as ever with her 'Christmas nonsense', supervising the tree decorations, the wreaths and winter flower arrangements. Shav gave her his usual gift of a valuable Blue John vase. New Year brought another happy feast among friends and family. She telephoned Rosemary to arrange to do some editing on their new book.

On the evening of 3 January 1960 as they sat around the dinner table at Winkfield, Connie was bubbling with ideas: for the garden, for Chelsea, for the schools and for another Christmas – 'Next year, I know what we'll do,' she laughed. Then, as she climbed the narrow stairs to her drawing-room after dinner, she suddenly stumbled and fell unconscious. She was carried to her bed, where within the hour she died.

'Dear, downright Connie,' wrote an old friend, 'I'm so glad her light went out without a long flicker. She wasn't one to dwindle into old age.'

Epilogue

Mourners remembered a cold, bleak funeral held on a bitter January day when even the massed white flowers and hundreds of tributes that poured in from all over the world could hardly cheer the mood. There was a sense of shock and of loss that Constance Spry had left so suddenly and unexpectedly. Friends rallied to breathe some warmth and gaiety back into her memory. On the day of her funeral her friend the journalist Ruth Drew spoke on the BBC *Today Programme*:

> Just three weeks ago, I spent a day with Constance. When she gave me a parting hug, I said, 'You've been a tonic, as usual!' Constance was always that. Her vitality – her versatility – her needle-sharp wit . . . all made her the most stimulating companion. What made her a true friend was her steady integrity and her generous sympathy.

National newspapers carried fulsome obituaries and early in February the BBC broadcast a tribute where friends and colleagues could recall their special memories of Connie. The horticultural journalist Roy Hay spoke first: 'Constance Spry was one of those rare beings who knew exactly what she was aiming at, did exactly what she wanted to do, and yet was able to inspire all those who worked with her to see things as she saw them.' Kitty Rich, a schoolfriend from Ireland, remembered how Connie Fletcher worked so hard to help people in need . . . how she also laughed and always dressed with flamboyance. Nancy Fairbairn (Ritchie), one of the first students at Winkfield, recalled happy days there 'some of the best of my life' and how ideas of all kinds 'constantly flowed from her. Graham Stuart Thomas described her as a great gardener and plantswoman who saved precious old roses from extinction. Helen Kirkpatrick spoke 'down the line' from New York:

> She had an insatiable curiosity and an extraordinary talent in arousing it in others. Her opposition to mediocrity in any form and a rollicking sense of humour made Constance a rare human being. She was always so alive and so full of fun and enthusiasm; we never noticed she was growing old.

Lady Sybil Eccles recalled the preparations for the coronation and said, 'No wonder she succeeded in so many ways; as a writer of meticulously accurate cookery and garden books, as an unaffected lecturer, as the gayest of teachers in her school near Windsor.' The designer Herman Schrijver recalled her artistry, her eye for different colours and for spacing and placing flowers so perfectly: 'I loved to watch her hands covered in rings and bracelets tinkling as she worked and chatted. One will always remember her, always.' The journalist Anne Scott James wrote an article in which she remembered her friend Connie:

> If you spent a day with her, she would cook a five course lunch which was a gastronomic poem, arrange a dozen vases of flowers while you carried in the lunch, make three varieties of scones for tea while you drank your coffee, write an article while you ate the scones and pick you a basket of flowers to take home while you read the article.

A collection of £900 was contributed to the Royal Gardeners' Orphan fund. Connie herself left £27,000 — hardly a fortune from such a hugely successful life — but she had never cared about profit and loss, only about creativity and freedom of expression. In 1961

David Austin started growing and selling old-fashioned roses commercially. He called his first hybrid 'Constance Spry' in memory of all that she had achieved with her beloved roses.

On 28 May 1962 Val Pirie married Shav Spry at Caxton Hall and became the second legal Mrs Spry. They divided their time between Winkfield and Ard Daraich. Shav became senile and took to walking round the school without his clothes, much to the consternation of the female students. He died in 1967 and Val made her home near Salisbury where she lived well into her nineties.

Constance Spry Ltd continued for some years under the chairmanship of Tony Marr at South Audley Street and the two other shops. In November 1973 the company decorated Westminster Abbey for Princess Anne's wedding. For a while Winkfield School continued to thrive under the care of Christine Dickie and Rosemary Hume. Sheila McQueen became a renowned lecturer and writer on flower arranging, receiving an RHS Victoria Medal of Honour and an MBE. She died in 2008 aged ninety-three.

Winkfield carried on under several different managements and in different premises until it finally closed in 2008. Tony Marr did not survive the first management change and, after marrying his second wife Vita, he retired to live mainly in Scotland and died in 1993.

The Cordon Bleu Cookery School still flourishes in Marylebone Road in London. It became fully integrated with the Cordon Bleu Group in 1990 and several other schools were opened in places such as Tokyo, Ottawa and Sydney. After successfully running the London Cordon Bleu school for most of her life, Rosemary Hume bought a house in the Kyles of Bute, Argyll, where she retired to live with her brother-in-law Dr Jan Nunn, with whom she had had a long relationship. She died in 1984.

In one of her last books Connie reproduced some verses from a 'sentimental poem' the name of whose author she had forgotten. The poem, 'Prayer', is by the American poet Louis Untermeyer and was published as part of *A Gospel for Restless Hearts*. It offers several clues to her character and one can see why she chose to quote it.

> *Open my eyes to visions girt*
> *With beauty, and with wonder lit —*
> *But let me always see the dirt*
> *And all that spawn and die in it.*
>
> *Open my ear to music — let*
> *Me thrill with spring's first*
> *Flutes and drums,*
> *But never let me dare forget*
> *The bitter ballads of the slums.*
>
> *From compromise and things half done*
> *Keep me with stern and stubborn pride;*
> *And when at last the fight is won,*
> *God keep me still unsatisfied.*

Acknowledgements

I particularly wish to thank Martine Frost, who ran the Constance Spry School until 2008. She generously gifted the school's archives to the Lindley Library and has been most generous in helping me with this book and for allowing me to quote from Constance Spry's books and reproduce photographs of flower arrangements. I am also indebted to the late Elizabeth Coxhead, whose research and interviews for her biography of Constance Spry, published in 1975, were an invaluable source.

I would like to thank several people who recalled for me their memories of training or working either at Winkfield or the Spry Flower School – in particular Rosamund Banks (Gould), Nancy Briggs (Ritchie), Alleyne Cook, Susie Edwards (Lunn), Gillian Hammick (Inchbold), Norma Howard (Fletcher), the late Sheila McQueen, Francis Monkman, Rex Murfitt, the late Vita Marr, Fred Wilkinson and Amanda Williams (Spence).

My thanks for help and for permission to use published and unpublished material to Lord Aberdeen, Griselda Barton, Hamish Bowles, Lord Eccles, Roy Gluckstein, Lord Haddo, Caroline Moorehead and Diana Souhami. My grateful thanks for permission to quote from the Cecil Beaton diaries and for permission to quote from Beverley Nichols. Extracts from *Vogue* magazine are by courtesy of Condé Nast Publications. Extracts from Beverley Nichols' *Garden Open Today* and *Down the Garden Path* are reprinted by permission of Timber Press Inc. (publisher of the current editions) and the Estate of Beverley Nichols (the copyright holder). Extracts from Cecil Beaton's diaries are reprinted by permission of the Literary Executors of the late Sir Cecil Beaton, 2010 and Rupert Crew Limited. Permission to reprint verses from the poem 'Prayer' has been granted by the Estate of Louise Untermeyer, Norma Anchin Untermeyer and Laurence S. Untermeyer, care of Professional Publishing Services, CT, USA. The drawings by Lesley Blanch of Constance Spry in her garden and the decorative chapter plates originally published in *Come into the Garden Cook* (1942) are reproduced by arrangement: Copyright the Estate of Lesley Blanch.

Librarians and archivists who were particularly helpful include Liz Gilbert at The Royal Horticultural Society Lindley Library, Brett Croft at the Condé Nast (*Vogue*) Archive, Louise North at the BBC Written Archives and Rose Cunnane at the Peamount Hospital Archives. I am also grateful to librarians at The Bristol University Theatre Library, The Bristol City Library, The London Library, The British Library, The Dorchester County Library, The Durham Mining Museum, The National Archives of Ireland, Dublin, The National Archives, Kew, The Archives of the British Red Cross, The Derbyshire Record Office, The Principal Registry of the Family Division and The National Association of Flower Arranging Societies.

My personal thanks to Georgina Morley, my brilliant editor at Macmillan, to my agent and dear friend Heather Holden-Brown and her assistant Elly James. I particularly wish to thank many friends who helped and supported me while I wrote this book, including Prosper Devas, Jemima Hunt, Fred Wilkinson, Tim and Joyce Jeal, Norrie and Anna Maclaren, Judy Preston, Tim Mowl, Christopher and Jane Francis, Loesje and Barrie Houghton, and Stewart and Catherine Boyd. My biggest thanks, as always, are reserved for my children Louisa and Joe and most of all for my husband, Ben, for thirty-five years of loving and sharing.

Select Bibliography and Sources

Books by Constance Spry in date order, all published by J.M. Dent

Flower Decoration (1934)
Flowers in House and Garden (1937)
A Garden Notebook (1940)
Come into the Garden, Cook (1942)
Summer and Autumn Flowers (1951)
Winter and Spring Flowers (1951)
How to Do the Flowers (1953)
Party Flowers (1955)
The Constance Spry Cookery Book, with Rosemary Hume (1956)
Simple Flowers (1957)
Favourite Flowers (1959)
Hostess, published posthumously, with Rosemary Hume and Anthony
    Marr (1961)

Journals and Newspapers

Country Life
Flower Arranger
Garden History, vol. 31, No. 1, 2003, pp. 80–94
Good Housekeeping
Harper's Bazaar
House and Home
Journal of the Royal Horticultural Society

The Garden
The Gardener's Chronicle
Tatler
Vogue

Books

Battersby, Martin, *The Decorative Thirties*. Studio Vista, London, 1969.

Beaton, Cecil, *Photobiography*. Odhams Press, London, 1951.

—*Diaries: The Wandering Years, 1922 –1939*. Weidenfeld & Nicolson, London, 1960.

Blacker, M.R., *Flora Domestica 1500 –1930*. The National Trust, London, 2000.

Cannadine, David, *Class in Britain*. Penguin Books, London, 2000.

Castle, Charles, *Oliver Messel: A Biography*. Thames & Hudson, 1986.

Cohen, Deborah, *Household Gods*. Yale University, 2006.

Connon, Bryan, *Beverley Nichols: A Life*. Timber Press, MA., USA, 2009.

Cooke D. and McNicol P., *A History of Flower Arranging*. Heinemann, London, 1989.

Coxhead, Elizabeth, *Constance Spry: A Biography*. W. Luscombe, London, 1975.

Duberman, M.B., Vicinus, M., and Chauncy, G., eds., *Hidden From History – Reclaiming the Gay and Lesbian Past*. Penguin Books, London, 1991.

Earle, Mrs C.W., *Pot-Pourri from a Surrey Garden*. Thomas Nelson, London, 1898.

Elliott, Brent, *The Royal Horticultural Society: A History 1804 –2004*. Phillimore & Co., Stroud, Glos., 2004.

Faderman, Lillian, *Surpassing the Love of Men: Romantic Friendship & Love Between Women from the Renaissance to the Present*. Junction Books, London, 1981.

Fisher, Richard B., *Syrie Maugham*. Duckworth, London, 1978.

Goode, Henrietta, *Camouflage and Art: Design and Deception in WW2*. Unicorn Press, London, 2007.

Hennessy, Peter, *Having it so Good: Britain in the Fifties*. Allen Lane, London, 2006.

Jekyll, Gertrude, *Flower Decoration in the House*. Country Life, London, 1907.

Keane, Maureen, *Ishbel: Lady Aberdeen in Ireland*. Colourpoint Books, Dublin, 1999.

Lyons, F.S.L., *Ireland Since The Famine*. Collins, 1971.

Malcolm, E. and Jones. E., eds., *Medicine and Disease and the State of Ireland. 1650–1940*. Cork University Press, 1999.

McKibbin, Ross, *Classes and Cultures: England 1918 –1951*. Oxford University Press, 1998.

McQueen-Pope, M., *The Footlights Flickered: The Story of the Theatre in 1920s*. Herbert Jenkins, London, 1959.

Moorehead, Caroline, *Sidney Bernstein: A Biography*. Jonathan Cape, London, 1984.

Morgan, J. and Richards, A., *A Paradise out of a Common Field: The Pleasures & Plenty of the Victorian Garden*. Random Century, 1990.

Nichols, Beverley, *Down the Garden Path*. Jonathan Cape, London, 1932.

—*Garden Open Today*. Jonathan Cape, London, 1963.

—*The Art of Flower Arranging*. Collins, London, 1967.

Nicolson, Nigel, *Diaries and Letters 1930–1939*. Collins, London, 1966.

Pimlott, Ben, *Queen. Elizabeth II and the Monarchy*. HarperCollins, London, 2002.

Pugh, Martin, *We Danced all Night: A Social History of Britain Between The Wars*. The Bodley Head, London, 2008.

Rhodes, James, ed., *Chips: The Diaries of Sir Henry Channon*. Weidenfeld & Nicolson, London, 1967.

Schiaparalli, E., *Shocking Life. Autobiography*. J.M. Dent, London, 1954.

Sissons, M., and French, P., *The Age of Austerity*. Penguin, London, 1964.

Souhami, Diana, *Gluck: Her Biography*. Weidenfeld & Nicolson, London, 1988.

Taylor, Barbara Lea, *Old-fashioned and David Austin Roses*. Firefly Books, Ontario, Canada, 2004.

Stuart Thomas, Graham, *Old Shrub Roses*. Sunningdale, Hampshire, 1955.

Vickers, Hugo, *Cecil Beaton: A Biography*. Weidenfeld & Nicolson, London, 2002.

Walsh, Seamus, *In the Shadow of the Comer Mines*. Castlecomer, Ireland, 1999.

Windsor, Wallis, *The Heart Has its Reasons: Memoirs by the Duchess of Windsor*. D. McKay, London, 1956.

Picture Acknowledgements

1. Connie aged about five (The Estate of Vita Marr); 2. Connie aged about sixteen (The Estate of Vita Marr); 3. Connie and her father with the Phoenix Caravan (Courtesy of the Peamount Hospital, Co. Dublin); 4. Connie's engagement photo (The Estate of Vita Marr); 5. James Heppell Marr et al (The Estate of Vita Marr); 6. Syrie Maugham (Copyright reserved/Millar and Harris); 7. Shav Spry (The Estate of Vita Marr); 8. Gluck (Courtesy of Roy Gluckstein); 9. Display for Atkinsons' window (Courtesy of Martine Frost); 10. 'Chromatic' by Gluck (Courtesy of Roy Gluckstein); 11. Rosemary Hume (The Estate of Vita Marr); 12. Val Pirie (Courtesy of Martine Frost); 13. Oliver Messel (Courtesy of the Dorchester Hotel); 14. Victor Stiebel and models (Getty Images); 15. Connie checking an arrangement (Copyright © The Estate of André Kertesz); 16. Decorative kale leaves (Courtesy of Martine Frost); 17. 'Blackamoor with whitewashed leaves' (Courtesy of Martine Frost); 18. The shop in South Audley Street (Courtesy of Martine Frost); 19. Staff in the shop (Getty Images); 20. A class in flower arranging (Courtesy of Martine Frost); 21. The wedding of the Duchess of Gloucester (Getty Images); 22. Helen Kirkpatrick (The Estate of Vita Marr); 23. Drawing of Connie in her garden by Lesley Blanch (Copyright © the Estate of Lesley Blanch, reproduced by arrangement); 24. Coolings Gallery in wartime (Courtesy of *The Times* Newspapers); 25. Floral decoration society meeting in Dorchester (Getty Images); 26. Connie judging at Dorchester (Getty Images); 27. Adding the finishing touches at Lancaster House (Getty Images); 28. Inspecting the floral decorations on the Coronation route (GettyImages); 29. A green table decoration (Courtesy Martine Frost); 30. Chrysanthemums with brown leaves (Courtesy Martine Frost); 31. Connie and Sheila McQueen in Brisbane (The Estate of Vita Marr); 32. Connie and Gilbert Harding (The Estate of Vita Marr); 33. Connie sewing (Getty Images); 34. A formal photograph of Connie (The Estate of Vita Marr); 35. The 'Bridal Rose' and lily of the valley (Courtesy Martine Frost).

Endpapers and drawings decorating chapter headings by Lesley Blanch, originally published in Connie's 1944 book, *Come Into the Garden, Cook*, copyright © the Estate of Lesley Blanch, reproduced by arrangement.

Index

CS indicates Constance Spry

Beaton, Nancy 187
Bedaux, Charles and Fern 193, 195
Bedford, Eric 297, 298, 299, 306
Beecham, Sir Thomas 119
Beerbohm, Max 119
Beeton, Isabella x, 236, 319
begonia 160
Bennett, Arnold 96, 119
Bérard, Christian 162, 181
bergamot 179–80
Bernstein, Sidney 82, 83, 94–5, 96,
  97, 111, 131, 176, 234, 239, 242
Billericay, Essex 73–4
Blair, Sir Robert 18, 22, 27, 68, 69,
  70, 84, 168
Blanch, Lesley 235–6, 239, 243, 324
Bliss, Arthur 149
Blitz, London 229–31, 235, 242, 244,
  300
bluebells 104
Book of Household Management (Beeton)
  319
Botanic Garden, Dublin 208, 209
Boudin, Stéphane 203
bougainvillea 104, 160, 163
Boulestin, Marcel 237
Bowles, Hamish 196
Bowles, Paul 163
Brains Trust, The 237–8
British Red Cross Society (BRCS) 54,
  56, 57, 58, 227, 232
Broadlands, Hampshire 110, 159–60,
  169, 213
Brompton Oratory 185
Brooklyn Botanic Garden 209
Brooks, Romaine 149
Buckhingham, Dora 266–7, 275
buddleia 5

cabbage leaves 122, 160,
camellia 89, 92, 102, 147, 179, 204,
  207, 262, 263, 268
carnations 25, 79, 91, 137, 160, 187,
  215, 276, 279, 280, 305, 314

Carter, Lady Violet Bonham 187, 220
ceanothus 19
cerastium 48
Channon, Henry 'Chips' 189
Château de Candé, France 193–4
Chelsea Flower Show xv, 141–4, 275,
  284, 305, 322, 325
Chinese lantern 92
chrysanthemum 80, 92, 102, 104,
  186, 230, 279, 322
church decorating 136, 184–8,
  279–80 *see also* weddings
Churchill, Clementine 314, 315
Churchill, Winston 117, 261, 283,
  295, 298, 308, 310
Claridge's Hotel, London 187, 202
clematis 6, 93, 139, 172, 176, 202,
  207, 243, 288
Clements, Julia 282
Cobham Hall, Kent 179–80
Cochran, Charles B. 'Cocky' 94, 95,
  112, 119, 120, 149
Cocteau, Jean 162, 163
Colefax, Lady Sybil 119, 124
Colney Park, Hertfordshire 139, 140,
  141, 158, 175, 176
Colville, 'Jock' 310
Colvin, Brenda 135
Come into the Garden, Cook (Spry) 239,
  241, 243–4
Conran, Sir Terence ix, xvi
Constance Spry Cookery Book, The (Spry/
  Hume) x, 317–20
Constance Spry Flower School, Curzon
  Street, London xiii, 181–2, 250
  later renamed The Modern School
  of Flower Work, London 184, 225
  see also Cordon Bleu Cookery and
  Flower School, London
Constance Spry Inc., New York
  212–22
Constance Spry Ltd, London 221,
  225, 229, 244, 262–4, 265–6
  shop renamed 221

corsages 101, 107, 201, 202, 215, 244

debutante customers 187, 201–2, 204

distressed furniture 126, 127

finances 98, 99, 131–2

gathering of flowers for 101–3, 104

grand customers 109–11, 119, 136, 137, 160, 161, 184–98

growth of 105, 106, 118–19, 141

lawsuit against 203, 213, 219–20

Limited company, becomes 183

renamed Constance Spry Ltd 221 *see also* Constance Spry Ltd

Second World War 219–20, 221

shop staff 98, 100, 101, 105–6, 107, 108–9, 119, 128, 130, 131, 133–4, 136, 137–8, 181, 191, 197, 202, 203–4, 212–13, 214, 215, 218, 225, 229

South Audley Street 180, 183–4, 201, 203, 213, 216, 218, 219–20, 225, 244, 263, 295

Wedding Room 203, 220

weddings 107, 184–8, 193–8, 203, 220

see also Constance Spry Inc. *and* Constance Spry Ltd

Flowers in House and Garden (Spry) 182–3, 208–10

Flowers in the Home (Watt) 206

Fogarty, Mary 35–6

forget-me-not 48, 205

Forrestal, Josephine 212, 214, 219

Fort Belvedere 188–9, 190, 192

Fortnum & Mason 124

Foss, George 108–9, 131, 141, 142, 143, 186–7, 263, 264, 280, 305, 315, 323

foxgloves 90, 102, 176, 204, 265

frangipani 309, 322

Frank, Jean-Michel 130

Fraser, Lovat 90, 94

fritillaries 176

fruit 101, 126, 143, 164, 205, 208, 211, 212, 216, 259, 289, 290, 314, 315

Garden Clubs of America 210

Garden Illustrated 226

Garden Notebook (Spry) 13, 226, 276

Garden That I Love (Karr) 49

Gardener's Chronicle 276, 277, 278, 283

gardenia 29, 102, 126, 207, 320

Garland, Madge 124

gentian 202

George V, King 188, 191

George VI, King 192–3, 197, 219, 295, 296

geranium 50, 160, 297–8, 306

Gerard, John 49

Gibbons, Grinling 211, 314

Gibbs, Vicary 140

Gielgud, Eleanor 130, 131, 134, 183

Gielgud, John 94, 111, 130, 236

gladioli 207, 230, 281, 305, 308, 315

Gloucester, Duke of 188

gloxinia 160

Gluck (Hannah Gluckstein) 147–53, 155–9, 160, 161, 162, 165, 167, 169–72

Good Housekeeping 66

Good Housekeeping Institute 66

Good Soups (Heath) 236

Gould, Ros 258

Granada cinemas 83, 84, 94–8, 105

grapes 101, 126, 164, 205, 290, 315

Gravetye Manor, Sussex 179

Greville, Mrs Ronald 119

Grimond, Jo 187

Grimond, Laura 187

Guardian ix, xv–xvi

Guildhall, London 204

gypsophila 91, 279

Habitat ix

Hackett, Eva 55, 58

Haddon, Norman 180
Hammamet, Tunisia 162, 163–5, 172,
208, 240, 241
Harding, Gilbert 284
Harlow, Jean 122
Harper's Bazaar 154, 209, 240, 283
Hartnell, Norman 94, 188, 197, 201,
303
Hatchet Restaurant, London 93, 103
hawthorn 176
Haxton, Gerald 121
Hay, Roy 283, 284, 322, 327
Heal, Ambrose 128
Heals, London 128–9, 131
helichrysum 92
hellebore 104, 126
Henderson, Keith xviii, 90–1
Henley Regatta 204
Henson, Jean 162, 163, 164, 208
Henson, Violet 162, 163–4, 208,
209, 240, 241
Hepburn, William 305, 306, 310
Hill, Oliver 119, 122, 151, 156
hippeastrums 315
hogweed 265
Holden, Daphne 255, 265, 315
Hole, Dean 79–80
hollyhock 104
Homerton and South Hackney Day
Continuation School, London
69–73, 78, 80, 83, 84, 100, 251,
252, 278
honeysuckle 92, 176
hops 91, 92, 93
Horlick, Betsan 186
hosta sieboldiana 268
Hostess (Spry/Hume) 324
House and Gardens 129, 209
Housewife Magazine 283
How to Do the Flowers (Spry) 290–1
Howard, Lady Alice 29
Hoyningen-Huene, George 163, 208
Hume, Rosemary x, 112–13, 181,
225, 234, 237, 241–2, 250, 251,

252, 254, 260, 261, 286, 300,
301, 302, 306, 307, 313, 316–17,
319, 320, 323, 324, 329
hyacinth 89, 101, 106, 125
hydrangea 123, 186, 269, 285, 291,
299, 306

ICI 261
ikebana 210
In a Gloucestershire Garden (Ellacombe)
49
Inchbald, Gill 257, 258
India-rubber plant 50
Ingwersen, Will 277, 278, 280
Inland Revenue 66, 67
Ireland 13, 17–26, 27, 28, 31–59, 63,
65, 69, 76, 189, 269–70, 317, 318
Irish Department of Agriculture and
Technical Instruction 18–19, 20,
28, 43
Irish Educational Review 35–6
Irish Gardening 20
Irish Industries Association 28
Irish Times 29
iris 47–8, 101, 143, 176, 207

J.M. Dent 154, 282, 283
James, Anne Scott 328
Japanese flower arranging 210
jasmine 207, 314
Jellico, Geoffrey 124
Johnstone, George 159
Journal of the Royal Horticultural Society
167
juniper 163

Kacew, Romain (Romain Gary) 236
kale xv, 37, 135, 160, 167, 187, 209,
243, 286
Karinska, Madame 162
Kew Gardens, London 315
King Edward's School, Moseley 11
King's College, London 26
Kirkpatrick (later Milbank), Helen

Index

Sinofranchetia chinensis 140

Sissinghurst, Kent 176, 287

skeletonised leaves 104, 133, 186, 188, 215, 218, 278, 283, 306, 308

Slainte 32, 33, 54

Smail, Bettie 232–3, 254

smilax 205

sorrel 176, 243

Souhami, Diana 150, 153, 166

Southwark Cathedral 186

Sparmannia Africana 226

spindleberry 176

Spry, Constance:

  accent 17, 282

  love for Shav Spry xii, 67, 76–7

  age, secretive about 324

  'All White' craze and 119–44, 180, 181, 221

  America, sets up shop in New York 212–222

  America, tour of 209–212

  appearance 21, 128, 214–15, 285, 322

  articles 154, 283, 320

  artificial effects and flowers, use of xiv, 100, 107, 133, 185, 212, 214, 215, 221, 263, 280, 305

  artistry xiii–xiv, 8, 22, 48, 82, 83, 89, 119, 123, 132, 133, 135, 172, 209, 258, 265, 291, 315, 328

  Australia, tour of 320–322

  birth 3

  books *see under individual book title*

  business, started 98–100 *see also* Flower Decorations, Constance Spry Inc., *and* Constance Spry Ltd

  bouquets 106–7, 185–8, 201,

  carpets, designs 'floral' 283

  charm 23, 33, 37, 41, 42, 96, 110–11, 138, 150, 214–15, 226, 297

  childhood xii, 3–13, 17–26, 175

Christmas, love of 6–7, 211, 215–16, 219, 324

Christmas decorations ('gew-gaws'), creates 6, 107, 211–12, 215–16

churches, decoration of 184–8, 279–80 *see also* weddings

colour, use of xiv, xvii, 89, 101–2, 107, 110, 118, 122, 123, 126, 127, 133–4, 135, 151, 159, 160, 163, 165, 167, 177, 178, 180, 181, 182, 183, 186, 190, 204, 205, 207, 208, 212, 219, 231, 233, 243, 249, 262, 263, 264, 268, 269, 276, 277, 278, 279, 280, 285, 289, 290, 297, 298, 299, 301, 302, 304, 305, 309, 312, 314–15, 318, 321, 328

containers (vases, urns, etc.), use of xv, 11, 36–7, 73, 92, 97–8, 103, 104, 107–8, 109, 123, 124, 129, 130, 131, 133, 137, 143, 160, 163, 164–5, 172, 185, 187, 189, 204, 205, 208, 216, 217, 219, 221, 255, 259, 264, 265, 273, 276, 279, 283, 291, 313, 315, 320, 324, 328

cookery 12–13, 23, 26, 41, 48–9, 50, 55, 73, 81, 236–45, 250–1, 252, 258, 259, 260–1, 281, 286, 300, 306, 317, 318–21, 328, 329

correspondence course on flower arranging 283

death 325, 327–8

defoliating flowers 104, 133, 186, 188, 215, 278, 283, 306, 308

democratic (blind to class difference) xi, xii, 17, 20–1, 24, 32, 36, 37, 76, 110–11, 119, 274, 278, 282

divorce xii, 77, 84

dried flowers, use of 92, 107, 212, 215, 217, 285

education, passion for xi, 8, 17, 25–6, 27, 31–8, 43, 44, 54,